DESIGN

'The author's command of the subject area is immaculate and the wide ranging references to contemporary design culture give the book a unique selling point.'

Julie Sheldon, Liverpool John Moores University

This is the student's essential guide to design – its practice, theory and history.

An easy-to-use and authoritative A–Z, *Design: The Key Concepts* will take you through such key topics as:

- International design – from Europe to Africa
- Design history – from Art Nouveau to Punk
- Sustainable design, recycling and green design
- Design theory – from semiotics to gender, to post-colonialism
- Design technology, graphic design and the web.

Fully cross-referenced, with up-to-date guides for further reading, *Design: The Key Concepts* is an indispensable reference for students of design, design history, fashion, art and visual culture.

Catherine McDermott is Professor in the School of Design at Kingston University, London, and a well-known writer and curator on contemporary design. Her current projects include work for the Design Council, the Crafts Council and curating in China and Africa.

ALSO AVAILABLE FROM ROUTLEDGE

Art History: The Basics
Grant Pooke and Diana Newall
978–0–415–37308–1

Art History: The Key Concepts
Jonathan Harris
978–0–415–31977–5

Key Writers on Art: From Antiquity to the Nineteenth Century
Edited by Chris Murray
978–0–415–24302–5

Key Writers on Art: The Twentieth Century
Edited by Chris Murray
978–0–415–22202–0

Cultural Theory: The Key Concepts
2nd Edition
Edited by Andrew Edgar and Peter Sedgwick
978–0–415–39939–5

Theory for Art History
Jae Emerling
978–0–415–97364–9

The Bible in Western Culture
Dee Dyas and Esther Hughes
978–0–415–32618–32618–6

DESIGN

The Key Concepts

Catherine McDermott

Routledge
Taylor & Francis Group

LONDON AND NEW YORK

First published 2007
by Routledge
2 Park Square, Milton Park, Abingdon, Oxon OX14 4RN

Simultaneously published in the USA and Canada
by Routledge
270 Madison Avenue, New York, NY 10016

Routledge is an imprint of the Taylor & Francis Group, an informa business

Typeset in Bembo by
Keystroke, 28 High Street, Tettenhall, Wolverhampton
Printed and bound in Great Britain by
TJ International Ltd, Padstow, Cornwall

British Library Cataloguing in Publication Data
A catalogue record for this book is available from the British Library

Library of Congress Cataloging in Publication Data
McDermott, Catherine.
Design : the key concepts / Catherine McDermott. – 1st ed.
p. cm.
Includes bibliographical references and index.
1. Design. I. Title.
NK1510.M56 2007
745.4–dc22
2007015236

ISBN10: 0–415–32015–1 (hbk)
ISBN10: 0–415–32016–X (pbk)
ISBN10: 0–203–96761–5 (ebk)

ISBN13: 978–0–415–32015–3 (hbk)
ISBN13: 978–0–415–32016–0 (pbk)
ISBN13: 978–0–203–96761–4 (ebk)

This book is dedicated to
Margaret Ainsworth 1952–2006

CONTENTS

LIST OF KEY CONCEPTS

advertising
aerodynamics
aesthetic movement
alternative design
alternative lifestyles
American design
animation
appropriate technology
appropriation
Art Deco
art furniture
artificial intelligence
Art Nouveau
arts and crafts movement
assemblage
Austrian design
automation
automotive design
avant-garde

Bauhaus
boutiques
British exhibitions

CAD
camp
capitalism
CCI
chaos
Chicago School

China
CIAM
classic design
classicism
commercial art
communication design
computer games
concept design
concurrent design
conservation
constructivism
consumer design
consumerism
consumption
contemporary style
convergent design
corporate culture
corporate identity
counterculture
craft
Cranbrook Academy
creative industries
creative salvage
critical design
cubism
cult objects
cultural analysis
cultural diversity in design
customizing
cybernetics

De Stijl
decoding
deconstruction
Design Academy, Eindhoven
Design and Industries
  Association (DIA)
design consultancies
Design Council
design education
design ethics
design exhibitions
Design for Disassembly (DfD)
design for need
design for recycling
design history
design magazines
design management
design museum
design policy
design research
designer labels
Deutsche Werkbund
DIY
Dutch design

eclecticism
ecocentrism
ecodesign
eco-efficiency
Ecole des Beaux Arts
embodied energy
emerging technology
engineering design
ergonomics
executive style
exoticism
experience design
experience economy
expressionism

fanzines
fascist design

fast-moving consumer
  goods
feminism
Festival of Britain, 1951
folk art
Fordism
found object
French design
functionalism
future forecasting
futurism

gender and design
geometric design
Glasgow style
globalization
Gothic revival
graffiti
Great Exhibition, 1851
green design
guilds of design

Habitat
heritage industry
high tech
historicism
Hollywood style

illustration
inclusive design
Independent Group (IG)
industrial design
Industrial Revolution
inflatable design
information design
innovation design
installation
interaction design
interdisciplinary design
interior design
international style
Italian design

Japanese design
Jugendstil

kitsch
Korean design

landscape design
Liberty's department store
lifestyle
lighting design

Machine Age design
MARS
Marxism
mass production
material culture
Memphis
Milan Triennale
military design
minimalism
Modern movement
Morris & Co.

nanotechnology
narrative design
naturalism
new age
new journalism
new look
New York World Fair, 1939
niche marketing
Novecento Movement

Omega workshops
op-art
organic design
ornament

packaging design
planned obsolescence
pop design
popular culture

post-colonialism
postmodernism
poststructuralism
primitive
product design
production design
prototype
psychedelic design
punk

Queen Anne revival
queer theory

radical chic
rationalism
ready-made
ready-to-wear
recycled design
retail design
retailing
robotics
Rococo revival
Royal College of Art
Russian design

satellite town
Scandinavian design
scientific materialism
screen design
semiotics
service design
shaker design
Smith, Adam
streamlining
structuralism
styling
subculture
surrealism
sustainability
sustainable design
systems theory

INTRODUCTION

Design: The Key Concepts is an accessible introduction to one of the 21st century's fastest growing areas of professional practice and research, that of international design and the creative industries. *Design* has been written not only for creative practitioners, academics and students but for anyone who needs a concise introduction to the field. *Design* also reflects the ambitions of this Routledge series, to be used as a reference source for professionals, designers and creatives working across different levels and for many different outcomes.

The entries offer quick insights into each term's range of meanings within the cultural context of design. The aim of each entry is to provide a simple definition of the term which includes consideration of its history and context, an analysis of key developments, an indication of important contributors and a review of the significance and impact for the 21st century.

Further reading references are listed to enable the reader to follow up ideas in more detail, and the diversity in these bibliographies can only suggest the huge research literature that design has initiated. The focus here, however, is to direct the user to the most important and recent books, articles, publications and websites. For this key element we have worked with Nicola Saliss, an experienced librarian whose subject specialism is design. Her detailed work has added a valuable research addition to the listed entries.

Design is an ever-expanding discipline within international business, which affects how each of us relates to the modern world. Global brands compete through design innovation, and the classic case study which reflects this model is the growth of Apple computers, led by the design superstar, Jonathan Ives, which turned around a failing business through the strategic use of design. Industry leaders who want to increase their competiveness, or even create a new market, appreciate the value of investing in design.

Major changes in terms of globalization, climate change and the development of communication industries have also transformed design. Design as a practice has undergone profound changes in the last twenty years, not least in terms of technology. The entries reflect these changes, which on the one hand have virtually eliminated some design practices, such as type design, and on the other have introduced a range of completely new design disciplines. A good example of a new defining discipline in the 21st century is interaction design, which includes the convergence of formally separate areas such as product, interior and graphic design. Interaction design is the all-important interface between the user and technology. Other new disciplines include experience design to deliver new insights into how brands are marketed, alongside new interdisciplinary practice areas such as information design, which integrates typography, graphic design, linguistics, psychology and applied ergonomics. Entries in the book also explore how the new materials and processes from cutting-edge science are impacting on future design practice. Typical here is the entry on nanotechnology and the emergence of complex contemporary areas of practice, such as sustainable design. A series of entries explores these new fields of practice research, reflecting the expertise of Dr Paul Micklewhaite, researcher in the Centre for Sustainable Design, Kingston University, in scoping out the range of new practice in this rapidly expanding field. In the 21st century green design will continue to impact across the entire design sector, from recent legislation banning old-style light bulbs to reduce greenhouse emissions to packaging recyclability.

The entries presented here are not restricted to a narrow definition of design. They range over both theoretical and practical concepts, and like design itself range across the interdisciplinary subjects that have helped shape and grow the discipline of design. These include, for example, sociology, semiotics, philosophy, business studies, engineering and ergonomics. Design was, and is, at the intersection of a range of disciplines and is placed here in the context of the wider economic, social and cultural forces that shape it. The book therefore has entries on Marxism and globalization, and the intention is to offer an insight into how these great ideas and events of the past 150 years have shaped and impacted on design culture. Indicated in bold in the text are cross-references to other entries which the reader can choose to explore, or not, as relevant.

Another key aspect in the choice of entries is the emphasis on the history of design to offer a context and framework for understanding such seminal movements and ideas as Arts and Crafts, the Modern Movement and Postmodernism, which shaped and continue to shape our contemporary visual world. Inevitably, some terms are missing. Like all dictionaries, the selection reflects an element of personal bias and focus, which Routledge and external reviewers have adjusted and improved. Finally, these design entries rely on updates, contributions and criticism from those working in and involved with the creative industries. They are warmly welcomed for the next edition.

DESIGN

The Key Concepts

ADVERTISING

The highly visible sign of a modern consumer culture promoting the sale of goods and services through a range of media, including newspapers, radio, television and the Internet. It has its modern origins in the development of the **Industrial Revolution**. Using advertisements to sell goods can, however, be traced back to Roman times: in Pompeii there are surviving images and text on the walls advertising products and services to a Roman audience. In the late 18th century pioneering British industrialists such as Josiah Wedgwood understood that simply producing goods was not enough; you had to market and advertise your products successfully. From the 1760s Wedgwood set in place most of the key elements of modern advertising we would recognize today. He used press ads and commissioned leading designers to design his catalogues so that customers could look at and order his ceramics in the comfort of their own homes. In the 19th century manufacturers understood the power of the single arresting image, and signs painted on to buildings became commonplace. These were followed by temporary paper posters and then purpose-built billboards, structures that have become more and more elaborate, so that in the Bund district of 21st-century Shanghai the sides of huge skyscraper buildings host advertisements for international companies.

By the beginning of the 20th century the use of magazine ads had become a key element for marketing campaigns, and the first experimental cinema advertisments had also come into play. The modern commercial world of advertising had begun. Cities now displayed an impressive amount of commercial visual imagery for which manufacturers had started to recruit some of the best-known artists of the day. Henri de Toulouse-Lautrec, Aubrey Beardsley and John Everett Millais are good examples of this trend, and some artists, such as Alphonse Mucha, were even destined to become better known for their advertisements than for their art. The term 'commercial art' came into being to describe the new importance of such advertising commissions. Perhaps the most important commercial artist of the 20th century was Adolphe Mouron Cassandre, whose **streamlined** posters of French ocean liners remain some of the most innovative graphic images ever created. His work epitomized advertising's shift away from being simply a source of product information to a new realm of aspirational lifestyles and the dream of escape. The key ideas underpinning this can be traced back to the revolutionary work in psychoanalysis of Sigmund Freud. Targeting the subconscious with powerful, and often sexual, marketing images became crucial to advertising. In this context, the ads made by the leading **Surrealist** artist of his day, Salvador Dalí, were groundbreaking and inspired many imitators. Dalí's work explored images that delved into the hidden desires of the viewer and removed objects from their usual context to produce in the viewer a shock that would facilitate the release of subconscious thoughts and desires. The lobster telephone is a classic example of this technique. In this way, Surrealist experiments were a blueprint for the emerging advertising industry, which now set out to promise much more than the commodity it tried to sell. The complex and sophisticated world of contemporary advertising therefore owes much to the Surrealist exploitation of the power of the erotic as a human impulse. Technology is the other key determiner of advertising, from the potential of neon signs, to the radio, cinema and television, to mobile phone messaging and the Internet. Advertising in the 21st century has come to be an entertainment industry in its own right.

Further reading:

Gibbons, Joan, *Art and Advertising*. London: I.B. Tauris, 2005.

Weill, Alain, *Graphics: A Century of Poster and Advertising Design*. London: Thames & Hudson, 2004.

Williamson, Judith, *Decoding Advertisements: Ideology and Meaning in Advertising*. London: Marion Boyars, 1978.

AERODYNAMICS

This is the study of airflow to find shapes which cause minimum resistance or turbulence, factors known to impede the speed of aircraft, trains, cars and ships. Early important experiments in aerodynamics included those of Sir George Cayley (1773–1857), an amateur scientist and a founder member of the British Association for the Advancement of Science, who explored the potential of manned flight. Gustave Eiffel (1832–1925) used his Eiffel Tower (1889) to carry out aerodynamic experiments and published two books on the subject. The first (1907) catalogued his Eiffel Tower experiments, while the second, the most important book on the subject, *Nouvelles Récherches sur la résistance de l'air faites au Laboratoire d'Auteuil* (1914), comprehensively documented the testing of scale-model aeroplanes in his wind-tunnel. This indicated that the principles of aerodynamic design were well understood by the early 20th century. The third yearbook of the **Deutsche Werkbund**, *Der Verkehr. Jahrbuch des deutschen Werkbundes* (1914), shows designs for motor cars, locomotives and aeroplanes as well as airships which demonstrate that aerodynamic principles were being absorbed by a wide range of designers. In the 1920s American commercial designers such as Norman Bel Geddes and Raymond Loewy exploited aerodynamic design in the form of **streamlining**. In 1932 Bel Geddes published *Horizons*, which contained a great deal of seductive propaganda in favour of streamlining. He and Loewy often looked to nature to support their theories of aerodynamics, citing, for example, the natural forms of ice floes. Aerodynamics retains a strong influence on **transport design** not only to improve performance but to enhance the aesthetics of vehicles through styling.

Further reading:

Bel Geddes, Norman, *Horizons*. New York: Dover, 1977 [1932].

Deutsche Werkbund, *Der Verkehr. Jahrbuch des Deutschen Werkbundes*. Jena: 1914.

Eiffel, Alexandre Gustave, *Récherches expérimentales sur la résistance de l'air exécutées à la Tour Eiffel*. Paris: 1907.

Eiffel, Alexandre Gustave, *Nouvelles Récherches sur la résistance de l'air faites au Laboratoire d'Auteuil*. Paris: H. Dunod et E. Pinat Editeurs, 1914.

Ledward, Kenneth S., *The Evolution of the 'Modern Airliner': From George Cayley to the Boeing Model 247*. London: Salt Oak, 1999.

Loewy, Raymond, *Industrial Design*. London: Fourth Estate, 1988 [1979].

AESTHETIC MOVEMENT

Term deriving from the title of the book *The Aesthetic Movement in England*, by Walter Hamilton, first published in 1882. Simon Jervis, an acknowledged authority on Victorian design, deliberately excluded an entry on the Aesthetic Movement in his pioneer *Dictionary of Design and Designers*, published in 1984. Presumably, he felt the term was too all embracing to be readily definable, encompassing, as it did, a taste for **Queen Anne Revivalism**, the cult of Japan and the latter-day Pre-Raphaelitism of Dante Gabriel Rossetti. In recent years, however, the Aesthetic Movement has been treated seriously as a term defining a stylistic movement. Designers and architects as diverse as Walter Crane, Lewis F. Day, Christopher Dresser, E. W. Godwin, Kate Greenaway, Thomas Jekyll, William **Morris**, W. Eden Nesfield, Richard Norman Shaw, Bruce Talbert and even Owen Jones can be accommodated within the category. It can be argued that there are considerable affinities between the early phase of the **Arts and Crafts Movement** and the

Aesthetic Movement. The years 1870 to 1895 can be said roughly to circumscribe the Aesthetic Movement.

Walter Pater (1839–94), in the famous conclusion to his *The Renaissance* (1868), sums up the ideals of the Aesthetic Movement: 'art comes to you proposing frankly to give nothing but the highest quality to your moments as they pass, and simply for those moments' sake'. Such thinking appears to have its origin in France in the writings of Théophile Gautier (1811–72), poet, novelist and journalist. Oscar Wilde (1854–1900), in the preface to *The Picture of Dorian Gray* (1891) in a series of witty epigrams, similarly rejects the idea that art may serve a moral purpose.

The word 'aesthetic' came to have a special meaning for the late 19th century, however, largely through George du Maurier's cartoons, which satirized the pretensions of smart society types who developed a taste for sunflowers, peacock feathers and Kate Greenaway **illustrations**. These people were considered to be 19th-century fashion victims and therefore were the subject of much ridicule and press comment. However, London's fashionable **Liberty's** department store marketed a range of Aesthetic clothes for women, and William Morris's daughter, May, as well as other members of the Arts and Crafts Movement wore these garments. The most high-profile figure was Oscar Wilde, who deliberately promoted himself as the centre of an Aesthetic taste that was slightly exaggerated, definitely exclusive and totally dedicated to the pursuit of art and beauty. Until his trial, Wilde carried the whole thing off as a wonderful performance piece, an attitude that found favour in British society, as he never appeared to take himself too seriously. Wilde the Aesthete brought to London a taste for Continental values and ultimately what Victorian society largely held to be Continental decadence. When he was sentenced to a term of imprisonment for homosexual activities that era of British style history was effectively closed until the revival of the male dandy in the post-Second World War period. The influence of Wilde remains strong in contemporary male fashion.

Further reading:

Aslin, Elizabeth, *The Aesthetic Movement: Prelude to Art Nouveau*. London: Elek, 1969.

Hamilton, Walter, *The Aesthetic Movement in England*. London: Reeves & Turner, 1882.

Jervis, Simon, *The Penguin Dictionary of Design and Designers*. Harmondsworth: Penguin, 1984.

Pater, Walter Horatio, *The Renaissance: Studies in Art and Poetry*. New York: Dover, 2005 [1868].

Spencer, Michael Clifford, *The Art Criticism of Théophile Gautier*. Geneva: Librairie Droz, 1969.

Wilde, Oscar, *The Picture of Dorian Gray*. London: Penguin, 2007 [1891].

ALTERNATIVE DESIGN

Alternative design developed less conventional products outside of mainstream manufacturing, which sought connections with both nature and the environment, and advocated a more economical use of resources. It signalled an opposition to excessive **consumerism** and the effects of waste and pollution on the environment. It was rooted in the 1960s development of **alternative lifestyles** which found strong expression in America as a counter-position to the country's post-war period of unprecedented economic growth and consumer spending, when the problems of pollution and environmental damage went largely unchecked by governments around the world. Although global waste problems were understood and recycling was a known concept, the general pattern was not to encourage Third World countries to develop their own tech-nological requirements. The trend was to impose Western technology (and Western lack of environmental standards) on developing countries. But high levels of conspicuous **consumption**, the unfair distribution of resources and sheer waste attracted strong opposition, and ever-more voices argued that these developments must be checked.

Among them was Victor Papanek, who developed the argument in *Design for the Real World* (1971). This book became a seminal text for a whole generation and was hugely influential. It posited the view that designers had a moral obligation not only to design responsibly in their own country but to apply their talents to solving problems in the developing world. Papanek, for example, illustrated his book with such ideas as low-tech radios, contrasting them with novelty products found in American small ads, such as parrot diapers and electrically heated **Queen Anne**-style footstools. *Design for the Real World* reflected a growing attraction for alternative technologies and alternative lifestyles away from the city, which led to the establishment of communities in isolated areas of the USA, notably in California.

In the early 1970s alternative design embraced anti-industrialized attitudes and images of self-sufficiency: for example, the American *Whole Earth Catalog* listed suppliers of geodesic domes, healing crystals, solar-power units and make-your-own-shoes kits. The idea of small being beautiful gained considerable ground, but only as a minority position. For example, when the environmental group Friends of the Earth was founded in the 1970s, it was seen as part of the alternative lifestyle movement, and its campaigns to save the whale and other endangered species were considered worthy but not mainstream. That situation had changed radically by the late 20th century, by which time such issues were high on the political agenda. Alternative design is now subsumed into the wider remit of **sustainable design**, and therefore 'alternative' is today part of mainstream design.

Further reading:

Papanek, Victor J., *Design for the Real World*. London: Thames & Hudson, 1985 [1971].
Whole Earth Catalog. Menlo Park, CA: Portola Institute, 1968–71.

ALTERNATIVE LIFESTYLES

A movement that stressed anti-materialism, peace and love, and encouraged individual lifestyles. During its heyday in the late 1960s and early 1970s, the word 'hippy' described sympathy for alternative values. Later, it became a term of abuse, and hippy ideas were dismissed as the self-indulgent attitudes of middle-class students who subsequently sold out to an Establishment they had once rejected. Undoubtedly, the movement's earnest introspection set it up for ridicule on a massive scale, but in the **New Age** 1990s hippy culture was given a more sympathetic evaluation.

Of major importance here is the hippy attitude to technology. Young people in the late 1960s began to oppose economic concepts such as **planned obsolescence** and the exploitation of natural resources. Hippy culture also challenged the design status quo. Design choices now became arbitrary and often bizarre, with the emphasis placed on individual lifestyles. Clothes were bought second-hand or from shops selling Afghan coats and embroidered Indian shirts. For women, the tailored clothes and obvious make-up of the early 1960s were discarded in favour of a more natural look and long hair. Furniture and **interior design** started recycling Victorian items, and propagated **DIY** ideas of building storage units from planks, bricks, beer crates and other discarded industrial materials. The norms of Western culture were regarded with deep suspicion, and alternative lifestyles and religions from the East, in theory at least, provided more attractive examples of how to live out the new social revolution.

Although serious principles underlay the hippy movement, its emphasis on free choice depended on the buoyant economy of the 1960s, and it did not survive the international oil crisis of 1973 and the massive recession which followed. The last vestiges of the movement were appropriated by wealthy, middle-class consumers who developed a taste for sushi, lentil loaves, personal growth and staying mellow. In 1977 Cyra McFadden's novel *The Serial* sent up the laid-back lifestyle in Mann County, California.

In the UK the success of the retailers Laura Ashley and **Habitat** offered the style to a wider market. Ashley, with her husband Bernard, began her business marketing Victorian-inspired clothes for middle-class hippies, and the sprigged fabrics from which they were made became her hallmark. Hers was a nostalgic, fantasy vision of urban life that suited the revivalism of the 1970s, with its obsession for stripped-pine Welsh dressers, country cottages and health food. Habitat also started to market a whole lifestyle based on this look, including curtains, wallpaper, furniture, lamps and other household items.

In this way alternative lifestyles made a mainstream contribution to popular design in the late 20th century. Alternative lifestyles in the 21st century are still strong but tend to be more focused towards downsizing homes and work alongside a continuing commitment to organic food and **sustainability**. The carbon footprint, a measure of impact on resources, has encouraged people to holiday at home, thus offering a different aspect to alternative lifestyles.

Further reading:

Fuad-Luke, Alastair, *The Eco-Design Handbook: A Complete Sourcebook for Home and Office*. London: Thames & Hudson, 2004 [2002].

McCleary, John Bassett, *The Hippie Dictionary: A Cultural Encyclopedia of the 1960s and 1970s*. Berkeley, CA.: Ten Speed, 2003 [2002].

McFadden, Cyra *The Serial: A Year in the Life of Marin County*. London: Prion, 2000 [1977].

Sebba, Anne, *Laura Ashley: A Life by Design*. London: Weidenfeld & Nicolson, 1990.

AMERICAN DESIGN

In the 21st century the USA is the only surviving world superpower, and the country's political and economic status is reflected by the high profile of American design. After the War of Independence in 1776,

American **design history** developed very quickly, and by the mid-19th century American industrialization was comparable with that of the most advanced European nations – Britain, France and Germany. As early as 1839, Septimus Norris of Philadelphia, America's largest producer of locomotives, was exporting rail vehicles to the Midland Railway in Britain. The victory of the Union over the Confederates in the American Civil War (1861–5) is invariably attributed to the advanced industrial technology of the North.

In the 19th century the huge territories of the United States were opened up by the mass immigration of European settlers. Before industrialization, farming communities produced the goods they needed; women spun, wove and made clothes, they consumed relatively few industrial products and they made their own essentials, such as candles and soap. By the end of the century, large corporations began to dominate the production and distribution of standardized, uniform products. The **Industrial Revolution** removed textile manufacture from the home and brought crafts like shoemaking, formerly done by independent craftspeople, into factories. Soap, lamp oil and cast-iron stoves came from local companies. Between 1890 and 1920 **mass production** and mass distribution brought new products and services, such as gas, electricity, prepared foods, **ready–made** clothing and factory-made furniture, to American families.

These innovations led to several particularly American responses, one of which was the appearance of numerous books on the subject of home management. The most famous and popular of these was *The American Woman's Home*, written in 1869 by Catharine Beecher and her sister Harriet Beecher Stowe, author of *Uncle Tom's Cabin*. It offered a complete guide to the management of the American home. Among the Beecher sisters' most important ideas were their detailed plans for the kitchen. They rationalized the space and designed storage areas, ideas that are claimed to have inspired the **Modern Movement**'s 'machine-for-living' concept. Their theories about the status of women in the home identified the American woman, at least in European eyes, as freethinking and independent. The American **Arts and Crafts Movement** was greatly influenced by the ideas of the Britons John Ruskin and William **Morris** but also included a reinterpretation of the American vernacular and simple homesteader furniture. This can be seen in the work of the Roycrofters, founded by Elbert Hubbard, who based his publishing business on the model of Morris's Kelmscott Press; and in the sturdy and functional furniture of Gustav and Albert Stickley, who were based in Binghamton, New York.

The USA would lead the way in other areas. For example, mail-order companies, such as Sears, Roebuck, were developed to deal with the problems of **retailing** throughout such a huge country. In addition, a new system of design was created, which incorporated standardized parts and methods of production, allowing products to be manufactured to a uniform standard across the country. This approach to design was called the 'American system', and it became part of an industrial process that ultimately led to the factory assembly lines of Henry **Ford**.

The 1920s and 1930s saw an American love affair with the new **Machine Age**, reflected in skyscraper architecture, the cinema, photography and **industrial design**. Notable exponents included: Busby Berkeley (1895–1976), **Hollywood** choreographer; Raymond Hood (1881–1934), architect and designer of the Rockefeller Center in New York; Edward McKnight Kauffer (1890–1954), poster and graphic designer, who mainly worked in London; Joseph Urban (1872–1933), architect, interior and set designer; John J. Wade (1893–?) and George J. Dietel (1876–1974), architects of City Hall, Buffalo, a major Art Deco building. In addition, a new breed of industrial designers appeared, including Norman Bel Geddes (1893–1958), Raymond Loewy (1893–1987) and Walter Dorwin Teague (1883–1960), who applied their new approach of **streamlining** to such diverse products as the Greyhound bus, Coca-Cola **packaging** and household objects.

The USA enjoyed a period of economic boom after the Depression years, and in 1939 it showed off its new prosperity at the **New York World Fair**. In the post-war period design remained an important issue for companies such as that of Herman Miller, who employed the furniture designers Charles and Ray Eames, Eero Saarinen and Harry Bertoia. Other American furniture companies such as Knoll also maintained a high design profile, while IBM led the field in industrial design. The European Modern Movement influenced the philosophies and attitudes of these companies, and their outlook was international. More homegrown was the design achievement of the 1950s. Encouraged by the consumer boom and a confident approach to styling, American design was exemplified by the car-styling work of Harley Earl for General Motors, a celebration of tail fins, bright colours and chrome. Other aspects of 1950s design included automat diners and Tupperware containers, a style sometimes called 'Populuxe'.

During the 1960s the emergence of **Pop** design encouraged writers such as Tom Wolfe to explore the creative world of **popular culture**. Although the 1970s brought a mood of conservatism, the USA introduced new directions in design with the emergence of **Post-**

modernism. Led by the example of leading Postmodernist architects, including Robert Venturi and Michael Graves, American design enjoyed a period of revived confidence. These developments were based in and around New York, but the West Coast also saw important changes. California became the centre of silicon-chip technology, and Apple computers, one of the most important companies in this powerful sector, renamed the area where it has its base Silicon Valley. At the northern end of the valley is Palo Alto, headquarters of the Hewlett Packard Company and the centre for the entrepreneurial American computer industry. In the 1980s Apple Mac transformed the approach to and practice of modern graphics, reflected in the work of West Coast designers such as April Greiman, and Zuzana Licko, who founded the **type design** magazine *Emigré*. Another Californian individualist destined to become an international design figure was the architect Frank Gehry, while design practices such as frog design and IDEO, based in Palo Alto, rose to prominence. IDEO pioneered new approaches to design practice: for example, brainstorming as a creative tool. Frog design was originally founded in Germany in 1969 and now works with over 500 clients, including Wega, Sony and Apple. It specializes in developing service and experience facilities.

The work of these designers meant American design continued to provide powerful inspiration for new directions in powerful economic trends. Apple has shaped the international consumer product market in terms of styling, marketing and technology with the phenomenal success of the iPod in the 20th century and the iPhone in the 21st. And other American products continue to set the consumer standard.

Further reading:

Aldersey-Williams, Hugh, *New American Design: Products and Graphics for a Post-Industrial Age*. New York: Rizzoli, 1988.

Beecher, Catharine E. and Beecher, Harriet, *The American Woman's Home*. Hartford, CT: Harriet Beecher Stowe Center, 2002 [1869].

Bel Geddes, Norman, *Horizons*. New York: Dover, 1977 [1932].

Champney, Freeman, *Art & Glory: The Story of Elbert Hubbard*. Kent, OH: Kent State University Press, 1983.

Hine, Thomas, *Populuxe*. New York: Alfred A. Knopf, 1986.

Kelley, T. and Littman, J., *The Art of Innovation: Lessons in Creativity from IDEO, America's Leading Design Firm*. London: HarperCollins, 2002.

Meikle, Jeffrey L., *Design in the USA*. Oxford: Oxford University Press, 2005.

Wolfe, Tom, *From Bauhaus to Our House*. London: Vintage, 1999 [1981].

Emigré, <http://www.emigre.com/>.

ANIMATION

A form of optical illusion where sequential images are shown in rapid succession so the viewer interprets them as a continuous movement. Early techniques of animation can be traced back to 19th-century novelty inventions for adults and children, which exploited the pheno-menon of human sight called the persistence of vision. In 1828 Paul Roget famously used a simple disc on a string, which had a bird on one side and a cage on the other. When the disc was spun it appeared to show the bird inside the cage. Early optical toys which created the illusion of movement include the phenakistiscope, invented by the French scientist Joseph Plateau (1801–83) and the Stampfer disc, invented by the Austrian Simon Stampfer (1792–1864). The zoetrope was invented in 1834 in England by George Horner. The principles which Horner employed are those used by the early animated pre-Disney films and continue to this day. The popularity of these novelties and subsequent, more elaborate inventions revealed an enduring human fascination for movement.

The development of animation was also closely aligned with early experiments with moving pictures. Notable here is the pioneer work of Kingston-born photographer Eadward Muybridge for Stanford University. The film industry offered the practical means for the discipline to develop and early cinemagoers saw drawings come to life for the first time. More sophisticated animation was soon developed, and the potential of animation to tell a story was quickly realized. The most famous advancements in the 1930s were by the Walt Disney Company, whose animated films of *Snow White* (1937) and *Bambi* (1942) became cinema milestones. These films required huge teams of artists drawing the pictures by hand, and so were labour intensive and costly to produce. Animation therefore became a specialist industry in which the individual found it hard to compete. However, in the 1960s Hanna–Barbera developed several animated cartoon programmes for children which used limited animation to cut costs and increase production.

Traditionally in films animation refers to a technique where each frame is produced individually and then photographed with a special animation camera. When the frames are played together the illusion of movement is created. Nowadays, though, computers have brought in a new era of animation. First, frames can be played together at a much faster speed, producing a more seamless sense of motion. Twelve frames per second is now the average speed used. Second, computer technology has permitted a move from 2D to 3D animation through use of its sophisticated programs. In 2D animation, all the effects had to be created by hand. Computers now allow animators to model an object so they can produce a more accurate 3D likeness. The animator can then chose from what angle to view this object, and can create different light sources for it, adding to the realism. The next stage is to render the object into 2D. This process is known as CGI (computer-generated imagery), and entire films can be produced in such a way. Key examples are *Jurassic Park*, the first film to use photorealistic CGI characters (dinosaurs), and *Toy Story*, the first CGI feature-length animation.

Recent developments in the field have meant that animators can create surfaces or skins for objects (e.g., fur) that can be programmed to move, stretch and reflect light as they would in real life, right down to individual hairs. As this process is time consuming it is expensive to produce, so the majority of work is still done through large studios: Dreamworks, Pixar and Disney. However, the rise of new, less expensive programs such as Flash means that more people can become involved, and independent studios can produce animation and distribute it over the Internet. Due to such advances, animation has been taken up by the music and **advertising** industries too, with independent animators like Bill Plympton finding success producing music videos, particularly with the popularity of MTV. Flash has proved popular for TV because it allows animators to save characters, props and movements to use again, thus simplifying the process. It is important here to emphasize the impact of Japanese animators, who have created a whole new aesthetic and look in their animated films in the last twenty years. Hayao Miyazaki Studio Gibli, founded in 1985, was one of the original creators of the manga comics and strip cartoons that have influenced animation all over the world.

The next challenge for animation is to create life-like movement and appearance in animated human bodies: 21st-century animation looks certain soon to succeed in creating work in which the viewer cannot distinguish between humans and animated characters.

Further reading:

Cavallaro, Dani, *The Anime Art of Hayao Miyazaki*. London: McFarland & Co., 2006.

Culhane, Shamus, *Animation: From Script to Screen*. London: Columbus, 1989.

Finch, Christopher, *The Art of Walt Disney: From Mickey Mouse to the Magic Kingdoms*. London: Virgin, 2004.

Wells, Paul, *Understanding Animation*. London: Routledge, 1988.

APPROPRIATE TECHNOLOGY

A term from the late 1960s used to describe design, products and equipment supplied to reflect and support local environmental, social and economic conditions. It was also called 'intermediate technology' in E.F. Schumacher's groundbreaking book *Small is Beautiful*. Such technology, it was argued, aimed to be appropriate to local needs, particularly in developing countries, and importantly did not impose the structure and approach of the West. It should be noted that the term in the 21st century is less precise and is interpreted amid the complexities of much wider research into **sustainable** studies. For the 1960s, however, appropriate technology involved adapting limited Third World resources to Third World needs. It aimed to support the economy of a particular area by using locally sourced materials and resources and by sustaining a diverse skill base in the local community.

Its principles still remain a sound template and basis for economic growth. One well-known example of appropriate technology is the wind-up radio designed in the mid-1990s by UK designer Trevor Bayliss. He responded to the situation in Africa where there is very limited electricity supply by inventing a radio that was powered by a simple hand-cranking device. Baygen Power was the company set up in South Africa to produce the radios, which have proved highly successful. Alongside such high-profile examples are a wide range of projects producing industrial machines to process water and fridges to hold essential vaccines and medicines, and generating income from cash crops. Architects for Aid is a major organization promoting appropriate technology for development projects using local resources, skill training and sharing.

Further reading:

Day, George and Croxton, Simon, 'Appropriate Technology, Participatory Technology, Design and the Environment'. *Journal of Design History* 6:3 (1993): 179–83.

Schumacher, E.F. (1973) *Small is Beautiful: A Study of Economics as if People Mattered*. London: Vintage, 1993.

APPROPRIATION

Postmodernist term for borrowing, quoting or using existing images, music and text to create a new design or art object. In terms of design, there are some iconic examples of appropriation from the history of art, which has deeply influenced the development of **product design**: Marcel Duchamp's **ready-mades**, for example, including his 1917 *Fountain* (simply a urinal), not only offered a process of working but a new aesthetic vision for the ordinary **found object**. In addition, Salvador Dalí's famous **Surrealist** objects, including his lobster telephone and lips sofa, offered a vision of the ordinary transformed into the extraordinary that inspired much **Pop** and Postmodernist design at the end of the century. Appropriation, however, is a step further than inspiration or quotation: it is the direct use of another's material in a completely different context to create new work.

Jean Baudrillard, Professor of Sociology at the University of Paris, explored the impact of **advertising** and consumer culture on contemporary society, and particularly challenged the idea of originality. He suggested that the notion of authenticity was essentially meaningless in an era when new technology facilitates the endless reproduction of information and images via television and faxes. These ideas found particular favour with designers in the 1980s, when images were appropriated freely from almost any source. Such borrowings are the graphic equivalent of the found object. Baudrillard called this process simulation. Something of a cult figure among a younger generation of designers, he provided an important intellectual justification for borrowing used images and deflecting attention away from the idea that design should always be original or new. A typical example from the art world would be the photographs of Sherri Levine. In terms of design, appropriation is perhaps most commonly used in fashion and graphic design, in the advertising work of Peter Saville and in Vivienne Westwood's use of 18th-century shirt patterns. However, it is important to note that appropriation is distinct from copying, and the intent is creative.

Further reading:

Baudrillard, Jean, *Selected Writings*. Oxford: Polity Press, 2001 [1988].

Irvin, Sherri, 'Appropriation and Authorship in Contemporary Art'. *British Journal of Aesthetics* April (2005): 123–37.

Kachur, Lewis, *Displaying the Marvelous: Marcel Duchamp, Salvador Dali and Surrealist Exhibition Installations*. Cambridge, MA: MIT Press, 2001.

ART DECO

A design style that derives its name from the famous Paris 1925 Exposition Internationale des Arts Décoratifs et Industriels Modernes.

It is sometimes said that the glamour of Art Deco was a reaction against the austerities of the First World War, and it quickly became widely popular. It could also easily be adopted by untrained designers. It is best seen as an amalgam of the complex visual changes affecting art and design prevalent in the pre-1914 era: **Cubism**, Orientalism, borrowings from African and Pre-Columbian (Aztec and Mayan), the bold colours of Fauvism, the discovery of the '**Primitive**' and of European **folk art**. Art Deco inherited many of the characteristics of **Art Nouveau**, and similarly revelled in the display of opulence. It was characterized by decorated surfaces, faceted forms and complex outlines, including a taste for wrap-around surfaces on furniture and in interiors. As a luxury style it is best seen in the work of the French *ébéniste* Jacques-Emile Ruhlmann (1879–1933), whose Paris workshop, Establissements Ruhlmann et Laurent, combined exotic materials such as ebony, shagreen, ivory and expensive veneers with refined **geometric** shapes. Another key French furniture-maker was Jean Dunand (1877–1942), who had learned the Japanese technique of lacquerwork and specialized in elaborate lacquered panels. France, with its high level of craft skills, dominated the international luxury market and French decorative arts and **interior design** were, by the 1920s, acknowledged to be the best in the world. Among the leading lights were: Édouard Benedictus (1878–1930), polymath and decorative designer; Édouard-Joseph (Djo) Bourgeois (1898–1937), architect and interior designer; Edgar Brandt (1880–1960), designer and artist in wrought iron; Cassandre (Adolphe Moujon) (1904–68), poster designer, typographer and painter; and Pierre Chareau (1883–1950), architect and designer.

Art Deco also reflected the new developments in 20th-century technology. Electricity, neon lighting and the reflective surface of smooth, chromium plating became standard components of an Art Deco style that can be seen in everything from cafés to local cinemas and smart international hotels. This popularization caused a number of contemporary commentators to coin the term 'Moderne' to indicate that Art Deco was a version, a mere pastiche, of something much more serious.

The popularization of Art Deco was particularly important in the United States. Everything from theatres to refrigerators got the treatment. **Hollywood** films turned the style into an enormous industry in the 1920s, while New York, the ultimate 20th-century city, celebrated Art Deco with some classic skyscrapers, including the Empire State Building and the Chrysler Building, as well as Donald Deskey's interiors for Radio City Music Hall. Art Deco style became universally popular, but it was particularly influential in jewellery design, where colour and flat geometric form could be shown off in custom-made quality pieces or cheap costume accessories. Decorative ceramics and tableware also picked up on the style, and it crossed all class divides in the 1930s.

The 1960s saw the first revival of Art Deco, with the famous London **boutique** Biba adopting a house style which used period black and gold, and in the 1970s **Postmodernist** architect Michael Graves reworked the vocabulary of Art Deco into his language of architectural components. In 2005 the **Victoria and Albert Museum** held a major exhibition on Art Deco, and the style was the subject of renewed interest and re-evaluation.

Further reading:

Benton, T., Benton, C. and Wood, G., *Art Deco 1910–1939*. London: V&A, 2003.

Brunhammer, Yvonne, *The Art Deco Style*. London: Academy Editions, 1983.

Duncan, Alastair, *Art Deco*. London: Thames & Hudson, 1988.

ART FURNITURE

A British term originally used in the 19th century to describe the furniture designed by Victorian architects which found a growing market in the expanding interest in art among the middle classes. Art Furniture was essentially a design reform movement, brought to public attention by the architecture writer Charles Locke Eastlake (1836–1906) in a series of magazine articles and books. The most popular of these, *Hints on Household Taste in Furniture, Upholstery and Other Details*, appeared in 1868, going to a fourth edition in England and to six editions in the USA. It was a manifesto in praise of overall rectilinear forms, honest construction and **geometric** ornament. Basically, the book adapted the style of designer–architects such as George Street (1824–81), Richard Norman Shaw (1831–1912) and William Burges (1827–81).

In 1867 the architect Edward William Godwin (1833–86) set up the Art Furniture Company, and ten years later he published *Art Furniture*. In this context Art Furniture now described the Anglo-Japanese style of the **Aesthetic Movement**.

In the 21st century the term might be due for a revival in a different context. There is much debate about the relationship between art and furniture, indeed between art and many design disciplines. One interesting example is an exhibition curated at the Cooper-Hewitt National Design Museum in New York in 2005 called Design ≠ Art which focused on little-known furniture pieces from the American **minimalist** artists Donald Judd, Scott Burton and Richard Tuttle and from other contemporary designers, whose work is intended for domestic and commercial use.

Further reading:

Bloemink, Barbara J., *Design ≠ Art: Functional Objects from Donald Judd to Rachel Whiteread*. London: Merrell, 2004.

Eastlake, Charles Lock, *Hints on Household Taste in Furniture, Upholstery and Other Details*. New York: Dover, 1969 [1868].

Godwin, Edward William, *Art Furniture*. London: Garland, 1978 [1877].

ARTIFICIAL INTELLIGENCE

A term used to describe the output of computers and in particular those developments which mimic human intelligence. It is the science and engineering of making intelligent machines, and especially intelligent computer programs, and is related to the similar task of using computers to understand human intelligence. AI does not have to confine itself to methods that are biologically observable but it is closely connected with a search for a robot and/or computer that can talk and communicate, an ongoing project that involves computer science, psychology and linguistics.

Further reading:

Saffer, Dan, *Designing for Interaction: Creating Smart Applications and Clever Devices*. Berkeley, CA: New Riders, 2007.

ART NOUVEAU

A sinuous, naturalistic style famous for its asymmetry and whiplash lines that was popular all over Europe at the turn of the 20th century and became the first international design style. It lasted from about 1895 to 1905, taking its name from a gallery called L'Art Nouveau, opened in Paris by Samuel Bing in 1895. Bing was a dedicated admirer of all things Japanese and had started his career selling Oriental imports. His influence was widespread, and in 1890 he organized his own pavilion at the Paris Exhibition. This was the first time that the style which would become known as Art Nouveau and its major exponents were shown to a wide audience. Later, Bing's gallery attracted international admirers and patrons, and exhibited the posters of Henri de Toulouse-Lautrec, jewellery by **Tiffany**, art glass by René Lalique and British wallpapers and fabrics by Charles Voysey and Walter Crane.

The French took the lead in embracing the style, with Emile Gallé (1846–1904) running a large workshop in Nancy that employed 300 craftsmen to produce furniture and glass. Gallé was a dedicated botanist who relished literal naturalistic details and he had a reverence for symbolism, which lay at the centre of his work. Louis Majorelle (1859–1926) also ran a factory in Nancy, and under Gallé's influence he changed his style from **Rococo Revival** to Art Nouveau. The other key French Art Nouveau exponent was Hector Guimard (1867–1942), now best remembered for his Paris Metro stations, which have come to evoke the city's *fin-de-siècle* taste. His style elaborated the theme of asymmetry and the flowing abstract ornamentation of swirls and scrolls. The most sophisticated exponent of Art Nouveau, however, was the Belgian architect Victor Horta (1861–1947), who designed all aspects of his buildings' interiors, including carpets, furniture and lighting. Horta, who designed the Belgian pavilion for the 1902 Turin Exhibition, single-handedly established Brussels as the most important European city for the new style.

Art Nouveau is now used as a general term to cover the last great 19th-century revival of the decorative arts that spread internationally from Europe to the USA. It is famous for flowing forms which derive their inspiration from nature and more than a glance backwards to the 18th-century taste for Rococo ornament. The movement acquired several names, including **Jugendstil** in Germany, Modernismo in Spain and Stile **Liberty** in Italy (the latter in honour of the London department store).

One of the most original versions of Art Nouveau can be seen in the work of the Catalan architect Antonio Gaudí (1852–1926). Working almost exclusively in and around his native city of Barcelona, Gaudí's work reflected Catalan nationalism with a highly original use of natural forms. His distinctive language of ornament established him as one of the great artist–architects of the 20th century. His original style can be seen at the Casa Battlo Apartments (1905–7), where mosaics of highly coloured glass are fully integrated into the essential structural elements of the curving roofline. Other exponents of the style include the **Glasgow School** led by Charles Rennie Mackintosh and Josef

Hoffmann and the **Wiener Werkstätte**. The German historian Nikolaus Pevsner put forward the thesis that the style had its roots in the British **Arts and Crafts Movement**, pointing to the origins of the whiplash motif in the designs of Arthur Mackmurdo (1851–1942) and Aubrey Beardsley (1872–98). The British, though, were less keen to be associated with another key element of Art Nouveau, namely the movement's sensual and often explicitly erotic imagery.

By 1905 the **avant-garde** had the movement in full retreat, and it was finally discredited by the **Modern Movement**. However, Art Nouveau's trademark elements – natural forms such as flowers and insects, the female nude and sexual symbolism – made it ideal for a 1960s revival. Reproduction posters of the style's great practitioners sold in huge numbers and were a reminder of the evocative power of sinuous decoration. This revival was particularly important for the graphics and textiles of **Psychedelia** in London and San Francisco and it continues into the 21st century.

Further reading:

Greenhalgh, Paul, *Essential Art Nouveau*. London: V&A, 2000.
Schmutzler, Robert, *Art Nouveau*. London: Thames & Hudson, 1978 [1962].

ARTS AND CRAFTS MOVEMENT

A design style and an ethical movement. The leaders of the Arts and Crafts Movement – John Ruskin (1819–1900), William **Morris** (1834–96), Walter Crane (1845–1915), R.W. Lethaby (1857–1931), Charles Robert Ashbee (1863–1942), W.A. Benson (1854–1924), Lewis Foreman Day (1845–1910), M.H. Baillie Scott (1865–1945), Charles Voysey (1857–1941) and Philip Webb (1831–1915) – and lesser figures like Ernest Gimson and A.H. Mackmurdo had grand ambitions to transform society. Increasingly, these designers saw industrialization only in terms of large, ugly cities, pollution and slum housing. They felt that the traditional values of human life were destroyed by industrial progress. This spirit of anti-industrialization was an instinctive reaction against the highly visible effects of industry.

The most important theorist and designer was William Morris. Despising the values of **capitalism** that could destroy the quality of people's lives, he became a committed socialist and the most influential thinker of his generation. Indeed, the heritage of his ideas remains with us to this day. Morris summed up his approach in a lecture at the

Birmingham Society of Arts and School of Design (19 February 1880) called 'The Beauty of Life': 'If you want a golden rule that will fit everybody, this is it: Have nothing in your houses that you do not know to be useful, or believe to be beautiful.' As a student at Oxford, he was inspired by the university architecture and the powerful romanticism of the Pre-Raphaelite painters. Some members of this group, Dante Gabriel Rossetti, Sir Edward Burne Jones and William Holman Hunt, were to remain his lifelong friends and collaborators. At first, Morris also saw himself as a painter, but soon he realized that his talents lay elsewhere. Contemporary accounts have left a picture of him as a deeply passionate man who was known for his charisma and volatile personality. His affluent family background meant that he could afford to commission furniture and architecture for his own home, and this led, in 1861, to the logical step of starting his own company, **Morris & Co.** whose first principles were truth to materials. Morris, and many likeminded designers, believed that every material has its own value: for example, the natural grain of wood or the glaze of a well-made pot. He revived traditional methods of production that in his lifetime had been superseded by new industrial processes. A workaholic who believed in hands-on experience, he spent hours teaching himself craft techniques like weaving and printing. He hated the garish synthetic dyes which had been developed by the chemical industry during the 1830s, so he set his own works at Merton Abbey in Surrey to reviving traditional vegetable dyes and printing techniques, like the discharge method used in famous prints such as *The Strawberry Thief.*

The Arts and Crafts Movement brought about a renaissance in British design and placed Britain at the heart of new design ideas. Information on the movement came in a series of exhibitions mounted by the Arts and Crafts Exhibition Society, the first of which was held in 1888 at the New Gallery in Regent Street, and in magazines like *The Studio*, which had an international readership. By 1900 the Arts and Crafts Movement had had an international impact, with Belgium and Holland being especially enthusiastic. In 1894, the Belgian writer Olivier Desirée published a study of the Pre-Raphaelites, which included an account of William Morris and Walter Crane. He concluded that only artistic developments in Britain took account of the needs of modern life. In Holland between 1898 and 1904, the architects K.P.C. de Bazel (1869–1923) and J.L.M. Lauweriks (1864–1932) published an illustrated magazine called *Bouw -en Sierkunst. Revue bimestrielle de l'art antique et moderne* in Dutch and French, which was directed to the same readership as *The Studio.* The Nederlandsche Ambachts en Nijverheids Kunst (Netherlands Association for the Crafts and Industrial Art) was founded in 1904 and published yearbooks between 1919 and 1931. *Die Togepaste Kunsten in Nederland (The Applied Arts in the Netherlands)*, a series of twenty-five illustrated monographs on the crafts, published between 1923 and 1935, demonstrates the vitality of the crafts in Holland. In Germany, the Darmstädter Künstler Kolonie (Darmstadt Artists' Colony) and the Deutsche Werkstätten für Handwerkskunst (German Handicraft Workshops) were essentially Arts and Crafts enterprises and closely resembled their British counterparts. The **Deutsche Werkbund**, though concerned primarily with large-scale industrial production, numbered many craftsmen and craftswomen among its members. The **Bauhaus**, founded in 1919, also had strong Arts and Crafts affinities, with courses organized around workshops – ceramics, metalwork, weaving and textiles, and woodwork. This entirely practical approach to the study of design was undoubtedly derived from Arts and Crafts exemplars including Lethaby's Central School of Arts and Crafts and the Birmingham School of Art. Russia also saw a series of design projects inspired by the Arts and Crafts Movement. These include Princess Marie Tenisheva's (1867–1928) Talashkino Craft Workshops and Museum, whose workshops endeavoured to revive the traditional crafts of Russian peasant society. Talashkino was, to an extent, modelled on the railway magnate Savva Mamantov's ideal cultural community of Abramtsevo, founded in the 1870s.

At the end of the nineteenth century Denmark, Finland, Norway and Sweden sought to establish distinctive artistic identities. In 1898 *Ateneum* appeared, a Finnish version of *The Studio* and the German *Pan*. In Vienna, in 1908, Swedish architects, including Bergsten, Boberg, Clason, Lallerstedt, Östberg, Tengbom, Westman and Wahlman, made a considerable impression at the International Exhibition of Architecture with designs which demonstrated a strong Arts and Crafts influence. As late as the 1930s designers and architects like Karna Asker (textiles), Gunnar Asplund (architecture, furniture and metalwork), Märtha Gahn (textiles), Wilhelm Käge (ceramics), Sigrid Kjellin (textiles), Orrefors (glass), Ragnar Östberg (architecture and interiors) and Eskil Sundahl (interiors) continued the British Arts and Crafts tradition. William Morris also influenced Switzerland, and in 1906 the Kunstgewerbe Museum in Zürich mounted an extensive exhibition of British Arts and Crafts textiles, ushering in a revival of Swiss decorative arts that was also reflected in the design curriculum at the Gewerbeschule in Zürich.

France did not develop a strong Arts and Crafts Movement. It had its own craft traditions without the ideological social underpinnings, and its great exhibition – Arts Décoratifs de Grande-Bretagne et d'Irlande – which opened in the Palais de Marsan, the Louvre, in April 1914, was obliterated by the outbreak of the Great War. Italy's response was also limited. Adolfo De Karolis, illustrator and wood-engraver, designed books for the writer Gabriele D'Annunzio which show the influence of William Morris's Kelmscott Press. Meanwhile, the architect Cavazzoni designed a number of villas in the pre-1914 era for the emerging class of industrialists which suggest that Italy was fully aware of developments in contemporary British domestic architecture. American architects such as Charles Sumner and Henry Mather Greene and the furniture designer Gustav Stickley used Morris to develop a native American Arts and Crafts style. In 1906 they completed a retirement home for the magnate David Gamble (of Procter and Gamble) in Pasadena, California, which reflected this style.

With the outbreak of the First World War the activities of the Arts and Crafts Movement came to a standstill, and in the following years the movement rapidly declined, but its ideas remain significant. The debates that so preoccupied these Victorians – craft versus machine production, and the purpose and function of design – are still important. Arts and Crafts' deep concern for social issues is also relevant. Morris saw himself as a socialist and revolutionary, and he held strong opinions that the designer has a moral responsibility in his or her work towards the greater good. He established himself as a great British figure whose ideas and designs are relevant to the our lives and to the future.

Further reading:

Naylor, Gillian, *The Arts and Crafts Movement: a Study of its Sources, Ideals and Influences on Design Theory*. London: Trefoil, 1990 [1971].
—— *William Morris by Himself: Designs and Writings*. London: Time Warner, 2004 [1988].
Todd, Pamela *The Arts and Crafts Companion*. London: Thames & Hudson, 2004.

ASSEMBLAGE

A fine-art technique, not a style, which combines two-dimensional materials and images and three-dimensional forms and objects. It became popular at the end of the 1950s in Europe and the USA. Assemblage attempts to erase the distinction between high and low art, imagery and materials. It was used to present the fragmented, diverse and rapidly expendable signs of the new consumer culture. The materials for assemblage could be natural or manufactured. The French

Nouveau-Réaliste artist Jean Dubuffet first used the term in 1953 for his assemblages of papier-mâché, scraps of wood and other debris. Other work from the Nouveau-Réaliste group included César's compressed cars, and Jean Tinqueley's mechanical assemblage, photomontage, **advertising** and **found objects**. Assemblage was particularly important in the work of American artists Robert Rauschenberg, Joseph Cornell and Louise Nevelson. This was part of the Dada revival of the late 1950s, and was used as both a tribute to and a critique of the new consumer-led society, a position that **Pop Art** was later to exploit.

Assemblage as a serious art movement was given official recognition in 1961 with the 'Art of Assemblage' show at the Museum of Modern Art in New York. The process of working with diverse objects and materials has remained central for many artists during the 1970s and 1980s, and remains a potent means of expression for the ecologically aware 21st century.

The techniques and attitudes of assemblage artworks have certainly influenced design. Most design students experiment with assemblage as a way of freeing the imagination, and several notable individualists in the areas of furniture and **interior design** employ the technique in their finished commercial work. The British architect Nigel Coates, for example, uses salvaged fragments, including aeroplanes, and recycled objects with specific references to mainstream culture in his interiors. And the Mozambican designer Kester famously used recycled guns for a series of **installation** pieces acquired by the British Museum for its new Africa Galleries in 2004.

Further reading:

Waldman, Diane, *Collage, Assemblage, and the Found Object*. London: Phaidon Press, 1992.

AUSTRIAN DESIGN

In the 19th century Vienna was at the centre of the Austrian Empire, and was famous for its flourishing cultural and intellectual life. It was also to make an important contribution to design, particularly on the difficult question of developing a style appropriate to the new 20th century. In 1873 Vienna staged a major international exhibition showing off the prevailing Austrian taste for florid **historicism**. Some ten years earlier the city had also established a museum of applied arts and a design school, following the example of the **Victoria and Albert**

Museum in London. It was not until the 1890s, however, that Viennese designers began to make a truly original contribution to design. In 1897, a breakaway group led by the painter Gustav Klimt (1862–1918) established itself as an independent artists' association. The following year Joseph Maria Olbrich designed the famous Secession Building, which became a visual symbol for progressive Austrian designers and architects. The group's magazine, *Ver Sacrum*, was also the name of a room designed by Josef Hoffmann in the 1898 Secession exhibition, and two years later the group's exhibition also included work by British designers Charles Rennie Mackintosh and Charles Ashbee. Mackintosh was to provide a particularly strong direction for progressive Austrian design, and for Hoffmann in particular.

The Österreichischer Werkbund (Austrian Work Federation), founded in 1912 with a substantial (20 per cent) female membership, was mainly concerned with the crafts. Ashbee and the **Guild** of Handicraft, meanwhile, inspired the establishment of a similar group of craftsmen and –women called the **Wiener Werkstätte** (Vienna Workshops). Hoffmann and Koloman Moser had visited the Guild in Chipping Camden and were so impressed that they persuaded a rich banker to back the Austrian equivalent. The Werkstätte's design work developed a rigorous **geometric** aesthetic, which none the less retained a place for decoration. In this respect Austrian design, until 1915, provided a significant bridge between 19th-century tradition and the **Modern Movement**.

Austria in the 21st century is a small, conservative country, but in terms of design it maintains a high profile with specialist products, such as outdoor sporting equipment, and promotes innovative education. The Academy of Fine Arts in Vienna is well known for its design teaching programmes in theory and practice, and for its studio system of teaching which has included Austrian architect and theorist Hans Hollein, the architectural practice Coop Himmelbrau and international figures such as Vivienne Westwood and Michele de Lucchi.

See also: **Wiener Werkstätte**

Further reading:

Brandstätter, Christian, *Wonderful Wiener Werkstätte: Design in Vienna, 1903–1932*. London: Thames & Hudson, 2003.
Vienne 1880–1938: L'Apocalypse joyeuse. Paris: Editions du Centre Georges Pompidou, 1986.

AUTOMATION

The replacement of human control by mechanical devices. Simple forms of mechanization include the use of computer terminals in offices, while more advanced forms allow entire production processes to be entirely controlled by machines. Processed food production, an industry which is now almost fully automated, uses the closed-loop technique, which means that raw materials are fed into one end of a machine and a finished product is delivered from the other end without any human intervention.

There are many social responses to automation. Some argue that because it reduces the number of employees needed in the workplace it contributes to unemployment. Others maintain that it de-skills a high proportion of the workforce and creates an elite who are trained to do the highly skilled design and maintenance of automated processes.

Further reading:

Braverman, Harry, *Labor and Monopoly Capital: The Degradation of Work in the Twentieth Century*. New York: Monthly Review, 1998 [1974].
Gill, Colin, *Work, Unemployment and the New Technology*. Cambridge: Polity, 1985.

AUTOMOTIVE DESIGN

This decides the important aspects of visual appearance in the design of passenger vehicles, trucks, buses and coaches. It includes both the exterior and the interior detailings, such as control panels and upholstered seating, and branding features, such as company logos and names.

According to statistics published in 2005 by the French International Organization of Motor Vehicle Manufacturers, the total world vehicle production in 2002 alone was a staggering 58,702,000. The influential design writer Victor Papanek described the impact of such automobile production on the environment as 'chilling'. Automotive design is an interdisciplinary profession requiring an understanding of styling, production engineering, metals and plastic technology and marketing. Although cars are objects with a primarily technological and functional purpose, they are much more than that for many of us: Roland Barthes called them 'purely magical'. Specialists in automotive and transport design are trained at the **Royal College of Art**, Coventry University, Pforzheim in Germany, the Center for Creative Studies in Detroit and the Art Center in Pasadena, among others.

Further reading:

Barthes, Roland, *Mythologies*. London: Vintage, 1993 [1957].
Batchelor, Ray, *Henry Ford: Mass Production, Modernism and Design*. Manchester: Manchester University Press, 1994.
Sparke, Penny, *A Century of Car Design*. London: Mitchell Beazley, 2002.
<www.autoindustry.co.uk/statistics/production/world>.

AVANT-GARDE

A French term to describe innovators and pioneers in art and design whose work is experimental or unconventional and is placed at the cutting edge of cultural practice. Avant-garde practitioners expressed themselves through innovative techniques and practice that offered difficult rather than easy modes of practice. Avant-garde work has come to be associated with outcomes that are forward thinking, ultramodern and ahead of their time. The phrase also carries more critical associations in that it can be used to describe work that is difficult to assess and elitist.

Further reading:

Belli, Gabriella (ed.), *1900–1919, The Avant-garde Movements: Art of the Twentieth Century*. London: Thames & Hudson, 2006.

BAUHAUS

A design school founded in Weimar, Germany, by Walter Gropius in 1919. It would become the most famous design school of the 20th century. Gropius changed the school from a local art academy to the Staatliches Bauhaus, and it became a centre for new ideas in both art and design. Later, it moved to Dessau, opening for business on 4 December 1926. The new buildings, confident and articulate manifestations of the new age, were designed by Gropius and they were his most important contribution to Modernism. The Dessau site provided a complete Modernist lifestyle for staff and students. The furnishings, including the studios and canteen, were tubular-steel designs created under the direction of Marcel Breuer, head of the joinery workshop. The lamp fittings, designed by Marianne Brandt, came from the school's metal workshops.

Gropius attracted some of the most important art and design practitioners of the **Modern Movement**, including Wassily Kandinsky, Johannes Itten, Paul Klee and Herbert Bayer. Post-war histories of the

Bauhaus stressed a single Modern Movement approach to design, a dedication to pure **geometric** forms based on the circle and the square, the primary colours of red, blue and yellow, modern materials and industrial production techniques. But that view edited out the complex and diverse arguments that beset the school, and the fact that the hardline Modernist position was always balanced by **Expressionist** theories, and in the case of Itten by a belief in mysticism and alternative religions. Furthermore, Gropius himself was deeply influenced by British **Arts and Crafts** thinking. The curriculum consisted of a broadly based foundation year, followed by craft specializations, a principle that is now the basis for **design education** all over the world.

The Bauhaus remained a small, exclusive training school until 1932, when the last director, Mies van der Rohe, took it to Berlin, where it continued for just one year. The Dessau complex subsequently became a training school for the Nazis. During its fourteen-year life the Bauhaus trained only 1,250 students, many of them foreigners, whose fees helped to support the school. With the rise of Nazism, many Bauhaus staff left to begin a new life in the USA. Gropius, for example, built some of his most important buildings in North America, and as Professor of Architecture at Harvard University his philosophy influenced an entire generation of American students. Van der Rohe settled in Chicago, as did László Moholy-Nagy. The latter founded the 'New Bauhaus' there in 1937. Teachers included Americans as well as former Bauhaus staff such as György Kepes. Serge Chermayeff succeeded Moholy-Nagy as director, followed in 1955 by the industrial designer Jay Doblin. Having been renamed the Institute of Design, the school is now part of the Illinois Institute of Technology.

After the war, Dessau became part of East Germany, and thus came under communist rule. Some of the Bauhaus buildings fell into dereliction, but one wing became a trade school. In 1976 the buildings were partially restored to become a hostel for visiting tourists. Then, in the autumn of 1989, the political tide turned. East and West Germany were unified, and the resulting liberalization resulted in the Bauhaus reopening as a design institution. Some fifty-six years after its forced closure, the new director, Professor Rolf Kuhn, announced plans to restore buildings, organize exhibitions and seminars, and open an experimental design workshop and a centre for new ideas and progressive design.

Further reading:

Smock, William, *The Bauhaus Ideal, Then and Now: An Illustrated Guide to Modern Design*. Chicago: Academy Chicago, 2004.

Whitford, Frank (ed.), *The Bauhaus: Masters & Students by Themselves*. London: Conran Octopus, 1992 [1984].

BOUTIQUES

Small, independent fashion shops that helped to revolutionize fashion **retailing** in the 1950s and 1960s. They introduced important new design trends in clothes, graphics and **interior design** to a wider public.

In 1964 the American magazine *Time* coined the phrase 'Swinging London' and published a tourist map which highlighted the city's new boutiques and nightclubs rather than the traditional tourist attractions. These new shops centred on three now legendary London streets – the King's Road, Carnaby Street and Kensington High Street – and they were given wacky names like Granny Takes a Trip, I Was Lord Kitchener's Valet, Hung on You and Gear.

The boutique has now come to represent the 1960s, with its explosion of youthful creativity and entrepreneurial spirit, but the retail revolution it represented had its roots in the 1940s. The name derives from the small shops of the Parisian Left Bank, which sold clothes of their own design. In the early 1950s British clothes, by contrast, were sold solely by department or chain stores. Fashion was the preserve of adults, and adolescent boys and girls were expected to dress like their parents. The emergence of teenage culture changed all that. In 1955 Mary Quant opened Bazaar, a shop selling her own clothes, on the King's Road. It was an immediate success and others quickly followed. Bill Green opened another pioneer shop called Vince in Foubert Place, off Regent Street, which sold imported Continental casual clothes. One of his assistants, John Stephens, went on to open a series of boutiques in Carnaby Street. These were the beginnings of the huge explosion of 1960s boutiques that started in London but quickly spread throughout Britain. By 1970, there were estimated to be 15,000 boutiques throughout the country.

As well as marketing the new clothes of the 1960s, boutiques contributed to important changes in interior design. Like stage sets, they were designed as **installations**, reflecting the new **Pop design**. They played pop music, employed young staff and aimed for a rapid turnover of stock. Barbara Hulanicki's Biba, with its dark, moody **Art Deco** interior, was particularly important because it marketed a complete design image. In 1968 John McConnell designed the famous black-and-gold Biba logo, inspired by Celtic imagery, with a mail-order catalogue in the same style. In 1969 Tommy Roberts asked designer Jon Wealleans to create a **Pop Art** interior, using inflatable false teeth and Disney characters, for his boutique Mr Freedom. Such innovations affected the way the more powerful department stores sold clothes. For instance, in 1967 Harrods opened its own boutique, called Way-In, with a keyhole logo designed by the international consultancy Minale Tattersfield.

The heritage of the boutiques survives in a series of specialized, luxury fashion shops. Notting Hill in London has several of these independent retail outlets, including Lulu Guinness and Matthew Williamson.

Further reading:

Fogg, Marnie, *Boutique: A '60s Cultural Phenomenon*. London: Mitchell Beazley, 2003.

Levy, Shawn, *Ready, Steady, Go! Swinging London and the Invention of Cool*. London: Fourth Estate, 2003.

BRITISH EXHIBITIONS

In the early 19th century Britain had no tradition of design exhibitions to compare with that of the Continent, particularly the successful Paris Exhibitions of the 1840s. In 1845, however, Prince Albert set up a committee to explore the possibilities. At first small events were organized, but in 1849 the Prince decided on a larger scheme, which eventually resulted in the **Great Exhibition** of 1851. Eleven years later London staged another international event, designed by Captain Fowke and decorated by J.G. Crace. This exhibition included a section on **Japan** and saw the emergence of a new, professional group of British designers, including R.N. Shaw, Philip Webb and William Burges. In retrospect, the exhibition of 1862 rather than that of 1851 marked the pinnacle of high Victorian design. It was followed by exhibitions of lesser importance in the early 1870s, and then the era of international exhibitions in Britain came to a halt. **Avant-garde** designers turned instead to the **Arts and Crafts** Exhibition Society as an outlet to show their work.

In the 20th century, however, British exhibitions enjoyed a revival. The most important official event was the 1924 British Empire Exhibition, held at Wembley in West London. Sir Laurence Weaver organized the displays, and one of the most popular exhibits was a life-size model of the Prince of Wales carved out of New Zealand butter. Inevitably, soon unfavourable comparisons were made with the ground-breaking Paris 1925 Exhibition, and it was felt that Britain's design lead, so strong in the 1890s, had slipped away.

In 1933 *Country Life* magazine sponsored the first exhibition of British **Modernism** with a **minimal** flat by Wells Coates and furniture by R.D. Russell. The **Design and Industries Association** also organized numerous design exhibitions, but the largest event of the 1930s was the 1938 Empire Exhibition held in Glasgow, which included over a hundred pavilions and palaces. The timing of this exhibition was hardly fortuitous, but the onset of the Second World War did not end Britain's plans for future design exhibitions. In 1944 the government set up the Council of **Industrial Design** to promote better standards of British products. Two years later, the **Victoria and Albert Museum** reopened its doors with an exhibition called Britain Can Make It (BCMI). This introduced the British public to the post-war belief that design was a key tool in the struggle to rebuild the country. It also promoted the novel idea that designers should step out of their traditional anonymous role and explain themselves and their activities to the public.

BCMI was organized on a shoestring budget, but just the opposite was the case with the exhibition that celebrated the centenary of the Great Exhibition. Called the **Festival of Britain**, it was built under the auspices of the Labour government on London's South Bank, with Sir Gerald Barry as director and Sir Hugh Casson in charge of design. It introduced the public to the idea of **Contemporary** style and proved to be a great popular success. Fifty years later, another Labour government staged a public exhibition in the Millennium Dome, but that event attracted much criticism and did not achieve anything like the attendance that had been predicted.

Further reading:

Hoffenberg, Peter, *An Empire on Display: English, Indian and Australian Exhibitions from the Crystal Palace to the Great War*. Berkeley: University of California Press, 2001.

CAD

Computer-aided design (CAD) is the use of programs to facilitate designers in the development of their work. It is a tool to design and develop products. Two associated terms are CAID (computer-aided **industrial design**) and CAAD (computer-aided architectural design).

CAD has transformed the design profession very quickly. As recently as the early 1990s, it was the responsibility of trained draftsmen to draw up detailed plans for buildings, products and machines before they were built. Design studios used traditional drawing boards and technical instruments, Rotring pens and measuring equipment to represent their ideas. Less than twenty years later, these have vanished from the design and manufacturing industries, replaced by the computers and software programs used by specialist designers and engineers.

CAD was pioneered in the 1970s by the space and aircraft industries, which first used the technique for commercial applications. The car industry followed suit, but only large companies could afford the technical investment needed at the time. These early experiments with CAD were limited to fairly simple 2D drawings, but in the 1980s solid modelling opened more potential. CAD now offers a diverse range of programs from 2D vector-based drafting systems to high-end 3D hybrid systems. Each of the design disciplines has embraced the potential of CAD, from pattern cutting in fashion to **interior design**. Here, CAD offers the client everything from concept drawings to final working drawings, which include CAD-generated, detailed electrical and structural specifications. High levels of visual analysis allow the designer to use CAD as a highly creative tool, and other facilities help to create images of the work, including the fly-through technique. CAD capabilities now range across freeform surface modelling, output of data straight to manufacturing facilities and rapid **prototyping** for industrial modules.

Product design is the design sector which has seen the greatest change through the introduction of CAD. Virtually all consumer goods are now produced using a CAD system at the visualization and rapid prototyping stages, and it allows standardized production in the global market. A product might now be designed in London, manufactured in Taiwan and sold in America. This international and standardized production and materials language is an essential element in getting products on to the market faster and at less cost.

Further reading:

Martegani, Paolo and Montenegro, Riccardo, *Digital Design: New Frontiers for the Objects*. Basel: Birkhäuser, 2000.

Peng, Chengzhi, *Design through Digital Interaction: Computing Communications and Collaboration on Design*. Bristol: Intellect, 2003.

CAMP

A design style that uses obvious bad taste in a spirit of mocking irony. Camp is perceived as having a gay sensibility and it is important for design because it contributed to a wider **Postmodernist** move to undermine traditional hierarchies of taste. Susan Sontag's essay 'Notes on Camp' (1964) is the most important piece of writing on the subject, defining the ultimate camp statement: 'it's good because it's awful'. Among the things Sontag cites as 'Camp' are: Aubrey Beardsley drawings, Edward Burne-Jones, Greta Garbo, Ernest B. Schoedsack's *King Kong* (1933) and **Tiffany** lamps. Sontag argues, 'Camp is the consistently aesthetic experience of the world. It incarnates a victory of "style" over content, over "aesthetics", over "morality", of irony over tragedy. Camp taste is by its nature possible only in affluent societies, in societies capable of experiencing the psychopathology of affluence.'

Camp is also used to describe the excessive behaviour associated with certain kinds of effeminate homosexuality. Male drag artists, for example, exploit it in their performances. On the other hand, the sumptuous **Art Deco** set designs of Erté reflect authentic theatrical camp, as do Salvador Dalí's set designs for *Salome*. Indeed, Camp design often involves an element of exaggerated theatricality. Fashionable interior decorators often work in a Camp idiom in that they make entirely inappropriate and overdramatic references in their designs. Camp design can also exploit the idea of using elements once considered beautiful or valid but now thought ridiculously sentimental or old fashioned. In this respect it overlaps with **kitsch**.

The use of Camp references often involves a knowing self-consciousness, noted in cult film director John Waters' ironic observation: 'In order to acquire bad taste one must first have very, very good taste.' Camp can often be an amusing dismissal of certain kinds of design and sensibility, so as a description it should be used with care because of the imprecision of its definition. In its purist form, however, it offers the territory of 'over-the-top', of design without rules, which challenges the status quo and as such has been explored by many Postmodernist designers.

Camp as a design sensibility may be seen in the world of **advertising** and marketing and somewhat less so in furniture and **product design**. It offers a kind of taste liberation. For other designers it is another aspect of social taste that includes irony and self-mockery. Such products are generally found in upmarket designer shops rather than in mass-market retailers such as Ikea. Camp celebrates the inept and the naïve – *Come Dancing, The Eurovision Song Contest, Riverdance, The Sound of Music* and faux-leopard-fur throws – but to perceive these as Camp relies on the attitude of the consumer.

Further reading:

Bergman, David (ed.), *Camp Grounds: Style and Homosexuality*. Amherst: University of Massachusetts Press, 1993.

Cleto, Fabio (ed.), *Camp: Queer Aesthetics and the Performing Subject: A Reader*. Edinburgh: Edinburgh University Press, 1999.

Sontag, Susan, *Against Interpretation and Other Essays*. London: Vintage, 1994 [1967].

CAPITALISM

The history of capitalism and the history of design are inter-woven. Design production and **consumption** can be seen as the outcomes of the capitalist system – an economic system characterized by a free market, commodity production, competition and profit, and controlled by the ownership of capital and the purchasing power to hire employees and run factories. The word was coined by Karl Marx in the 19th century as a term of abuse, and this negative meaning continued throughout the 20th century.

Since the **Industrial Revolution**, discussion has focused on the role of the worker in the capitalist system. **Adam Smith** described a process called 'division of labour', which the American economist Harry Braverman used as the starting point for his left-wing theory in 1974. Braverman argued that capitalist production aims to deprive workers of control in the labour process and give it to managers. The work is subdivided into small tasks, so workers, even white-collar staff, are progressively de-skilled. The workers' struggle in the workplace is not so much a concern with wages as with attempts to retain their skill and control over production. The German philosopher Herbert Marcuse (1898–1979) put forward another view. He argued that 20th-century society generated artificial needs, and that industrial capitalism did not allow the existence of the individual or a full spiritual life for the working class.

However, with the changing political landscape in China and the break-up in the 1990s of the Soviet Union, old positions have changed. It is now argued that an efficient, modern economic system that does not allow the potential to exploit workers can raise standards of living. In the 21st century 'capitalism' is now used to describe the potential freedom and opportunities it can offer, and design is part of that new world.

Further reading:

Braverman, Harry, *Labor and Monopoly Capital: The Degradation of Work in the Twentieth Century*. New York: Monthly Review, 1998 [1974].

Marcuse, Herbert, *The Aesthetic Dimension: Toward a Critique of Marxist Aesthetics*. London: Macmillan, 1979.

Marx, Karl, *The Communist Manifesto*. London: Penguin, 2003 [1848].

Smith, Adam, *The Wealth of Nations*. New York: Random House, 2003 [1776].

CCI

Centre de Création Industrielle, now widely known as the Pompidou Centre, is the design showplace of Paris. Designed by Richard Rogers and Renzo Piano in 1977 and named after a former French president, its purpose is to educate the public and schoolchildren about the designed environment. Its first director was the writer François Burckhart, former head of IDZ-Berlin, Germany's government-sponsored showcase for modern design. In recent years the Pompidou Centre has mounted an important series of exhibitions exploring both **design history** and contemporary issues. Particularly notable among these has been a series highlighting the cultural achievements of individual cities, including Vienna and Berlin.

Further reading:

Silver, Nathan, *The Making of Beaubourg: A Building Biography of the Centre Pompidou*, Paris. Cambridge, MA: MIT Press, 1994.

CHAOS

A theory deriving from the scientific world, but which has also been explored as an attitude to design. The theories and ideas of chaos were developed at Harvard University from the 1960s onwards. This scientific community included David Ruelle, Edward Lorenz, Mitchell Feigenbaum, Steve Smale and James A. Yorke. Chaos is a mathematical theory of nonlinear dynamical systems that describes strange attractors and chaotic motions. In simple terms, it suggests that we have only just begun to understand the complex chain reactions of events and natural phenomena present in nature. The classic example of such complexity is generally cited as the 'butterfly effect': when a butterfly flaps its wings on one continent it can have unexpected final effects on another. Such ideas are the paradigm of, for example, the rational world of Newtonian physics. One of the best-known publications on the subject is *The Practical Geometry of Nature* (1980) by Harvard scientist Benoit B. Mandelbrot.

Literary concepts of chaos go back even further than the 1960s. In the 19th century the French poet Charles Baudelaire referred to 'moving chaos' in one of his poems. In the 1920s *Ulysses*, by the Irish novelist James Joyce, was accused of being chaotic, while Dadaists talked about returning to 'some kind of chaos'. This tradition was kept alive by the Situationists in the 1960s, and **Punk** inherited some of that way of thinking in the Sex Pistols' slogan 'Cash from Chaos'.

Increasingly, it has become fashionable to apply the attitude, rather than perhaps the methodology, of chaos to the world of design. The term 'creative chaos' began to be used in the 1980s for a position against a single and ordered view of design. One notable theorist in this area is the 1960s activist Marshall Berman, who wrote the influential *All That is Solid Melts into Air* (1982). Berman mixed literary, sociological and architectural studies in his reappraisal of the city. His pluralist approach suggested to many designers that one should go with and exploit the cultural flow of chaos; indeed, that chaos could be a much richer source of ideas than any attempt to impose order and structure.

The resonance of creative chaos can now be seen throughout the world. For example, it is a theme in the work of Japanese architects and designers such as Arata Isozaki and Shiro Kuramata, as well as in the American Frank Gehry's Guggenheim Museum in Bilbao, Spain. Elsewhere in Europe, creative chaos as a theme can be identified in the work of many contemporary architects and designers, including Zaha Hadid and Michele de Lucchi. Chaos is not a design movement in itself but one aspect of the pluralism implied by **Postmodernism** and its relationship to cultural history in general.

Further reading:

Berman, Marshall, *All That is Solid Melts into Air: The Experience of Modernity*. New York: Simon & Schuster, 1982.

Lorenz, Edward N., *The Essence of Chaos*. London: UCL Press, 1995.

Mandelbrot, Benoit B., *The Fractal Geometry of Nature*. Oxford: Freeman, 1982.

Marcus, Greil, *Lipstick Traces: A Secret History of the Twentieth Century*. London: Picador, 1997 [1989].

Ruelle, David, *Chance and Chaos*. Harmondsworth: Penguin, 1993 [1991].

CHICAGO SCHOOL

A group of architects who built the first skyscrapers in Chicago between 1880 and 1900. The term also refers to the buildings and influence of Frank Lloyd Wright, although he concentrated on private commissions for houses rather than high-rise buildings. After the great fire of 1871 in Chicago attention was paid to making architecture safe and suitable for the city's fast-growing reputation as a commercial centre. William Lebaron Jenney and Louis Sullivan developed a version of high-rise functional **classicism** that was ultimately replaced by a taste for the Beaux Arts style and **Art Deco**. The city, however, continued to enjoy a reputation for progress and modernity. In 1933–4 it held the Chicago Century of Progress Exposition, which, although affected by the economic recession, offered a vision of the future via the potential of technology and design that caught the public imagination and further enhanced the reputation of the city.

Further reading:

Peisch, Mark L., *The Chicago School of Architecture: Early Followers of Sullivan and Wright*. London: Phaidon Press, 1964.

CHINA

The history of China in the last fifty years has been violent and tragic, as the country has struggled to come to terms with historic problems alongside the rapid development of a modern industrial and consumer society. Its staggering rate of growth is reflected in the claim that China is now the second-largest economy in the world.

Historically, Chinese architecture and design have shaped the world, along with Chinese arts and sciences. In the 20th century the Communists under Mao Zedong established strict controls over people, trade and culture, and China's economy was a centrally planned system including collectivized agriculture, largely closed to international trade. After 1978, Mao's successor, Deng Xiaoping, allowed a market-oriented economy and a burgeoning private sector, a diversified banking system, stock markets, foreign trade and investment, all of which contributed to the country's dynamic economic growth. This phenomenon is reflected in China's capacity to manufacture consumer goods, clothes, cars, domestic appliances and so on. 'Made in China' is now marked on the majority of everyday objects in Western homes.

Contemporary Chinese design has a much lower profile. There has been significant investment in **design education** and cultural institutions, but as yet there are no distinctive Chinese global brands or well-known Chinese designers. However, there have been high-profile achievements in art and film, and in 1993, for the first time, a group of contemporary Chinese artists showed their work at the Venice Biennale. Meanwhile, Chinese fashion designers beginning to establish a worldwide reputation include Wu Haiyan, Zhang Tian'ai (with Tian Art) and Zhang Zhaoda (with his brand Mark Cheung). In 2006 Bund 18, a 1923 neo-classical bank, won a Unesco heritage award for its conversion into a high-end fashion store, including Lavie, Ji Cheng's fashion label and Lu Kun's menswear label Lukan. There is also a group of designers who have trained and now work abroad but retain a keen sense of Chinese identity in interior, product and graphic design. Best known is the Hong Kong designer Alan Chan (Chen You Ian), whose company Alan Chan Design is listed by *Graphis* magazine in its top ten design companies in the world. Steve Leung (Lang Haitian) is famous for his **minimal interior design** inspired by the simplicity of China's Ming Dynasty designs. Deng Kunyan is an architect from Taiwan whose studio is located in Shanghai's new cultural quarter along the Suzhou River, which imitates the loft developments of SoHo in New York. Han Jiaying's posters are used for *Frontiers* magazine and have won several international awards. And Shao Fan, an artist and furniture designer who combines classical Chinese design with contemporary work, was the only Chinese designer at the 2004 Salon du Meuble de Paris.

China has rapidly expanded its design education: the first Design programme was launched at Hunan University in the early 1980s, but now over 400 Chinese schools offer similar courses including Qinghua University, China's premier institution, which has a huge building of 60,000 square metres for its Design students, and Art Academic in Guangzhou, which teaches 3,000 Design students. In 2001 China also set up a national award called the China Enterprise Products Creative Design Award and a forum for **industrial design** in Shenzhen.

One key problem for China has been the lack of national product brands in the market, but this is starting to change. Bird is a successful Chinese mobile phone company which has become an international brand in the sector; Lenovo dominates the domestic personal computer market; and Haier, China's biggest manufacturer of domestic appliances, aims to build partnerships with Sanyo and Samsung to achieve wider global recognition. Fashion brands such as Anta and Great Wall have yet to impact on the international market, but they look likely to lead a distinctly Chinese approach to design. It seems certain that the label

'Designed in China' will soon be almost as familiar as the ubiquitous 'Made in China'.

Further reading:

Hutton, Will, *The Writing on the Wall: China and the West in the 21st Century*. London: Little, Brown, 2007.
Leece, Sharon, *China Modern*. Hong Kong: Tuttle, 2002.
Smith, Karen, *Nine Lives: The Birth of Avant-Garde Art in New China*. Zurich: Scalo, 2005.

CIAM

The Congrès Internationaux d'Architecture Moderne was an international congress of architects which was active from 1928 to 1953. Its members included the architects, apostles and teachers of the **Modern Movement**, who debated and established the movement's ideas. In all, ten conferences were held, including most notably Frankfurt (1929), Brussels (1930), Athens (1933) and Paris (1937). The subjects under discussion were always rigorously modern, such as mass housing schemes, the planning of cities and the standardization of furniture. The Swiss architect Karl Moser (1860–1936) was the first CIAM president, with Le Corbusier, Mart Stam, Gerrit Rietveld and El Lissitsky among its first members.

Further reading:

Mumford, Eric, *The CIAM Discourse on Urbanism, 1928–1960*. Cambridge, MA: MIT Press, 2000.

CLASSIC DESIGN

A modern label which seeks to identify the enduring objects of 20th- and 21st-century design, those which have stood the test of time and critical approval. The term also includes objects from earlier periods: Thonet bentwood chairs and **Shaker** objects, for example. These objects all share common elements: they reflect a set of approved models and suggest values outside the vagaries of fashion. Classic, however, can also have other, very different meanings. In the 19th century, when **scientific materialism** was having a profound intellectual impact, Darwin's theory about survival of the fittest was applied to design, with the idea that certain objects deserved to survive on merit alone. Although the word 'classic' was not used by the Victorians, its sense was implied, and this viewpoint underlay Nikolaus Pevsner's book *Pioneers of Modern Design* (1936). The **Modern Movement** also subscribed to this view in that leading architects and designers selected objects they felt embodied the values of excellence. Le Corbusier, for example, revered Thonet's mass-produced bentwood chair and used it in a number of his interiors. From the 1930s onwards this attitude was also reflected in the collecting policy of the Museum of Modern Art in New York.

The concept of classic was also used to commercial ends by manufacturers who saw a market for reproductions of the work of 20th-century designers such as Charles Rennie Mackintosh and Marcel Breuer. The furniture company Cassina has produced a series of reproductions, including Gerrit Rietveld's red–blue chair and copies of Eileen Gray and Christopher Dresser pieces. This category of classic, however, is still reliant on contemporary taste rather than an absolute standard. None the less, 'classic' implies that the object has stepped out of the issues of style and taste and that its integrity survives within the wider context of the century. These qualities are strong marketing tools, and in the 1990s there was a proliferation of designer shops selling 'classic' products. The Museum of Modern Art shop in New York is an interesting example: objects ranging from pens to tableware are automatically granted classic status simply by appearing there. International auction houses such Philips de Pury and Luxembourg now have New York 21st-century design departments to sell classic designs by Ron Arad and Marc Newson. The term 'classic' is used by such companies to imply investment potential.

See also: **cult objects**

Further reading:

Camden Arts Centre, *Classics of Modern Design: A Camden Arts Centre Exhibition, 28 October–18 December 1977*. London: Arkwright Arts Trust, 1977.

Pevsner, Nikolaus, *Pioneers of Modern Design: From William Morris to Walter Gropius*. London: Yale University Press, 2005 [1936].

CLASSICISM

A reverence for the architecture and art of Greece and Rome has always been a key element in Western design. During the 18th century archaeological discoveries such as Pompeii helped to spark off a new interpretation of the style, often referred to as Neo-classicism. This was seen in the designs of Robert Adam, Thomas Chippendale and Thomas Hope. Although Classicism was not popular after the mid-19th century, it none the less remained a constant source of inspiration and ideas for designers. In the early 20th century Classicism was a theme in the work of Modernist designers such as Le Corbusier and Walter Gropius, and was an important element in the work of Mies van der Rohe. More recently, Classicism has emerged as an important source for contemporary architects and designers developing an aesthetic for the 21st century. Notable here is the architect Norman Foster and his range of international high-rise buildings inspired by the Classical tradition.

Further reading:

Jenkins, David (ed.), *On Foster – Foster on*. London: Prestel, 2000.

COMMERCIAL ART

An obsolete term for what is now described as poster, **packaging**, display and **advertising** design. The term itself was an uneasy Victorian invention, the word 'commercial' being intended to relegate these areas of graphic design to a lowly status. Its use, however, survived well into the 20th century. The magazine *Commercial Art*, founded in 1922, survived into the 1930s.

COMMUNICATION DESIGN

The transfer of information using visual language. Communication design is a relatively new term now widely used in **design education** to describe the expanded role of the old-style graphic designer. As communication needs become increasingly complex, communication design describes a design process that extends the possibilities of visual communication to develop new skills using both traditional and current technologies. Communication design responds to the new digital communication environment that is both global and multi-disciplinary in order to meet the needs of evolving cultural networks.

The communication inventions and developments of the 20th century – including the refinement of 19th-century inventions – have transformed all but the most remote parts of the world. The telephone, for example, invented in 1876 by Alexander Graham Bell, has now developed into the mobile phone revolution of the 21st century. The typewriter, invented by Latham Schools in 1866 and first manufactured by Remington, transformed not only the centuries-old reliance on pen and ink but the organization of the office, and facilitated the drive towards increased speed and efficiency. Nowadays, the typewriter survives as the keyboard attached to a personal computer with the same QWERTY letter layout; however, with the introduction of voice recognition and scanning its future looks uncertain. Public broadcasting, the cinema, television and the ability to play and record music in the home also brought fundamental and dramatic change in the 20th century. In 1896 Guglielmo Marconi patented a system that used a wireless connection. By the 1920s, this had led to the establishment of the British Broadcasting Corporation in the UK. From the large, cumbersome radio sets of the 1930s evolved the transistors of the 1950s and the recent generation of MP3 players.

Few technological advances have played such a decisive role as computers. Initially, these offered very limited options and were designed to solve specific problems. A famous pioneer was Charles Babbage (1791–1871), whose 'analytical engine' was the earliest example of a programmable computer. In 1840, Ada Byron, Countess of Lovelace (Byron's daughter), wrote a program for this machine and can therefore be termed the world's first computer programmer. A century later, digital computers accepted the input of numbers, processed these by means of programs, and presented their output in the form of numbers. These cumbersome machines were slowly refined, with the invention of the silicon chip in the 1960s enabling cheap and portable computer technology to develop.

Communication design as a design discipline stresses the importance of experimentation within the framework of the contemporary design profession and the redefinition of traditional design areas, exploring new relationships between text, image and new technologies. It also encompasses **information design**, which focuses on making complex information, such as that required for forms, spreadsheets and databases, easier to understand.

Further reading:

Horn, Robert E., *Visual Language: Global Communication for the 21st Century*. Bainbridge Island, D.C.: MacroVu Press, 1998.

Poynor, Rick, *Design without Boundaries: Visual Communication in Transition*. London: Booth-Clibborn, 2002.

COMPUTER GAMES

In 2004, PriceWaterhouseCoopers, the international consulting firm, identified the computer and video games industries as the fastest-growing sector in a $1.3 trillion global entertainments industry.

The computer and video game design industry is still relatively new. It can be traced to the 1950s and 1960s, and the work of pioneers including William Higginbotham and Steve Russell. Higginbotham created one of the first video games in 1958, while he was the head of the Instrumentation Division at the American Brookhaven National Laboratory, to entertain visitors during open days. Russell used an MIT PDP-1 mainframe computer to design *SpaceWar!*, the first game intended for computer use, in 1962. In 1972, Nolan Bushnell, widely credited as the originator of computer games, and Ted Dabney set up Atari Computers and created the first arcade game, based on *Spacewar!* The same year, the first commercial video game console, programmed with twelve games that could be played in the home, the Odyssey, was released by Magnavox. Its designer was Ralph Baer. In the 1960s, he had written the first video game played on a television set while working for Sanders Associates, a military electronics firm. Further technological landmarks came with the development of electronic systems that utilized the new microchip, invented by Robert Noyce for the Fairchild Semiconductor Corporation. On 17 June 1980, Atari's *Asteroids* and *Lunar Lander* were launched as the first two video games for arcade use.

The development of the culture and technology of computer and video game designs has been incredibly rapid. The design, production, marketing and socio-cultural impacts of interactive entertainment and communication are all important areas: Computer games have benefited from advances in **artificial intelligence** research; the development of computer graphics and sound technology; the evolution of techniques and genres of computer game design; business competition; the micro-computer revolution; networked gaming; the continued evolution of software and hardware; marketing innovation; gendering of games and game play; simulation; and technology transfer (and military simulations). The evolution and popularity of computer games is closely linked to the emergence of the Nintendo GameBoy and Sony PlayStation in the 1990s.

Further reading:

Curran, Steve, *Game Plan: Ten Designs that Changed the Face of Computer Gaming*. Hove: RotoVision, 2004.

McCarthy, D., Curran, S. and Byron, S., *The Complete Guide to Game Development, Art, and Design*. Lewes: Ilex, 2005.

CONCEPT DESIGN

The stage in the process of designing and manufacturing products between the initial design proposal and **prototyping**. While the concept design embodies the designer's idea and intention, at this stage its appearance, form and function may not be fully resolved. The term also refers to non-functioning design models for promotional purposes, used by manufacturers as marketing devices in exhibitions and publications. Concept designs are models that look like mass-produced items but are not put into production and are intended to publicize and promote the company's strategies and brand. In this respect they have a long history: concept designs manufactured to show off a company's vision and ambition can be traced back to extravagant products displayed in the **Great Exhibition** of 1851. Concept designs that engage the consumer with tantalizing glimpses of the future have always been a popular element at trade shows, particularly for **transport design** and products for the home. Car design is an area in which concept designs are widely used to enhance a manufacturer's image. An example is Marc Newson's 021C concept car for the **Ford** Motor Company, launched at the International Furniture Fair (2000) in Milan. The focus of the 021C was publicity, not car production, with car interiors designed by Newson and produced by B&B Italia, including custom-made luggage in orange patent leather by Prada. This concept design did its job by attracting huge media coverage.

Further reading:

Keinonen, T., Takala, R. and Jaasko, V. (eds), *Product Concept Design: A Review of the Conceptual Design of Products in Industry*. London: Springer, 2005.

CONCURRENT DESIGN

A recent term describing a design and development approach for manufacturers that combines design, technology and engineering services. It suggests to the client a holistic and more efficient service for commercial and industrial products.

CONSERVATION

The protection and preservation of our architectural heritage. In recent years conservation has become a powerful political issue, but these concerns go back to the 19th century, which saw the growth of numerous societies and organizations dedicated to the conservation of old buildings and the landscape. The Society for the Conservation of Ancient Buildings was founded in 1877 following a letter to *The Times* from William Morris. Currently, the most important British conservation body is the National Trust, now the largest landowner in Britain, with 540,000 acres and 292 properties open to the public, 87 of them large houses. It was formally registered in 1895 and acquired its first property four years later. Other conservation bodies followed in its wake: the Ancient Monuments Society (1921), the Council for the Protection of Rural England (1926) and the Georgian Group (1937). In the postwar period the conservation brief on buildings was widened to include Victorian architecture, and the Victorian Society, founded in 1957, was particularly important in this work. In 1979, the Thirties Society was established, and more recently campaigns have been launched by the Twentieth Century Society to save important examples of 1950s and 1960s architecture.

Although the preservation of heritage buildings is essential, many people argue for a balance and do not subscribe to the opinion that any building more than fifty years old is better than a modern one. This fierce debate found a focus in a 1980s test case in which Peter Palumbo attempted to redevelop a site in the City of London. The unremarkable Victorian architecture he proposed to replace with a Modernist office block was passionately defended by many people, with the resulted being that Palumbo's planning applications were blocked. This was a prime example of conservation impeding the development of contemporary architecture.

Further reading:

Larkham, Peter J., *Conservation and the City*. London: Routledge, 1996.

CONSTRUCTIVISM

The principal Russian contribution to the ideas of the **Modern Movement**. After the 1917 Revolution in Russia the Bolsheviks deprived landowners and landlords of their property and abolished the previous capitalist system of production and distribution of goods. They sought the means to feed, clothe and adequately maintain the huge population of the Soviet Union as befitted the new workers' state. Thus, socially organized production was coupled with democratic planning through soviets (workers' committees). These organizations had developed during the Revolution as the most democratic means of decision-making. Delegates from local soviets would represent their views at regional and national levels, but they were subject to recall and replacement by the locality. Using this system, the production of goods could be related to the needs of the population at local and national levels.

The Revolution led to a huge burst of energy in all the arts, with a range of styles given free rein. Art and design were seen as linked, along with architecture, film, theatre and photography. Painters and sculptors who had previously worked within the confines of their own discipline now worked alongside designers and architects in helping to rebuild the new society. However, few large projects were realized in the early days as the Soviet Union suffered invasion, civil war and terrible economic problems. The provision of food and shelter, together with defence of the Revolution, had to be prioritized above cultural activity. Constructivist work, however, did play a key role in the development of European Modernism, with Russian designers communicating closely with the Dutch **De Stijl** group, as well as contributing to published journals and exhibitions. Constructivists also left Russia to work abroad, at the **Bauhaus**, for instance. In 1925 the Paris Exposition des Arts Décoratifs was a rare international showcase for Russian design. Konstantin Melnikov (1890–1974) designed the USSR pavilion, which contained Rodchenko's design for a workers' club, with distinctive interior and furnishings that drew wide admiration for their original and confident approach.

Russia, however, was moving towards a political situation that would not encourage the **avant-garde**. Finally, this led to the rise of the bureaucracy and its political representative, Josef Stalin. Brutal Stalinist repression sounded the death knell of the social and artistic aspirations of the Russian Revolution. Nearly eighty years later, however, Russian Constructivism remains a powerful force in modern design. In the late 1970s a series of books and exhibitions brought this work to the attention of Western designers, and contemporary graphic designers continue to be inspired by the work of female designers Liubov Popova (1889–1924) and Varvara Stepanova (1894–1958), as well as Aleksandr Rodchenko (1891–1956), El Lissitzky (1890–1941) and Kasimir Malevich (1878–1935). The sheer brilliance of the work of these

Constructivists, largely unbuilt and hardly seen outside a small circle, also continues to inspire architects like Zaha Hadid and Daniel Libeskind.

Further reading:

Gough, Maria, *The Artist as Producer: Russian Constructivism in Revolution*. Berkeley: University of California Press, 2005.

CONSUMER DESIGN

Term referring to commodities or objects bought for use in the home. Consumer goods, sometimes called consumer durables, include televisions, videos, cameras and kitchen equipment. The term also refers to products bought and used by the customer for final **consumption**, such as food, beer and newspapers, and is sometimes used instead of **industrial design**. However, the latter also includes products designed for use outside the home, such as industrial or military hardware.

Further reading:

Forty, Adrian, *Objects of Desire: Design and Society since 1750*. London: Thames & Hudson, 1995.

CONSUMERISM

Modern consumerism is rooted in the powerful changes that occurred in, and the wealth of, 19th-century industrial centres, including Welsh mining communities, Clydeside shipbuilding and Lancashire cotton mills. The 19th century was a period of great achievements and progress epitomized by the inventions of the age – railways, photography, the telegraph, cars, telephones, electricity and aeroplanes – alongside the appearance of the first mass-produced products, department stores, **advertising** hoardings and mail-order catalogues. Great deprivation contrasted with staggering affluence, and set against this backdrop the energy and confidence with which the production of goods developed make it a fascinating era to study.

The twentieth century saw an important shift of emphasis in design from the production of goods to their **consumption**. New ideas of lifestyle, the birth of mass consumer goods, the emergence of new consumer groups (such as the teenager) and a general increase in disposable income brought about this important change. The **Post-modern** era of the last forty years has introduced a multicultural consumerist culture, typified by both an **eclecticism** of style and the viable democratization of design. Postmodernism stressed the search for personal identity, a response to Modernity's destruction of the autonomous individual. This theory highlights the loss of emphasis placed by Modernism on production and the growing power of contemporary consumer culture. Consequently, consumerism in Postmodern terms is more easily understood as lifestyle and reflects the image construction of the individual, with the home an extension of individual identity.

Anti-consumerism has its roots in the 1950s, starting in the USA with Vance Packard's (b. 1914) attacks on the automobile industry and its development of inbuilt obsolescence. In the early 1950s Packard began to investigate the work of the Institute for Motivational Research in New York State. His observations on the new world of American supermarkets and television advertisements were published in 1957 in *The Hidden Persuaders*, a populist exposé of the world of hard selling which became a bestseller. Packard overturned the formal conventions of the serious sociology book by using the language of the popular press. Typical of his style was a chapter describing research that measured the rate of eye-blinks of housewives in supermarkets which suggested the shoppers fell into a state of light hypnosis. The chapter was titled 'Babes in Consumerland'. Packard was a prolific writer and went on to publish a series of critiques on consumer culture, including *The Status Seekers* (1959), *The Waste Makers* (1960), *The Pyramid Climbers* (1962) and *The Naked Society* (1964).

Further reading:

Packard, Vance, *The Hidden Persuaders*. Harmondsworth: Penguin, 1981 [1957].
—— *The Naked Society*. London: Longmans, 1964.
—— *The Pyramid Climbers*. London: Longmans, 1962.
—— *The Status Seekers: An Exploration of Class Behavior in America*. London: Longmans, 1959.
—— *The Waste Makers*. London: Longmans, 1960.

CONSUMPTION

Widely regarded as a benchmark of economic success and the mark of a growing economy. Thorstein Veblen (1857–1929) was an American economist who coined the term 'conspicuous consumption' in his influential book *The Theory of the Leisure Class* (1899) to describe the behaviour of the fabulously wealthy American dynasties at the turn of the twentieth century. The term describes spending which satisfies no real need but is a mark of prestige. Veblen's work on **cultural analysis** provides a key description of the mode of behaviour by which a leisure class maintains its separate cultural identity; in this case by indulging in the excesses of that gilded age. He was a populist radical who attacked the ostentation of the rich and their design accoutrements. Most importantly, he became a prominent source of dissenting American economic theory in the 20th century, and his ideas went on to influence post-war design commentators such as Vance Packard and Victor Papanek. It is rather ironic, however, that in the 1980s Veblen's thoughts on conspicuous consumption were appropriated to rather different ends by the prevalent consumer culture.

Further reading:

Veblen, Thorstein, *The Instinct of Workmanship and the State of the Industrial Arts*. New York: Cosimo, 2006 [1914].
—— *The Theory of the Leisure Class*. New York: Dover, 1994 [1899].

CONTEMPORARY STYLE

For the 1950s, Contemporary was more than a new design style; it was a vision of the future. This international movement was a natural reaction against the oppression of war, with its drabness, regimentation and shortages: Contemporary was symbolic of a new tomorrow. Its priorities were colour, lightness and organic shapes and, with the help of technology, it aimed to be democratically accessible. During the war years chemical dyes were virtually unobtainable, so it is not hard to see why the designers and consumers of the 1950s loved colour combinations, which included hot pinks, sizzling orange, bright blues and canary yellows. These new colours found their way into cheerful, abstract patterns, which appeared on the wallpapers, textiles and carpets of post-war homes, cafés and hotels. The new interest in design can be clearly seen in the 1950s magazines about the home and in the boom in do-it-yourself.

Contemporary design also introduced new shapes, with objects from chairs to electric fires becoming lighter and more curved. This organic quality was inspired by fine-art developments such as the mobiles of Alexander Calder and the sculptures of Henry Moore, but it was made possible by technological advances developed during the war. Plywood, for example, had become much more versatile with the invention of synthetic glues and new kiln techniques. Originally used in the manufacture of bomber planes, it could now be bent into dramatic sculptural shapes. The American designer Charles Eames had started working with the material for splints for wounded servicemen, but went on to design a series of classic plywood chairs.

In England Contemporary design was first shown at the 1951 **Festival of Britain**. For the event, Ernest Race designed the Antelope chair, using spindly metal legs with bobble feet and a brightly coloured, machine-formed plywood seat. Designers were commissioned to produce new objects for post-war homes, which were now smaller and more compact. Furniture needed to be flexible and to respond to social change, hence the introduction of the tele-chair, the convertible bed-settee and the room divider. There was also an important ideology underlying Contemporary design. The war had left a feeling of common purpose and of working together for a better future. In this context Contemporary was not an exclusive, upmarket design style, but a democratic development that would provide well-designed objects for everyone. In Norway the government provided grants for young married couples to buy modern furniture, and Scandinavian design developed and marketed an inspired version of the new style. In Britain the **Design Council** furnished show houses in new towns and ran features in popular magazines outlining the advantages of Contemporary design. There was a great deal of talk about it being classless, and in the early 1950s there was an attempt to **mass-produce** it at a moderate price.

Contemporary style coincided with an economic boom, experienced first in the USA and then in Europe. During the decade the American **advertising** industry invented a marketing strategy of adding the suffix 'luxe' to many products. For example, 'de luxe', implying elegance and superiority, was applied to everything from cars to vacuum cleaners. Populuxe, a combination of populism and luxury, is a 1980s invention to describe design from the American consumer boom years of 1954 to 1964, reflecting a period when jobs were relatively easy to find, and consumer spending, which had disappeared in Europe from 1939 to 1952, gradually returned. Contemporary design was a celebration of that spending power. By the end of the decade, however, Contemporary had lost its monopoly on progressive thinking. It had become just another style, and its clichés were replaced by other powerful forces, including **Pop design**, in the 1960s.

Further reading:

Hoskins, Lesley, *Fiftiestyle: Home Decoration and Furnishing from the 1950s*. London: Middlesex University Press, 2004.

CONVERGENT DESIGN

Increasingly, designers are asked to contribute to the overall strategy for promotion of a product. This element of 'convergence' is typically represented by the work of the designer Jonathan Ives for Apple computers. Convergent design brings together practitioners and processes that traditionally were thought of as separate categories and activities, including **product design**, **advertising** and marketing. The end of the 20th century saw this important new term being coined to describe shifts in the design process that were to change the profession. Now the understanding of what product design involves has broadened in scope to include corporate and strategic consulting and brand development. A company image is still defined by its products but increasingly also through advertising and branding. In this convergence, product design becomes the old-style brand message and now seamlessly combines innovative technology with advertising campaigns. Convergent design means that product design and advertising share the same process and communicate the same identity, quality, function and significance of the object. They employ a common visual vocabulary and by working together achieve more market success.

The launch of Apple's iPod is the single most successful example of convergent design – the integration of object, copy and advertising image. In the 21st century this and the merging of advertising and design is the model for practice in the majority of the creative industries. The word 'convergent' is also widely used to describe changes in the communications industry in which separate services – fax, email, telephone, video, etc. – are now supplied in a single machine.

Further reading:

Curran, Steve, *Convergence Design: Creating the User Experience for Interactive Television, Wireless and Broadband*. Gloucester, MA: Rockport, 2003.

CORPORATE CULTURE

Not strictly a design term, but a company ethos that permeates many large manufacturing companies. It originally took off in the USA, with office size and furniture being determined by an employee's status on the company ladder. Other perks, such as company cars and keys to the executive washroom, were allocated on the same basis. Corporate culture is satirized in the classic 1960s comedy film *The Apartment*, starring Jack Lemmon, which criticized a perceived American national need for conformity during the 1950s and 1960s. The stereotyped executive man got a bad press in the 1960s and 1970s, as did his Japanese equivalent, forever associated with company songs and slogans, dedicated worker loyalty and twelve-hour days.

More recently, the idea of corporate culture has been treated more favourably. It is now seen less in the context of staff perks and rituals than as a recognizable business approach to increase profitability. The strength of corporate culture when applied to design can be seen in the architecture, **packaging** and graphics of global companies such as the McDonald's hamburger chain. More and more companies are encouraging the idea of business identity as a marketing strategy to increase their customer base and profitability. Corporate culture has also been subsumed into the wider umbrella of branding and **experience design**, which focus more on the consumer experience that on staff employment.

Further reading:

Klein, Naomi, *No Logo: No Space, No Choice, No Jobs*. London: Flamingo, 2001 [1999].

CORPORATE IDENTITY

The name given to a company's graphic image. The tradition of designed company names, or logos, goes back to the 19th century. They have been used to reinforce a strong brand identity, usually for food and drink products, including Kellogg's cereals, Quaker Oats, Campbell's soups and most famously Coca-Cola. In the 20th century the idea of an even more powerful corporate image took hold, and corporate identity was born.

The father of corporate identity is usually held to be the German designer Peter Behrens, who worked for the electrical company AEG in the inter-war years, but it was in the post-war USA that the design of corporate identities became a profession in itself. Indeed, the identity designed for the American company IBM in the 1950s by Eliot Noyes and Paul Rand is regarded as a model of its kind. Noyes went on to apply corporate identity schemes to other blue-chip American companies such as Westinghouse, Mobil Oil and Pan American World Airways. By the 1960s, a series of **design consultancies** specializing in corporate identity had been established in the USA, including Lippincott & Margulies, Anspach Grossman Portugal, and Saul Bass. These industry pioneers replaced names with strong graphic symbols, which the customer can instantly identify. The large 'M' for McDonald's and the track sign for British Rail are two examples of this trend. European firms quickly followed suit, including the high-profile British consultancy the Wolff Olins Partnership, which devised the hugely successful brand identity for the Tate Modern in 1999. Corporate identity as an industry term has now been replaced by brand consultancy, which aims for a similar transformational effect on markets but has widened the focus from simply the design and application of a brand identity to all aspects of marketing, including **packaging** and **advertising**.

Further reading:

Buddensieg, Tilmann, *Industriekultur: Peter Behrens and the AEG, 1907–1914*. Cambridge, MA: MIT Press, 1984.
Andres, Clay and Fishel, Catharine, *Identity Design Sourcebook: Successful IDs Deconstructed and Revealed*. Gloucester, MA: Rockport, 2004.
Olins, Wally, *Corporate Identity: Making Business Strategy Visible through Design*. London: Thames & Hudson, 1989.

COUNTERCULTURE

A 1960s term used to define unconventional theories about traditional institutions such as marriage and family life that offer alternatives to any social mainstream. Counterculture stressed the need for opposition and for people to express their individual creativity. Each historical period reflected this in shared but different ways: for example, in the 1960s the focus was on experimenting with drugs and, in the contemporary vernacular, in 'dropping out and doing your own thing'. Design and **advertising** were interested in counterculture because it reflected the aspirations and concerns of a generation which could be used to inspire and market a wide range of products. Design could therefore reflect counterculture and bring it back into the mainstream. The **appro-priation** of anarchic **Punk** clothes and graphics by mainstream design is an example of this process. In 2004, Queen Elizabeth's granddaughter was photographed with her tongue pierced, and street fashion at Ascot is another example of the influence of counterculture on the Esta-blishment.

Further reading:

Green, Jonathon, *All Dressed up: The Sixties and the Counter Culture*. London: Pimlico, 1999.

CRAFT

Making objects by hand is one of the defining human characteristics, and craftwork has a long history of expertise and technique. The creation of craft objects requires skill in the use of traditional materials, wood, metal, glass and textiles. Craft might be viewed as two separate but connected strands: worldwide, there is the survival of traditional craft skills, such as the production of Inuit leather clothing; however, there is also a return to, or revival of, craft techniques to produce con-temporary and new items. This second strand has an established history connected to a self-conscious rejection of the industrial techniques of the late 18th and 19th centuries. Britain, which led this period of dramatic technological change, also inspired its response in the British **Arts and Crafts Movement**, led by William **Morris**. In the 20th century, the potter Bernard Leach provided a role model for the craftsperson, working in dedicated, rural isolation and struggling to achieve a complete understanding of his craft. The lure of the simple life was irresistible in the early 1970s to a generation of young crafts-people who often seemed to feel that good work could only be pro-duced in a derelict Victorian church or a renovated 17th-century barn.

The Crafts Council was established in 1971 as the national agency for crafts; it was granted a Royal Charter in 1982. It initially supported the role of the artist-craftsperson, but gradually came under increasing pressure to broaden its terms of reference. While the traditional role for the crafts remains strong, a rather different profile emerged in the 1980s. The term 'designer-maker' appeared in the late 1970s as a way of describing the new role craftspeople were developing for themselves. This can be seen in the work of John Makepeace and Richard LaTrobe Bateman in furniture, Wendy Ramshaw in jewellery, and potters John

Leach, Alison Britten and Kate Malone. The old idea of craft as a sort of **guild** activity, handing down skills in making traditional, vernacular items such as ladderback chairs and woven baskets, no longer held true. Jewellery was a particularly important area in this respect. In the early 1980s, jewellery-makers looked to new materials, forms and techniques to make decorative pieces that broke with the conventions of traditional jewellery. They wanted the creative designing aspect of their activity to be recognized alongside their role as makers.

The USA led the way with new aesthetic ideas applied to glass, wood and iron. In Britain, young makers began to challenge the whole basis of the craft aesthetic, encouraged by the culture of **Punk** and its belief in the power of **do-it-yourself**. A change of direction can be traced through two important exhibitions organized by the Crafts Council. The first, in 1982, was 'The Maker's Eye', which helped to broaden the concept of what a craft object might be by including such things as letter boxes and motorcycles. Then, in 1987, 'The New Spirit in Craft and Design' looked at the influence of **youth culture** on London's new makers, including Judy Blame (b. 1960), Tom Dixon (b. 1958), André Dubreuil (b. 1951), and Fric and Frack (Fritz Soloman and Alan MacDonald, est. 1985). These young furniture-makers, jewellers and metalsmiths recycled scavenged materials and obsolete artefacts from the streets of urban London – Dalston, Clerkenwell, Hackney and Portobello – and they challenged the conventional boundaries of craft production. They took up an extreme position, but they forced the crafts to re-examine their role and future.

More recently, traditional craft values, which never truly disappeared, have revived. Crafts are no longer peripheral and marginal activities, and their new central role is influencing the whole spectrum of the visual arts and design.

Further reading:

Crafts Council, *The New Spirit in Craft and Design*. London: Crafts Council, 1987.

Greenhalgh, Paul, *The Persistence of Craft: The Applied Arts Today*. London: A. & C. Black, 2002.

CRANBROOK ACADEMY

Cranbrook Academy of Art, in the Detroit suburb of Bloomfield Hills, was the result of a collaboration between George Gough Booth, a

Detroit newspaper publisher and philanthropist, and the Finnish architect Eliel Saarinen. Their intention was to establish an American school that would train artists and designers in the community. It was an experiment based on **Arts and Crafts** ideas, which sought to integrate creative life into the everyday and aspired to Utopian ideas of community life with art at its centre for the benefit of all. Under Saarinen, the academy developed a distinctly Scandinavian approach, which alongside Booth's ambitious cultural vision for American design meant that Cranbrook quickly became one of America's most prestigious schools.

Saarinen pioneered modern American design and architecture at the academy, including the Saarinen House and Garden, the home and studio he built for himself and his wife, the noted textile designer Loja Saarinen. He was Cranbrook's resident architect from 1925 to 1950, and by the early 1930s had brought together a highly talented community of teachers and craftsmen to work at the school. These included Harry Bertoia, Charles Eames, Maija Grotell, Eero Saarinen and Florence Knoll, all designers who subsequently went on to have a major impact on American art, design and architecture.

With Booth's death in 1949, and Saarinen's the following year, the school temporarily lost its direction. In recent years, however, it has once more become an important centre for **design education**, led in the 1980s by Katherine and Michael McCoy. The academy is now the only US institution dedicated solely to graduate education in the visual arts, architecture and design, it has an ambitious exhibition and gallery programme, and the building itself has become a tourist attraction, as have additional buildings by Rafael Moneo. Since 1996, its director has been Gerhardt Knodel, a former Cranbrook art graduate.

Further reading:

Design in America: The Cranbrook Vision, 1925–50. New York: Abrams in association with the Detroit Institute of Arts and the Metropolitan Museum of Art, 1983.

CREATIVE INDUSTRIES

A widely cited definition of creative industries is that used by the UK government: 'those industries which have their origin in individual creativity, skill and talent and which have a potential for wealth and job creation through the generation and exploitation of intellectual property'. The sector, as defined by the UK Department of Culture, Media and Sport, includes **advertising**, architecture, the art and antiques market, crafts, design, designer fashion, film and video, interactive leisure software, music, the performing arts, publishing, software and computer games, television and radio. Other sectors identified as having a close relationship to the creative industries include heritage, hospitality, museums and galleries, sport and tourism.

There is, however, considerable debate regarding the inclusion of some of these in this definition, particularly those related to information technology. Many leading figures object that the term 'creative industries' is far too generalized. In the UK, for example, it does not make a distinction between those design industries subsidized by the state, such as film, and those that do not receive government funding. There is also some confusion regarding the boundaries between the creative industries and the culture and entertainment industries: the former are generally regarded as delivering value to the national economy through the generation of jobs and revenue. However, 'creative industries' is now applied to a wide spectrum of design, culture and media activities.

Further reading:

Cox, Sir George, *The Cox Review of Creativity in Business*. 2005. Available at: <http://www.hm-treasury.gov.uk/independent_reviews/cox_review/coxreview_index.cfm>.
Hartley, John (ed.), *Creative Industries*. Oxford: Blackwell, 2004.

CREATIVE SALVAGE

A 1980s design style based on making items from Britain's industrial leftovers. It was a kind of recycled skip culture and inspired a wave of metal furniture and objects from such designers as Ron Arad, Tom Dixon, Danny Lane and Jon Mills. In their hands, creative salvage was an urban-inspired rejection of Japanese, matt-black stereo systems and Milanese designer chic. Arad's One-Off Gallery in Covent Garden had distressed walls, a concrete staircase and chairs made from old Rover car seats; Dixon opened a studio in Notting Hill Gate, where he welded bizarre metal furniture; and Lane made chairs from pieces of broken glass. In 1985 a group called Mutoid Waste started to put on performance pieces based on the new aesthetic, while Crucial, a well-known gallery in Notting Hill, started exhibiting and selling Creative Salvage objects. Creative Salvage as a design process is still ongoing, but it is now integrated into **sustainable design** and recycling processes.

Further reading:

Addis, William, *Building with Reclaimed Components and Materials: A Design Handbook for Reuse and Recycling.* London: Earthscan, 2006.

CRITICAL DESIGN

A field of study in which designed objects are employed as research tools. Critical design is associated particularly with research programmes at the **Royal College of Art**, expressed in the work of Anthony Dunne and Fiona Raby. Other practices use the term to describe their work. Diller Scofidio + Renfro (founded as D+S by Elizabeth Diller and Ricardo Scofidio in 1979) is an interdisciplinary studio that fuses architecture, the visual arts and the performing arts. Its work takes the form of architectural commissions, temporary and permanent site-specific **installations**, multi-media theatre, electronic media and print. The objects produced are often original configurations of familiar products, such as videos, radios and televisions, intended to engage critically with the social, cultural and practical aspects of established technologies. Such designs are rarely intended for **mass production** but instead are described as 'critical interventions'.

Dunne & Raby also explore the ways in which design practice can challenge the culture of relentless innovation to develop more critical thinking on the wider role of design in everyday life. Architecture and furniture design have operated in the context of cultural experimentation for some time, but **product design**'s strong ties to the market place have meant less focus on the cultural function of electronic products. Critical design suggests that as more of our social and cultural experiences are mediated by electronic products, designers need to develop ways of exploring how such products might enrich people's everyday lives. Dunne & Raby aim to stimulate discussion and debate among designers, industry and the public about the quality of this electronically mediated life, and to develop effective tools for disseminating conceptual design proposals that engage people's imaginations about the future of electronic products. In 1999 they produced *Hertzian Tales*, which combined critical essays with design proposals. More recently they have applied the methodology of critical design to other areas, such as biotechnology.

Meanwhile, DS+R have contributed to the development of critical design in a series of books, including *Flesh* and *Blur*. These publications reflect the trio's strong academic backgrounds: Elizabeth Diller is Professor of Architecture at Princeton University; Ricardo Scofidio is Professor of Architecture at the Cooper Union; and Charles Renfro is on the faculty of Columbia University's School of Architecture.

Further reading:

Betsky, Aaron, *Scanning: The Aberrant Architectures of Diller + Scofidio*. New York: Whitney Museum of American Art, 2003.

Diller, Elizabeth and Scofidio, Ricardo, *Blur: The Making of Nothing*. New York: Harry N. Abrams, 2002.

Diller, Elizabeth and Scofidio, Ricardo, *Flesh: Architectural Probes: The Mutant Body of Architecture*. London: Triangle Architectural Publishing, 1994.

Dunne, Anthony, *Hertzian Tales: Electronic Products, Aesthetic Experience and Critical Design*. Cambridge, MA: MIT Press, 2005 [1999].

CUBISM

In the inter-war period Cubism simultaneously became a style, a movement and a set of aesthetic principles. Although painting was its primary focus of activity, it also affected design and architecture. It was pioneered by a small group of artists working in Paris around 1905–8. These artists formed two separate groups, working more or less independently of each other, but sometimes overlapping. The first group, which included Picasso (1881–1973), Braque (1882–1963), Gris (1887–1927) and Léger (1881–1955), was centred on Kahnweiler's Gallery and Picasso's studio in Montmartre. The second group, which included Robert and Sonia Delaunay, met in the cafés of Montparnasse and at the house of Marcel Duchamp (1887–1968) in suburban Puteaux. It was the second group that gained initial notoriety as the Cubist Movement, launching their work at the 1911 Paris Salon des Indépendants, where it was greeted with derision. None the less, their fame spread to other European cities and New York. In the meantime, the art dealer Kahnweiler had secured a faithful clientele for the painters he represented and began to establish a reputation for them as the true pioneers of Cubism. By 1914, if not before, the ascendancy of Picasso and Braque over the movement as a whole was established.

The paintings from this period had formal characteristics in common, which distinguished Cubism as a style. The first was the use of 'multiple perspective': the subject viewed from different angles at the same time. The second was an overall pictorial composition in which the subject was broken up, which diminished the illusion of space and solid. The third was a restricted palette of colours to avoid the sharp tonal contrasts that would interrupt the overall composition of the painting.

This set of aesthetic principles also had a wider application to the new ideas emerging under the wider terms of reference of Modernism. First there was a growing concern on the part of technically radical artists in the pre-1914 decade to acknowledge the specificity of the visual medium and art practice in question. For the Cubists, this ranged from Picasso's celebration of the artifice of art to Léger's attempt to find pictorial equivalents for modern, urban visual experience. Artists wanted to engage with the experience of modernity in both its positive and negative aspects. For the Cubists, this was summarized in the concept of simultaneity, which referred to the collective experience of city life, the multiplicity of visual perception or the simultaneous contrast of colours. Accompanying their interest in modernity, however, was a commitment to artistic tradition and appreciation of the need for the new to build on the old. This ranged from a concern to update **Classicism** to a sympathetic adaptation of popular and vernacular images and practices. In this way Cubist theory has a direct link to Modernist experiments in architecture and design. In this search for painting, buildings, furniture and products the heritage of Cubism is identified in Czech Cubism and the work of Pavel Janák, Josef Gočár, Vlastislav Hofman, Josef Chochol and Emil Králíček.

Further reading:

Cottington, David, *Cubism and its Histories*. Manchester: Manchester University Press, 2004.
Golding, John, *Cubism: A History and an Analysis, 1907–1914*. London: Faber, 1988 [1959].

CULT OBJECTS

This term covers a wide range of artefacts which reflect the style preferences of individual groups. It became a popular concept in the 1980s when a series of fashionable objects came to express lifestyle aspirations. In the world of 1980s clothes, the Burberry mackintosh, the Barbour waxed cotton jacket, original Levi 501s and the Gucci loafer shoe enjoyed status as cult objects. One of the best known items of the period is the Filofax personal organizer, which came to represent the consumer culture of the decade. It was the essential accessory of the successful graphic designer or journalist, before being challenged by the Psion computer version and now the Blackberry in the 21st century. Drink **packaging** is another cult marker. Both Coca–Cola and Perrier make the grade, together with a changing array of designer beer bottles and cans.

If, in theory at least, classic design aspires to permanence and longevity, cult objects are about fashion and change. Every mall and smart shopping street has a specialist shop selling cult objects, such as Moss, the New York SoHo store run by Murray Moss. Here permanence is less important than the fashion and style preferences of a new, upwardly mobile and affluent group of consumers who want to buy into the myth of designer lifestyles. Young consumers look to design to define a stylish and distinctive identity. Fashion encourages a reverence for the designer label; it is more important who you wear than what you wear to establish your identity and status. However, these consumerist values that were so strong in the late 20th century are now being challenged as new attitudes about resources and social values take a more critical view of design. Nevertheless, new cult objects have continued to appear in the 21st century, with Apple's iPod being elevated to cult status as soon as it was launched.

Further reading:

Sudjic, Deyan, *Cult Objects: The Complete Guide to Having it All*. London: Paladin, 1985.

CULTURAL ANALYSIS

An interdisciplinary process investigating contemporary culture. Research in this area is concentrated in several universities, including Berkeley, California, which publishes a journal of the same name, and the Centre for Cultural Analysis at Leeds, which explores contemporary culture through conferences, debate and research.

Further reading:

<http://socrates.berkeley.edu/~caforum/>.

CULTURAL DIVERSITY IN DESIGN

Cultural diversity in design involves understanding how people live in different cultural and social contexts. This works on two levels: the first to increase the potential market for products and services; and the second to help local economies. The study of cultural diversity helps to explain not only how people live but what they want. It utilizes social research, anthropology and economics to identify people's values, aesthetic preferences and lifestyles on a global basis. Cultural diversity in design terms includes class, faith, sexuality, disability and gender differences, as well as race or ethnicity, and its study uses methodologies derived from recent research into **inclusive** and transgenerational design. This work has had a significant impact on the way companies plan to position themselves in the market place.

Any contemporary discussion of design creativity in the 21st century has to take on board issues of cultural diversity, which, for instance, clearly contributes to London's status as a global capital of the creative industries. In 2004, the Mayor of London's groundbreaking report identified the capital's culturally diverse nature as key to its flourishing creative economy. Cultural diversity is now recognized as a distinctive element in British design, which reflects a uniquely rich history of multicultural settlement, immigration and movement in UK society. Understanding and expressing this cultural diversity is now seen as a key asset for contemporary design and offers the potential to address a uniquely broad range of issues, materials, production, style and **consumption**.

'British' design, as it is displayed and promoted in museums, government exhibitions, magazines and books, is very diverse in terms of nationality. It boasts, for example: the designer Onkar Singh Kular; the son of Asian immigrants to Yorkshire; Macedonian-born Marjan Pejoski, famous for the swan dress he designed for Björk; and Israeli-born furniture designer Ron Arad. The economic potential of culturally diverse design is vast, but it also enriches the quality of people's experiences and connects different worlds and communities.

Further reading:

Mayor of London, *London: Cultural Captial: Realising the Potential of a World-class City*. London: Greater London Auhority, 2004.

Smiers, Joost, *Arts under Pressure: Promoting Cultural Diversity in the Age of Globalization*. London: Zed, 2003.

CUSTOMIZING

A popular extension of custom-making, whereby an expensive product is made to order following customer specifications. Typical examples of this are Rolls-Royce cars and pleasure yachts fitted out with luxury extras, but standard, mass-produced items can also be given this personal touch. For example, Levi jeans may be embroidered and leather jackets may be decorated with studs. Customizing in this sense has turned into a kind of **folk art**. Such treatment of standardized objects is not exclusive to Western culture. In the Philippines the basic American jeep is turned into a highly decorated vehicle called a Jeepney. Customizing has thus emerged as a contemporary creative art form that has inspired numerous exhibitions and books.

More recently, customization has been a modern technological response to increasingly fragmented markets, so a retail store can log a customer's purchases and then provide them with offers linked to their personal taste and previous spending patterns. Mobile phones also customize information tailored to individual tastes, texting details of upcoming classical music concerts or sports fixtures, for example. These marketing ploys will undoubtedly increase in range and sophistication. Customizing will harness technology to offer the consumer a feeling of personal service and greater choice in the market place.

Further reading:

Aoki, Shoichi, *Fresh Fruits*. London: Phaidon, 2005.
McKell, Iain and Farrelly, Liz, *Fashion Forever: 30 Years of Subculture*. London: Immprint, 2004.

CYBERNETICS

The study of electronic communications and automatic control systems designed to replace tasks previously done by humans. The term was popularized in a 1948 book by the American scientist Norbert Wiener, who helped to establish the study of cybernetics throughout the world and generated considerable debate over the social and interdisciplinary implications of the term. Cybernetics is now generally regarded less as a science than as a vision of the future, associated with robots and science fiction.

Further reading:

Wiener, Norbert, *Cybernetics: Or Control and Communication in the Animal and the Machine.* London: John Wiley, 1948.

DE STIJL

A Dutch art and design movement and one of the most influential Modernist groups of the 20th century. The De Stijl group was committed to the efficiency and precision of machine-made form as a celebration of modernity. It took its name from a magazine founded in 1917 by the architect and painter Theo van Doesburg (1883–1931). The magazine was a vehicle to publicize the group's design work but also published serious theoretical writings which stressed an intense mysticism. De Stijl was particularly interested in theosophy, a religious system that believed in a direct communication between God and the soul, which would also appear as an influence at the **Bauhaus**.

Founder members of De Stijl included the painter Piet Mondrian (1872–1944) and the architect J.J.P. Oud (1890–1963), but the group soon expanded. The best known new member was the designer Gerrit Rietveld (1888–1964). De Stijl promoted a rigorous modern aesthetic which used the primary colours of red, blue and yellow, as well as black, grey and white, restricted to flat planes and strong **geometric** shapes. In design terms the purest example of De Stijl is Rietveld's famous red–blue chair, manufactured in 1918 by van de Groneken. This chair, built on a series of horizontal and vertical planes, has become a design classic of the **Modern Movement**. Along with Rietveld's Schröder House at Utrecht (1924), it provides a clear and eloquent expression of the group's original ideals. The members of De Stijl rejected any form of **naturalism** in favour of a formal abstraction that allied the movement with Russian **Constructivism**. Links with Moscow during this early period were strong. El Lissitzky, a Constructivist, featured in *De Stijl* magazine in 1926, and he returned the favour with a Russian article on Rietveld. The magazine was important because it provided a sense of community for such international and diverse groups as Dada and the Bauhaus as well as the Constructivists. By the end of the 1920s, though, the De Stijl Movement had effectively broken up. Nevertheless, its influence remained strong. In the Netherlands, the design tradition it created is revered, and on an international level the visual style of the movement has influenced everything from graphic design to interiors.

Further reading:

Overy, Paul, *De Stijl*. London: Thames & Hudson, 1991.
Padovan, Richard, *Towards Universality: Le Corbusier, Mies and De Stijl*. London: Routledge, 2002.

DECODING

A word originally appropriated by sociologists from military intelligence, where it means translating enemy coded messages. In design terms it is used to describe the ideas of **Deconstruction**, attempting to reveal the complex layers of meaning hidden in any image. In 1978 Judith Williamson published *Decoding Advertisements: Ideology and Meaning in Advertising*, which applied the methods of **semiotics** and post-Freudian analysis to analyse and interpret graphic design. Decoding is widely used in design discourse to signal that designed objects have complex meanings that function on different levels.

Further reading:

Williamson, Judith, *Decoding Advertisements: Ideology and Meaning in Advertising*. London: Marion Boyars, 1978.

DECONSTRUCTION

A form of critical analysis associated mainly with the theories of the French philosopher Jacques Derrida (b. 1930) from the late 1960s. It deconstructs social stereotypes and clichés about gender and the status quo, which are communicated by the mass media. Deconstruction reveals the complex layers of meaning of an image which Derrida felt could be understood only by exploring the systems that govern us and the opposition activated by those systems. Therefore, an **advertising** campaign for baby food would have different readings for different women that reveal political and social meanings dependent on the individual. Deconstruction implies that we can analyse an image and reveal its visual, cultural and linguistic meanings by applying scientific principles derived from **semiotics**. The term '**decoding**' is also used to express this process. Designers in the late 1980s became very interested in this idea of layers of meanings, but did not claim to explore Deconstruction in its purist form because design still remains an intuitive activity that cannot be reduced to a set of scientific principles.

Derrida's writings on the visual arts in the late 1970s were also influential. However, in terms of design, the concept of Deconstruction has been particularly significant in European and American architecture since the early 1980s. This Deconstructionist (also sometimes referred to as 'Deconstructivist') movement in architecture came to prominence in an exhibition in 1988 at the Museum of Modern Art, New York, organized by the American architect Philip Johnson. Architectural practitioners and theorists such as Peter Eisenman (b. 1932) and Bernard Tschumi (b. 1944) have used a Deconstructionist approach to examine the nature and function of architecture, in particular the relationship between 'inside' and 'outside', characterized by overlapping, fragmented forms. In this context Deconstruction has been identified as a strand of **Postmodernism**. Examples include Tschumi's masterplan and designs (1982) for the Parc de la Villette in Paris, which came close to Derrida's ideas as it was laid out without a clear structure of paths and with buildings that had no obvious function.

In the late 1980s Deconstruction was applied to the experimental **typography** of a number of young graphic designers who 'took apart' traditional letterforms having been inspired by the possibilities of the new computer revolution. The term was also applied to the innovative cut and tailoring of a number of fashion designers whose work seemingly crossed the boundaries between art and fashion. Included in this list are: Hussein Chalayan, Issey Miyake and Comme des Garcons.

Further reading:

Brunette, Peter and Wills, David (eds), *Deconstruction and the Visual Arts: Art, Media, Architecture*. Cambridge: Cambridge University Press, 1994.

Royale, Nicholas, *Jacques Derrida*. London: Routledge, 2003.

Tschumi, Bernard, *Cinégramme Folie: le Parc de la Villette*. Sevenoaks: Butterworths, 1987.

DESIGN ACADEMY, EINDHOVEN

This academy enjoys a reputation for pioneering a new conceptual approach to **design education** that has proved highly influential. It remains small, at around sixty postgraduate students each year. Established in 1947 as the Akademie Industriële Vormgeving Eindhoven, it is widely regarded as one of the most important contemporary design schools in Europe. The academy's alumni have done much to regenerate

Dutch design in the 1990s. They include members of the country's best-known design practice, Droog, such as Hella Jongerius, Jurgen Bey, Tord Boontje, Job Smeets and Richard Hutten. The academy occupies a well-known building in the city, a former Modernist factory called De Witte Dame (the White Lady), which hosts the graduate show each year during Dutch Design Week – a feature in the European design calendar. Promotion is the key to the Eindhoven strategy, and the final show is professionally shot and styled, presented at Milan Fiera each year and hugely influential.

Since 1991, the academy's director has been Li Edelkoort, who pioneered trend forecasting as a profession as well as an important aspect of social commentary. Edelkoort has also promoted **sustainable** partnerships with companies such as Dyson, Unilever and Nike. The Eindhoven design approach is to focus on specific disciplines within a bigger cultural agenda, for example calling the product programme 'Man and Living' and **transport design** 'Man and Mobility'. This is reflected in the academy's approach to teaching. One key contributor to its success is the range of high-profile and creative tutors, many of whom are academy graduates, but the staff also includes UK theorist John Thackera and magazine stylist Ilse Crawford. Recently, the academy has suggested a change of emphasis from conceptual work to the needs of industry, but it remains a unique educational centre for design. In 2005 the stylish New York design store Moss chose Eindhoven graduate Maarten Baas's burnt furniture for a solo exhibition.

DESIGN AND INDUSTRIES ASSOCIATION (DIA)

The English equivalent of the **Deutsche Werkbund**, a group that linked design with industry. In the years before the First World War a number of British designers were becoming increasingly aware that European design developments were taking the lead. In particular, the activities of the Deutsche Werkbund indicated that the **Arts and Crafts Movement** was lagging behind the times. In 1915 a small group of British designers, including Harold Stabler, Harry Peach of the Leicestershire Dryad Works and Ambrose Heal, founder of the well-known furniture store, launched the Design and Industries Association, which operated from the Art Workers' **Guild** premises in Queen Square, London. The DIA's slogan was 'Nothing Need Be Ugly'. Another guiding figure in the association was W.R. Lethaby, then Professor of Design at the **Royal College of Art**. Although the expressed aim of the group was to create a closer link between design and industry, the profile of the DIA was closely allied with the Arts and Crafts establishment, and there was little to suggest in the early 1920s that it was responding to the European **Modern Movement**. The group's conservative approach is reflected in the DIA yearbooks published between 1922 and 1930. These volumes are full of photographs of Dryad cane furniture, Brown Betty teapots and Jaeger sports clothes. None the less, there were subtle signs of change, most notably a series of transcribed radio talks on Modernism for the BBC in 1932, and a short-lived magazine, *Design in Industry*, edited by Maxwell Fry. That magazine's successor, *Design for Today* (1933–5), illustrated the work of leading British Modernists, including Raymond McGrath and Wells Coates. The year 1933 also saw an important exhibition of British **industrial design** held at Dorland Hall, and the new confidence this encouraged led to a rise in the DIA's membership. In 1944 the establishment of the government-supported Council of Industrial Design effectively took over the work of the DIA, but the latter still supports design exhibitions, lectures and publications.

Further reading:

Plummer, Raymond, *Nothing Need Be Ugly: The First 70 Years of the Design & Industries Association*. London: Design & Industries Association, 1985.

DESIGN CONSULTANCIES

The design practice, or consultancy, is a 20th-century phenomenon. Designers started working from their own offices, in the manner of such other professionals as accountants and solicitors, in the USA during the 1920s. Before then, they had worked together, for example in the **Wiener Werkstätte** and the British **Guilds of Design**, but in a more unstructured way. The role of the independent designer has a longer history. It is known, for example, that in the 1760s Josiah Wedgwood paid for freelance ceramic designs to extend his factory's range of products. By the 19th century, the concept of a staff designer within a manufacturing industry was becoming more familiar. The United States provided a different model for the design profession, with the pioneering work of Raymond Loewy, Norman Bel Geddes, Walter Dorwin Teague and Henry Dreyfuss. These American industrial designers were direct products of the changes in the American economy in the 1920s, and in particular the effects of the Depression. To stimulate economic growth, manufacturers wanted new products and they looked to the emerging design profession to supply them. Teague is usually considered the first full-time professional designer. He set up his office in 1926 at 210 Madison Avenue and his first commission was a camera for Eastman-Kodak. Bel Geddes worked for the Toledo Scale Company, and the surviving correspondence between designer and client reveals a great deal about early working methods. In particular, Bel Geddes was keen to promote the use of his own name as a marketing device for the product. This showed the new status and power accorded to designers; to reinforce this, American designers produced serious books on design. Self-promotion was the forte of Raymond Loewy, famous for designing the Gestetner duplicating machine, the Lucky Strike cigarette packet and the Greyhound bus. Glamorous and charismatic, Loewy's lifestyle resembled that of a movie star. The designers of this era, sometimes called the **Machine Age**, produced a style called **streamlining** and established the models for European design consultancies.

In Britain, the **Design Research** Unit was founded in the 1930s by Milner Gray and Misha Black. By the late 1940s, they had become the largest design practice in the UK. Crawford's, best known as an **advertising** agency, developed a design office around the same time, but the real expansion of design consultancies took place in the post-war period. In the 1960s, several British consultancies were formed that went on to build international reputations, including Conran Design, Pentagram, Wolff Olins, Minale Tattersfield and Kenneth Grange. All of these tried to distance themselves from the idea that design was associated with styling, priding themselves on providing a complete service for the prospective client. A new generation of consultancies emerged with the retail boom of the late 1970s, including Stewart McColl, David Davies, Michael Peters, Fitch Benoy and Din Associates. For design practices, these were halcyon days. Several went public on the Stock Exchange and overnight their founding partners became millionaires; in the 1980s, designers like Terence Conran and Rodney Fitch featured in the UK's rich list for the first time.

Since then, the creative industries have continued to grow. In 2003, they contributed £11.6 billion to the UK's balance of trade. In the preceding six years they had grown by an average of 6 per cent per annum, three times the rate of the economy as a whole.

Further reading:

Bel Geddes, Norman, *Horizons*. New York: Dover, 1977 [1932].

Blake, Avril, *Misha Black*. London: Design Council, 1984.

—— *Milner Gray*. London: Design Council, 1986.

Cox, Sir George, *The Cox Review of Creativity in Business*. 2005. Available at: <http://www.hm-treasury.gov.uk/independent_reviews/cox_review/coxreview_index.cfm>.

Dreyfuss, Henry, *Designing for People*. New York: Allworth Press, 2003 [1955].

Loewy, Raymond, *Industrial Design*. London: Fourth Estate, 1988 [1979].

Teague, Walter Dorwin, *Design This Day: The Technique of Order in the Machine Age*. London: Studio Publications, 1947 [1940].

DESIGN COUNCIL

A body founded to encourage manufacturers to use designers, to raise the profile of design in British industry and to improve levels of public taste. It began life on 19 December 1944 as the Council of **Industrial Design** (COID), with its arrival announced by Hugh Dalton, President of the Board of Trade. Although the name was changed in 1960 to the Design Council, its brief remained the same.

The COID's first job was to organize an exhibition called 'Britain Can Make It', held at the **Victoria and Albert Museum** in 1946. This event was extremely successful, attracting nearly 1.5 million visitors, and marked the beginning of an exhibition programme in design which continued until 1995. Gordon Russell, whose furniture company of the same name promoted a safe and very British version of Modernism, was COID's director from 1947 to 1960, its most influential period. In these post-war years the idea that design should be democratic and could play an important role in reconstructing British life was widely held, and COID promoted the view that modern design, called 'contemporary design' in the 1950s, had a key social function, even going so far as to suggest that it could undermine class differences. It pursued a vigorous publicity strategy – which included the launch in 1949 of an in-house magazine, *Design*, as well as books and educational material on the subject – and effectively targeted the media. The BBC selected COID-approved furniture for its television programmes, while popular magazines such as *Woman* regularly ran features in collaboration with it.

However, this popularity came to an end in the 1960s, with the challenge of **Pop design**, and the Design Council gradually became less of a central force. The 1970s and 1980s saw four directors: Lord Reilly, Keith Grant, Ivor Owen and Andrew Summer. None of them was able to guide the organization into a new role, and it only narrowly escaped closure. In the 1990s, though, the Design Council radically changed when it moved to Bow Street in Covent Garden. Under a new director, David Kester, it is now playing an energized role in the development of

British design, developing ambitious research and strategy initiatives, such as a very successful website, www.designcouncil.org.uk

Further reading:

Howard, Debra, *50 Years of Design, Schools and the Design Council*. London: Design Council, 1994.

Woodham, Jonathan, 'Managing British Design Reform: Fresh Perspectives on the Early Years of the Council of Industrial Design', *Journal of Design History* 9(1) (1996): 55–65.

—— 'The Question of Taste', *Crafts* 172 (2001): 46–9.

DESIGN EDUCATION

Design education, as is the case with every other discipline, has been shaped by history and economic need. In a modern sense it is a direct response to the needs of a country to enhance its economic prosperity through nurturing its design talent. Historically, though, there have been many ways to acquire a design education. For example, in the artisan craft tradition the Sèvres porcelain factory provided practical training for craftsmen. Architectural training was another well-established route to becoming a designer, while during the **Industrial Revolution** new programmes were set up to train designers for industry. The creation of a rational set of rules for ornament and design suggested new training methods from which the design student could usefully learn. Leading educationalists believed that exercises in simple **geometric** design developed the hand and eye, as well as the manipulative skills needed in the modern industrial world. Such ideas became extremely fashionable. Prince Albert, for example, encouraged his children to mix mortar and lay bricks, while educationalist Frederick Froebel introduced the concept of constructive play by creating building blocks for children. These ideas have retained their popularity over the years. Games like Lego work on the same principle, and even such advanced schools as the Bauhaus in the 1920s reintroduced simple geometric exercises for its students. However, the **Bauhaus** also encouraged more experimentation, as did the American **Cranbrook Academy** and, in the post-war period, **Ulm** in Germany and the **Royal College of Art** in the UK.

Design education is now provided all over the world. In the UK in 2003–4, 140,000 students completed a design course. The debate about what direction such education should take remains focused on the needs of the profession versus the quality of experience offered to the students. In a **Design Council** survey, professional designers expressed concern that current design education was not providing the right skills for the 21st century.

Further reading:

International Journal of Art & Design Education. Available at: <http://www.blackwellpublishing.com/journal.asp?ref=1476-8062>.

DESIGN ETHICS

In the 21st century it is increasingly accepted that businesses should acknowledge their role in the wider community and companies have begun to report on their social and environmental performance. These developments suggest an ethical position in which the designer plays a key role, but while design ethics are widely discussed in the design profession and often connected with social responsibility there are no established or agreed definitions. Design ethics at present suggests a more critically rigorous appraisal of designing and designs as they impact on users and communities. It encourages the application of socially responsible criteria as integral aspects of design and promotes an ethical, and hence professional basis, for evaluating design priorities and practical outcomes. Currently in the UK legislation restrains manufacturers and designers, for example on issues of safety and liability. The international design profession, however, does not have a clear ethical code to compare with that of, for example, the legal or medical profession.

DESIGN EXHIBITIONS

Lavish, large-scale design exhibitions were features of the 19th century. The published catalogues of these events provide an important chronicle of contemporary design developments. They reflect the aspirations, achievements and ambitions of the age, and even though the exhibitions presented a specialized view of design, they provided a forum in which to air key arguments and debates on quality, style, taste, education, industry and commerce.

Exhibitions showing the history of design started in France, and soon spread to the rest of the Continent. The first French government trade show, called Exposition de l'Industrie, was organized in 1798, and there were eleven more over the next fifty years. Thereafter, France continued to mount exhibitions, the most notable of which was the one in 1889 in Paris, with the Eiffel Tower as its centrepiece. In **design history** terms these French exhibitions were the most important of the century, but also significant was the exhibition in Philadelphia in 1876. And just after the turn of the century, in 1901, Turin staged one of the most impressive exhibitions to date.

The best-known international design exhibitions of the 20th century include the 1925 Paris Exposition des Arts Décoratifs, the 1929 exhibition in Barcelona, the 1930 International Modern Style exhibition in Stockholm, the 1939 **New York World Fair**, the 1958 exhibition in Brussels and the 1960 exhibition in Osaka. The Montreal Expo of 1967 was notable for Otto Frei's German pavilion, with its steel mesh roofs, and for Buckminster Fuller's geodesic domes for the USA pavilion. In 2008 China will host its first World Fair in Shanghai.

Further reading:

Greenhalgh, Paul, *Ephemeral Vistas: The Expositions Universelles, Great Exhibitions and World's Fairs*, 1851–1939. Manchester: Manchester University Press, 1990.

Velarde, Giles, *Designing Exhibitions: Museums, Heritage, Trade and World Fairs*. Aldershot: Ashgate Press, 2001 [1987].

DESIGN FOR DISASSEMBLY (DfD)

Sustainability is now not merely a personal ideology but a highly respected research and development activity at the heart of economic growth. Research communities around the world have sought to establish clear methodologies to establish the new discipline of **sustainable design**, and a new range of terms and descriptions for the processes of sustainable design has been developed. DfD is such a term, introduced in the late 1990s as a design strategy.

This functional and pragmatic approach to design has a long history, which can be traced back to 19th-century American products such as the Colt gun and the Singer sewing machine, which incorporated standardized parts that could be easily obtained, replaced and repaired. These designs were responses to the huge geographical scale of America, which required such flexibility. In the 21st century, however, DfD has come to have a specific meaning in relation to contemporary manufacturing and design needs. It refers to a product whose parts can be easily repaired, reused, remanufactured or recycled at the end of its life. The point of such design is that it allows the easy replacement of failed parts, thereby extending the product's life and offering an alternative to inbuilt obsolescence. Manufacturers understand that products are only likely to be recycled if they can be disassembled and sorted easily and effectively, so that process must be fully integrated into the company's trading and marketing strategies.

The American company Xerox, one of the biggest office appliance manufacturers in the world, offers an interesting DfD case study. In 1938, Chester Carlson, a patent attorney and part-time inventor, made the Xerox first machine in a makeshift laboratory in Astoria, New York City. Thereafter, he spent years trying to sell his invention without success. Finally, in 1948, though, the Xerox 914, the first automatic office copier to use ordinary paper, was manufactured, and millions were sold all over the world. The Xerox 914 is now part of American design history, and is included in the permanent collection at the Smithsonian Institution.

In the 1990s Xerox made a key business decision to design all of its new products for disassembly so that they can be easily repaired and upgraded. The company is also a pioneer in designing and building 'waste-free' products. All Xerox–designed copiers and printers are now developed to be remanufactured at the end of their initial life cycles. They all have replaceable print cartridges, which can be returned free of charge to be reused, remanufactured or recycled; and for some Xerox products the return programme even includes waste toner – a first for the industry.

Further reading:

Dowie-Bhamra, Tracy, 'Design for Disassembly', *Co-Design* 5/6 (1996): 28–33.
Industry Council for Electronic Equipment Recycling. See: <http://www.icer.org.uk/>.

DESIGN FOR NEED

Design for Need was developed in the late 1960s as a socially led approach to design. It was a movement arguing for a fair and equitable distribution of resources across the world, but its success has been limited. In the 21st century, for example, 85 per cent of the world's energy is used by only 25 per cent of the world's population.

Design for Need carries with it a strong social message that was first proposed in a series of design debates in the late 1950s. The visionary thinker and designer Richard Buckminster Fuller (1895–1983) is the most important theoretician of the movement. He suggested an alternative direction for architecture and design in the late 20th century which continues to be an inspiration to an entire generation concerned with human needs and the environment.

Victor Papanek (1925–98), an internationally renowned designer, anthropologist and teacher, did a great deal to popularize these ideas. He wrote a number of design-related books – including *Design for the Real World* (1971), *Nomadic Furniture* (1973), *Nomadic Furniture 2* (1974), *How Things Don't Work* (1977), *Design for Human Scale* (1983) and *Viewing the World Whole* (1983) – that became the standard texts for the movement. Papanek was a pioneer of a more human, ecological and ethically centred design, and his primary concern was using **alternative design** in developing countries. Born in Vienna, he emigrated to the USA as a child in 1932 and graduated in 1948 in architecture and **industrial design** from the Cooper Union. He then studied at MIT under America's most influential architect, Frank Lloyd Wright. He opened his own consulting office in 1953, and later became dean of the School of Design at the California Institute of the Arts, and chairman of Design at the Kansas City Art Institute. Of all his books, *Design for the Real World*, published as a pocket-sized paperback, was the most influential, becoming an immediate success. It remains one of the world's most widely read books on design, and has been translated into twenty-three languages. Fundamentally, it is a plea for design to be seen as a moral activity, not as a marketing device, and in this context the book's subtitle, 'Human Ecology and Social Change', is particularly revealing. Papanek effectively challenged the world of mainstream commercial design by putting it under ethical and political scrutiny. He suggested that young designers should dedicate themselves not to designing another fridge or sofa, but to directing their talents to help the disadvantaged and the underprivileged; advocated **design for recycling**, the use of natural forms and closer relationships between designers, sociologists and anthropologists; and proposed the adoption of a morally responsible and holistic approach to design, adapting technology to the individual's needs and respecting the experience and traditional practice of other cultures, particularly in the developing world. Papanek himself studied Inuit and Native American designs in a bid to understand basic human relationships to the environment. Such research was dismissed at the time, but it is now central to practice within **sustainable design**. The design strategies of traditional forms are key points of reference for alternative design and they remain so for newer forms of **ecodesign**.

Further reading:

Papanek, Victor J., *Design for the Real World*. London: Thames & Hudson, 1985 [1971].

DESIGN FOR RECYCLING

Design for Recycling (DfR) is a design approach which aims to reuse as much of a product as possible when it reaches the end of its life. ('End of life' is now widely used to describe the products a consumer has used and then thrown away.) DfR offers an increasingly successful approach to recycling as a **sustainable** approach to design, manufacturing and disposal. It should be thought of as an integrated design strategy, starting with suitable material selection for a design at its initial stages. Getting the material right helps with its identification and recycling at the end of a product's life. When DfR is built into the beginning of the manufacturing and design process it enhances a product's potential for **disassembly**, reuse and refurbishment, and supports a product's function and market success. So DfR not only saves resources but makes sound business and economic sense.

Several international companies have led the field of DfR research and tackled the key problem of ensuring that materials are labelled to identify them and kept them separate for easy reclamation. Once the material has been located it can then be prepared for reuse by cleaning, grading, shredding or blending before being reintroduced into the manufacturing cycle. 'Recyclate' is the technical term for a new material made from recycled elements.

The Japanese car company Toyota offers an interesting case study. In 1998 it claimed to be the industry's first manufacturer to introduce recycling strategies of easy removal at the design stage. Seven years later, Toyota's Eco-VAS programme introduced an environmental evaluation system that included life-cycle assessment (LCA) from the development process through to production, use and disposal. Toyota claims up to 83 per cent of their vehicles are now recycled. Notable here is the research and investment the company made in the reduction of processing the shredder residue generated by end-of-life vehicles. Another successful innovation is its car-bumper and recycling scheme to recover materials and components, which Toyoto rolled out throughout its Japanese distribution centres.

Another key strategy for successful DfR is the use of a single type of material (mono-material components) in a product. A good example is the plastic drinks bottle, which previously comprised separate and incompatible plastics for the bottle itself, screw top and sleeve. By introducing a bottle using only one plastic for all three elements, nothing is thrown away after recycling and the material collected is pure-grade PET. This simple idea means that it is no longer necessary to separate the collected material or use chemical separating treatments. The ecobottle is also an example of design aiding DfR, because its conical shape means that bottles can be screwed inside each other and piled up for easy storage before recycling. The low neck of the ecobottles also means that the pile increases by only 1.5 cm for each bottle added.

New legislation to determine DfR targets within the consumer electronics industry will also shape the future of the design profession. DfR will be given a new impetus to set targets for the safe disposal, recovery, recycling and reuse of electrical and electronic components.

Further reading:

Reclaimed: Recycling in Contemporary British Craft and Design. London: British Council, 1999.

DESIGN HISTORY

When the Design History Society was established in Britain in 1977, it marked a small but significant development in the study of design. Before this date the history of consumer products was generally called the history of decorative arts or the the history of applied arts. Study in this area was the territory of museums or antiques collectors. It was not possible to read Design in the conventional British university sense, and Design History as a subject did not exist, except as a small ancillary part in History of Art and Architecture courses.

In the early 20th century, however, there had been two pioneers of design history: Sigfried Giedion (1888–1964) and Nikolaus Pevsner (1902–83). In 1948 Giedion's book *Mechanization Takes Command* argued that the modern world and its artefacts were continuously affected by scientific and industrial progress. He was the first to argue that the anonymous technical aspects of history are just as important as the history of creative individuals, which had dominated, and still dominates, much of the history of design. This view, which suggested a wider cultural approach to design, was deeply influential. *Mechanization Takes Command* looked at developments in Chicago slaughter-houses, and suggested that their use of conveyor belts could be applied to modern industry. Other case studies included the Yale lock and the Colt gun. Giedion had trained as an art historian under Heinrich Wolfflin before becoming a defender of **Modern Movement** principles, and he devoted much of his professional life to promoting modern architecture. In 1928 he became the secretary of ClAM, and in the 1940s his Harvard lectures on the theme of Modernism were published as *Space, Time and Architecture*.

Nikolaus Pevsner arrived in Britain as a refugee in 1936, and went on to become the country's most important writer on architecture and design. He also virtually invented the history of architecture and the history of design as subjects worthy of serious academic study. His book *The Pioneers of Modern Design*, first published in 1936, has become standard reading for many design undergraduates. This book's success, due in a large part to its accessible and rational approach, has given Pevsner a legendary status in the field of design studies. It is much more than a simple history, having helped to create a popular perception of design history which has shaped common tastes and ideas. Pevsner saw the development of design as a road that led to Modernism and Walter Gropius, and his book espoused a single and powerful ideology.

Pevsner was born in Leipzig, the son of academic Jewish parents. In the early 1930s he taught at Göttingen University, and after fleeing to England he introduced rigorous German methods to British academic life. His first job, at Birmingham University, was to prepare a research report into the role of design in British industry. It made sobering reading. After the war he was appointed Slade Professor of Fine Art at Cambridge, a post he held from 1949 to 1955. During the 1960s and 1970s he worked on his mammoth survey of the buildings of England. Inevitably, his pre-eminence and his defence of Modern Movement principles have come in for criticism. No one, however, can challenge his position as one of the great historians of the 20th century.

Another early British pioneer in the development of design history was Herbert Read (1893–1968), Britain's foremost **avant-garde** critic of art, literature and design from the 1930s to the 1960s. He was the only British critic of his generation who worked out an all-embracing view of art and design. Although most of his writings were concerned with a defence of modern art, one of his most important books concentrated on design, *Art and Industry* (1934). At that time he was living in

Hampstead, a stone's throw from Henry Moore, Barbara Hepworth and Ben Nicholson, and during that period he met Piet Mondrian, László Moholy-Nagy and Walter Gropius. In *Art and Industry* Read helped to popularize design, or 'machine art', as he so tellingly called it. Although he profoundly disliked industrial culture, he championed the idea that utilitarian objects, such as metal operating tables, could and should be beautiful. For a whole generation of 1930s British designers Read's book was a significant turning point. It was not surprising, then, that when Milner Gray set up one of the country's first design practices, the **Design Research** Unit, Read was invited to become its first director. In the post-war period, however, his popularity diminished. The new generation of **Pop** writers and critics took exception to his idea that the artist was the sole possessor of eternal truths and to his implicit rejection of the world of **popular culture** to which they were so strongly committed.

The emergence of design history as a separate area of study was a direct response to changes in British art and **design education** in the 1960s. An overhaul was long overdue and the Coldstream Report recommended that the old diploma qualification for a designer should be upgraded to a degree, in line with wider university education. Rightly or wrongly, part of this upgrading was a compulsory element of contextual studies, which traditionally occupied 15 per cent of the student's time and accounted for 20 per cent of their final marks.

When these changes were implemented, Art History departments in British art schools and polytechnics underwent an expansion, and design students in the areas of graphics, **industrial design** and fashion started to demand teaching in their own subject histories. Academic staff therefore had to develop new courses, often with little in the way of resources to help them. In the 1970s books on design history were thin on the ground, so students learned directly from hands-on experience of the objects and from such series as the post-war Faber guides, which were really aimed at the antiques collectors' market. However, Gillian Naylor's book *The Arts and Crafts Movement* appeared in 1971, and Tim and Charlotte Benton developed an early Open University Design History course. The Bentons did a great deal to bring together young UK art school lecturers and encourage them to build up the new subject area of Design History. They were not, however, among the founder members of the Design History Society. Those included Penny Sparke, now at Kingston University and author of several important books on design, Stephen Bayley, the first director of the **Design Museum**, Dorothy Bosomworth, Alan Crawford, Jonathan Woodham and Catherine McDermott, who became the society's chairperson in the early 1980s. The society organized a newsletter, lectures and conferences, and built up a network of members interested in design history which has expanded into an international organization with annual conferences and the *Journal of Design History*, published by Oxford University Press.

Gradually the new subject gained ground. Several universities, including Brighton, Staffordshire and Newcastle, offered degrees in Design History and publishers started to commission books on the subject. There were, however, criticisms of these developments from some distinguished museum curators who felt that they were the guardians of the subject. Simon Jervis, then a curator at the **Victoria and Albert Museum**, described the focus on design after the **Industrial Revolution** as blinkered. Unfortunately, the development of design history in Britain coincided with a period of educational cutbacks, so the possibilities for sabbaticals and research grants were virtually non-existent. By and large, polytechnic lecturers did not have the resources or the time to forge a strong intellectual base to the subject, but the analytical methods they developed were important. These include the use of methodologies that are also used in sociology, philosophy and anthropology. Critically important in this have been the theories of the French philosopher Roland Barthes, who provided an intellectual element and methodology to design history that many felt it had previously lacked.

In Britain a series of books exploring issues of style and design were written by graduates and teachers at Birmingham University's Centre for Contemporary Studies, with a pioneer of the genre being Dick Hebdige in his *Subculture: The Meaning of Style* (1979). In addition, the writings of university academics in economics and the history of technology have enriched the understanding of design. In this context American academics have made a significant contribution to design history, and their work has helped to broaden the field, with interdisciplinary connections to women's studies, **visual culture** and the social sciences. From that perspective have come definitive accounts of the home, shopping, housework and the fashion industries, and the journal *Design Issues* has been influential. Design history is now recognized as a key element within design education and has become an accepted subject area and an established part of the educational agenda.

Further reading:

Design Issues. See: <http://mitpress.mit.edu/catalog/item/default.asp?ttype=4&tid=19>.

Giedion, Sigfried, *Mechanization Takes Command: A Contribution to Anonymous History*. New York: Norton, 1969 [1948].

—— *Space, Time and Architecture: The Growth of a New Tradition*. Cambridge, MA: Harvard University Press, 1967 [1941].

Hebdige, Dick, *Subculture: The Meaning of Style*. London: Routledge, 2002 [1979].

Journal of Design History. See: <http://jdh.oxfordjournals.org/>.

Naylor, Gillian, *The Arts and Crafts Movement: A Study of its Sources, Ideals and Influences on Design Theory*. London: Trefoil, 1990 [1971].

Pevsner, Nikolaus, *Pioneers of Modern Design: From William Morris to Walter Gropius*. London: Yale University Press, 2005 [1936].

Read, Herbert, *Art and Industry: The Principles of Industrial Design*. London: Faber and Faber, 1966 [1934].

DESIGN MAGAZINES

The development of a specialist design press really took off after the Second World War. *British Design* magazine, launched in 1949 as the house publication of the **Design Council**, is a good example of this, but the history of design publications is actually much longer. However, during the 18th and 19th centuries publicizing rising stars and shaping public opinion and taste in the area of design remained the preserve of books until the end of the Victorian era. A range of home-improvement periodicals had already appeared by then, but the first journal dedicated to profiling innovative design was *Studio* magazine, which began in 1893.

Financed by a Yorkshire businessman, Charles Holmes (1848–1922), *Studio*'s editorial policy was to focus on progressive artists and designers: its first issue featured Aubrey Beardsley, and it published a lengthy profile of Charles Rennie Mackintosh in 1897. It numbered many European designers and architects among its subscribers, and constituted essential reading for them, much as *Domus* did later. An American edition was launched in 1897, the *Studio Yearbooks* were published from 1907, and there was a series of special issues, including one in 1906 called 'The Art Revival in Austria', which introduced the work of the **Wiener Werkstätte**.

Although individual groups of designers published their own magazines, as did design organizations such as the **Deutsche Werkbund** and the **Design and Industries Association**, the concept of a distinctive, specialized design press did not really take off until the 1960s. Then, for the first time, design journalism made an appearance, in the

USA with the writings of Tom Wolfe (b. 1931), and in Britain with those of Peter Reyner Banham (1922–88), Britain's most important post-war design writer.

A founder member of the **Independent Group**, Banham was closely involved in the 1950s with the new **Pop** aesthetic. In some respects, he was a conventional academic: his Ph.D. thesis on the **Modern Movement**, which he wrote under Nikolaus Pevsner's supervision, was later published as *Theory and Design in the First Machine Age*. From 1958 to 1975, however, he wrote many pieces for the *New Statesman* dealing with design, technology, the mass media and **popular culture**. Those articles covered a diverse range of subjects, including customized Minis, household gadgets, the cult film *Barbarella*, the children's puppet programme *Thunderbirds*, sunglasses and **folk art**, and they made a major contribution to **Pop design** theory. Banham developed a theoretical basis for Pop in terms of its cultural relevance to the 1960s, and gave the era its first informed critique of Pop design. His writing was witty and accessible, and challenged the traditional hierarchy of high versus low culture. He dismissed the idea that architectural theory and writing provided the only basis from which to discuss such disciplines as **interior design** and furniture, and his insights on contemporary culture reshaped the world of design writing:

Tom Wolfe is part of the post-war generation of writers on design. He is also the inventor of a new style of design writing called '**New Journalism**', which emerged in the USA during the 1960s as the journalistic equivalent of Pop design. The idea was to use an accessible writing style that picked up on slang, **advertising** jargon and the vernacular. The approach is suggested by the titles and subjects of some of his most famous books, *The Kandy-Kolored Tangerine-Flake Streamlined Baby* and *The Electric Kool-Aid Acid Test*, both published in 1968. Wolfe's books became essential reading during the sixties, and his influence as a writer and critic has proved enduring. Wolfe invented the phrase the 'me-decade' to describe the 1970s, but his satire on social aspirations shifted to architecture in the 1980s with the popular critique *From Bauhaus to Our House* (1981). More recently, he has developed into a serious writer of fiction. The publication of his novel exploring the social mores of New York life, *Bonfire of the Vanities* (1988), caused a sensation. This savage satire was Wolfe's attempt to write a novel with the style and scope of Victorian writers such as Dickens and Thackeray.

When Wolfe was making his name in America in the 1960s, newspapers in Britain started to use regular design correspondents for the first time. One such was Fiona McCarthy, who worked for the *Guardian*. These initiatives were abandoned with the recession of the 1970s, but they reappeared with a vengeance in the 1980s. In Britain alone the 'designer decade' saw the launch of *Creative Review, Designers' Journal, Interior Design, Designer, Eye, Design Week* and perhaps the best known of all, *Blueprint*. Launched in 1984, *Blueprint* was edited by Deyan Sudjic, who later became the editor of *Domus*. Using a distinctive layout and photography, it charted the major international trends of the 1980s.

Another key journalist of the time was Peter York (real name Peter Wallis), a well-known writer and broadcaster on British style and society. In the early 1980s he wrote a series of articles for the society magazine *Harpers & Queen* in which he coined the phrase 'Sloane Ranger' to describe a certain type of woman and her upmarket accoutrements: Barbour jackets, Hermès headscarves and green wellington boots. York went on to identify the Princess of Wales as the perfect example of the species and later wrote a bestselling book, *The Official Sloane Ranger Handbook*, described by Tom Wolfe as a 'seminal sociological study'. York developed a writing style in the manner of Wolfe and still writes for leading newspapers.

In the 21st century design journalism is a specialized area of writing that appears in many of the world's quality newspapers. Chief exponents include Stephen Bayley for the *Observer* and Alice Rawsthorn for the *Herald Tribune*.

Further reading:

Banham, Peter Reyner, *Theory and Design in the First Machine Age*. Cambridge, MA: MIT Press, 1980 [1960].

Barr, Ann and York, Peter, *The Official Sloane Ranger Handbook: The First Guide to What Really Matters in Life*. London: Ebury, 1982.

Wolfe, Tom, *From Bauhaus to Our House*. London: Vintage, 1999 [1981].

—— *The Bonfire of the Vanities*. London: Picador, 1999 [1988].

—— *The Kandy-Kolored Tangerine-Flake Streamlined Baby*. London: Vintage, 2005 [1968].

—— *The Electric Kool-Aid Acid Test*. New York: Bantam Books, 1999 [1968].

—— *The New Journalism*. London: Pan, 1975.

DESIGN MANAGEMENT

Design management seeks to position design as an essential part of business strategy. In 1975 the Design Management Institute (DMI) was founded in America to support the growing move to professionalize design and integrate it in a serious way into business and industry. It followed the establishment of a series of Design Management post-graduate courses at US universities.

Design management has a long history as a theory devised to impose rational organization on factories and offices. This began in the early 20th century with Frederick Taylor, whose pioneering attempts became known as **Taylorism**. Design management is now firmly on the agenda of every successful company. In the post-war period it grew with the rise of middle managers, outlined by Alfred Chandler in *The Visible Hand: The Managerial Revolution in American Business*, a book that won the prestigious Pulitzer Prize in 1977 and rooted management technology firmly in the sphere of business history. More recent work on design management theory has been less thorough, generating a debased 'airport paperback' genre that relies on anecdotal evidence, which makes the task of defining design management more difficult. However, although the theory can often result in generalization and a blinkered view of design, it is rising up the management agenda, even though the efforts of management theorists to incorporate design into their theories have not been entirely successful. There is also a move to change the name of design management to design strategy or **design policy**, with the aim being to locate design at the heart of new business development.

Further reading:

Chandler, Alfred D., *The Visible Hand: The Managerial Revolution in American Business*. Cambridge, MA: Harvard University Press, 1977.

Sebastian, Rizal, 'The Interface between Design and Management', *Design Issues*, Winter (2005): 81–93.

Taylor, Frederick Winslow, *The Principles of Scientific Management*. London: Harper & Bros., 1911.

DESIGN MUSEUM

Officially opened in 1989 by the then Prime Minister, Margaret Thatcher, the museum was the brainchild of Sir Terence Conran, founder of the **Habitat** retail group. In 1981 he established the Conran Foundation as a charitable institution to fund and run the new museum, the first of its kind. Conran had been thinking about a project to promote design in this way for several years, and in 1979 he met Stephen Bayley, then a young university lecturer, whom he appointed to oversee his plans. At first the project was given space in the old boiler rooms of the **Victoria and Albert Museum**, which Conran converted into a gleaming white exhibition space in return for a five-year lease. From 1982 to 1987, the Boilerhouse, as it was called, put on a series of contemporary design exhibitions on such subjects as Sony, Philippe Garner, **Memphis**, National Characteristics of Design and **Youth Culture**. Shortly after the new museum opened in Butlers Wharf, Bayley resigned to work as a design researcher and journalist.

The museum is now established on the design map, also running an innovative MA programme titled Curating Contemporary Design, training the next generation of young design curators. In 2006 Deyan Sudjic, then Dean of Design at Kingston University, was invited to steer the museum into a programme of expansion for 2012 which will see it moving to a new location alongside the Tate Modern on London's Southbank.

Further reading:

McDermott, Catherine, *Design Museum: 20th Century Design*. New York: Overlook Press, 2000.

DESIGN POLICY

Design policy has become more strategically important as part of economic planning, and there has been a serious move to integrate its strategies into business development. Long considered a useful but optional element in business, design policies are now commonly seen as essential, and not having one is viewed as a major oversight in any forward-thinking, modern company. In this way the role of design is formalized, even in some instances professionalized, within large companies and organizations.

Design Policy is a subject explored by leading business schools and universities as part of the training required for a new generation of managers, financiers and entrepreneurs. Importantly, it is also seen as part of government thinking. Gordon Brown, when Chancellor of the Exchequer, in 2005 commissioned the Cox Report, an important study which set out to establish UK design policy for the 21st century.

Further reading:

Cox, Sir George, *The Cox Review of Creativity in Business*. 2005. Available at: <http://www.hm-treasury.gov.uk/independent_reviews/cox_review/coxreview_index.cfm>.

DESIGN RESEARCH

Design research has a long history, but over the last ten years it has been given a new focus and meaning as it has become an independent activity within the university sector. In the past, the body of writing on design has tended to be subsumed within the parent disciplines of art and architecture. Typical of historically important design writings is *The Analysis of Beauty* (1756), a defence of the **Rococo** decorative style by the painter William Hogarth.

In the 18th century design publications took the form of pattern books or treatises, which included theories on such contemporary issues as the sublime and the picturesque. The first modern books on design theory started to appear in the 19th century and generally fell into two categories. The first were linked to the new theories of **design education** and centred on the School of Design (later the **Royal College of Art**). These writings include the work of Owen Jones (1809–74) and Christopher Dresser (1834–1904), who advocated a **geometric** approach to ornament based on nature and the study of the past, including Islamic and Classical forms. The second group of books comprised responses to the effects of the **Industrial Revolution**, and among them the writings of the architect Augustus Pugin (1812–52) are particularly important. Like Pugin, John Ruskin (1819–1900) and Gottfried Semper (1803–79) also linked design to architecture in the 19th century. However, by far the largest body of design theory came from the British **Arts and Crafts Movement** led by William **Morris**. He was the most important design writer of the century, and, together with many of his followers, he published his thesis that design should be related to social theory. The designers of the Arts and Crafts Movement continued to publish books and essays right into the 1920s, and their views were widely read and imitated.

In the early 20th century manifestos from practitioners of the **Modern Movement** focused on art and architecture, but design as a key component of the new **Machine Age** was also included. Le Corbusier's writings praised the values of **mass production** and standardized objects like the Thonet bentwood chair, which he named '*objets-types*'. The most far-reaching ideas on design theory came from Walter Gropius, director of the **Bauhaus**. He had read the works of Morris and followed Hermann Muthesius's campaign at the **Deutsche Werkbund** for standardization. The tradition of designers themselves writing about design was taken up in the USA by the newly emerging **industrial design** profession of the 1920s and 1930s. It was then that

Norman Bel Geddes published his book *Horizons* in praise of the machine.

After the Second World War design theory allied itself to the new theories of business management and scientific methodology. **Ergonomics**, developed during the war as a scientific attempt to design machinery with human comfort and efficiency taken into full account, became fashionable. 'Design Methods' was the name for a movement that looked at a systemic method to design. Important here is **Ulm**, the German school of design, and in the 1960s at the **Royal College of Art** the work of British academic Bruce Archer and later Christopher Jones and Nigel Cross. This was an attempt to break down the stages of design in order to make the process accessible and easy to understand and to enable design to work with disciplines such as behavioural pyschology and anthropology.

Alongside these developments, design theory and criticism were becoming more interdisciplinary and eclectic. Its sources included the works of the French philosopher Roland Barthes, and it borrowed from disciplines including sociology, anthropology and art history. Design research and theory have also benefited in the last twenty years from the emergence of new areas of study, particularly those dealing with minorities, including women, ethnic and sexual minorities. The area of women's studies, for example, has informed important new ideas about kitchen planning and management.

By the 1990s, the aim of design research was to develop a critical body of knowledge to enhance the discipline and raise its status to that of other practice fields, such as architecture and engineering. Design research has sought to develop a working methodology to understand design processes and applications in the widest possible context in order to promote best practice and problem-solving methods to increase the economic success of design. It therefore has considerable potential for improving our use and management of design. Since the 1990s, in the UK government research funding has provided new opportunities for design researchers, and the field has continued to grow. In 1993 Professor Christopher Frayling identified three types of academic research in art and design which helped to define the field: research into art and design; research through art and design; and research for art and design.

Design research has developed a rich interdisciplinary culture, with designers working alongside social scientists, psychologists, marketing and management specialists. The United Kingdom is now recognized as having a leading role in the international design research community. In the 21st century there is a diverse design research programme within universities that is 'open source'. Central to the academic approach is that research findings are accessible to the international community via journals such as the *Design Journal*, books, conferences and online networks. Many university design research centres also promote Knowledge Transfer Partnerships (KTP) to offer consultancy and research support to external organizations. Design research can be divided into several key areas, including: continuing research and development by design companies which have a technical or product focus on specific materials or processes; individual designers and organizations who theorize and write about design; the academic world, centred on international universities, which produces studies in design that attempt to construct theoretical frameworks for design questions; research into specific design problems, such as those to do with childcare or **sustainability**; exploration of user needs; and **design management**. It should, however, be noted that tensions between the design profession and academics can still be identified.

Further reading:

Hogarth, William, *The Analysis of Beauty*. New Haven, CT: Yale University Press, 1997 [1753].

Laurel, Brenda (ed.), *Design Research: Methods and Perspectives*. Cambridge, MA: MIT Press, 2003.

DESIGNER LABELS

Literally the tapes sewn into a garment to identify a particular maker or fashion house, but also signifiers of the wearer's lifestyle. Designer labels have therefore always been in a hierarchy, but in the late 20th century they developed into a major retail phenomenon. Well-informed customers always knew perfectly well that a Savile Row suit by Anderson and Shepherd was a more valuable and higher-status item than a Burton's off-the-peg version. However, in the 1980s designer labels no longer only indicated quality but suggested style and became desirable for the labels themselves. This phenomenon had been sparked in the previous decade by the craze for designer denim jeans. Such fashion items became **cult objects** not because they were better made than other brands but because they carried a designer label. Designer-label goods were therefore expensive not because of their costly materials but because of their associated lifestyle. The importance of the label for **Postmodern** styling means that it connects you to any number of **subcultures** or lifestyles.

In retail terms 'label' is interchangeable nowadays with the term 'brand'. Designers are expected to brand or label not only their signature products, say Vivienne Westwood clothes, but a range of products including spectacles, baby clothes, perfume, pet accessories and even food.

Further reading:

Breward, Christopher, *Fashion*. Oxford: Oxford University Press, 2003.
Ewing, Elizabeth and Mackrell, Alice, *History of 20th Century Fashion*. London: Batsford, 2005 [1974].

DEUTSCHE WERKBUND

A German organization founded in 1906 to promote design and industry. It was loosely modelled on the British design **guilds**, but with an important distinction. The Werkbund was not a social experiment or an exclusive designer club but was established to promote the interests of manufacturers, industrialists, artists and designers. Very quickly it became a much more important organization in Germany than its UK equivalent, the **Design and Industries Association**, did in Britain. Founder members of the Werkbund included Peter Behrens (1896–1940), the Austrians Josef Hoffmann (1870–1956) and Joseph Maria Olbrich (1867–1908), Bruno Paul (1874–1968) and Richard Riemerschmid (1868–1957). Significantly, important manufacturers were also involved in founding the group.

In 1907 Hermann Muthesius (1861–1927), author of the influential *Das englische Haus* (1904–5) and superintendent of the Prussian Board of Trade for Schools of Arts and Crafts, made a speech at the newly founded Commercial College in Berlin in which he set out the problems facing German industry. He stressed that if Germany wished to achieve industrial supremacy, it was essential to produce soundly designed and well-manufactured goods. He also warned of an economic recession if designs were simply copied from the 'form-treasury' of the past century. While Muthesius's views aroused some opposition, particularly from the German arts and crafts establishment, he was supported by a number of influential figures, including Peter Bruckmann, a prominent manufacturer of silverware.

The declared aim of the Deutsche Werkbund was 'The improvement of industrial products through the combined efforts of artists, industrialists and craftsmen,' but it was concerned not only with craft objects but with mass-produced items and the latest forms of transportation. The Werkbund yearbooks illustrate examples of locomotives, aircraft, motor cars, ocean liners and urban transport systems, all of which are considered from the practical as well as the aesthetic standpoint.

Peter Behrens is the best known of the designers associated with the Werkbund. In 1906 he was invited to design publicity material for the electrical company AEG by its far-sighted managing director, Walter Rathenau. The following year he was appointed coordinating architect to AEG. In this capacity he designed not only buildings, including a famous turbine factory (1908–9), but electric lighting systems, fans, kettles, ovens, clocks, typefaces and shop-fronts. He continued to design for the company until the outbreak of war in 1914.

The best example of the Werkbund's self-confidence was the large-scale exhibition it mounted at Cologne in 1914. This included buildings by Behrens, Walter Gropius, Muthesius, Hoffmann, Paul, Bruno Taut and Henri van de Velde. Gropius's model factory and Taut's glass pavilion have entered the folklore of the **Modern Movement**. The buoyant confidence in industry displayed at Cologne may be contrasted with the 'backward-looking' approach of the British **Arts and Crafts** Exhibition which opened in Paris at exactly the same time.

After the 1914–18 war, the Werkbund became less concerned with **industrial design**. In 1920 a designer and friend of Mies van der Rohe, Lilly Reich, became the group's first woman director, and she organized an exhibition of German design at the Museum of Art in Newark, USA. This inspired a new interest in America in product aesthetics. In 1927, now under the direction of van der Rohe himself, the Werkbund organized an exhibition devoted to housing in Stuttgart. The Weissenhof Seidlung, an ideal suburb, was the outcome. In 1934, in the face of Nazi disapproval, the Werkbund was disbanded. However, it was revived after the Second World War and is still in existence today.

Further reading:

Campbell, Joan, *The German Werkbund: The Politics of Reform in the Applied Arts.* Princeton: Princeton University Press, 1978.

Schwartz, Frederic J., *The Werkbund: Design Theory and Mass Culture before the First World War.* New Haven, CT: Yale University Press, 1996. www. deutscher-werkbund.de

DIY

Do-it-yourself is a long and proud tradition of amateur making, which gathered force in the middle of the 20th century as men attempted home-improvement projects. By the 1950s, there was a network of clubs, magazines and television programmes teaching men to build garden sheds, modernize Victorian houses and turn them into contemporary interiors, and make their own furniture. DIY carries with it nostalgic and innocent connotations for a particular generation born just after the war. At the heart of this culture is an idealized view of the father, the family and the domestic home. In the 1970s, however, the term was upturned by the same generation and came to mark the subversive and anarchic ambitions of **Punk**. Jamie Reid used DIY in the form of ransom-note lettering on the cover of the Sex Pistols' *Never Mind the Bollocks* album, to stand for the power of people to make music, design and art without the support of big business and mainstream culture. DIY stood for individualism and rebellion, and the potential to invent one's own culture.

In the 1990s youth activism again gave DIY a new meaning as it came to represent the potential of technology to liberate entertainment. Rave parties, a phenomenon of the decade, were made possible by rapidly circulated text messages which would announce a venue, and a party would take place before the police could intervene. But DIY's meaning was not confined to hedonistic party opportunities. Groups with serious political ambitions, such as the Eco Warriors, used DIY strategies of self-organization and consequently had a significant impact.

Further reading:

Conran, Terence, *Terence Conran's DIY by Design*. London: Conran Octopus, 1989.
McKay, George (ed.), *DiY Culture: Party and Protest in Nineties Britain*. London: Verso, 1998.

DUTCH DESIGN

The Netherlands has enjoyed a rich design tradition since the 16th century, when the country was an important trading power. The craft tradition extended well into the 19th century with, for example, the ceramics of the Koninklikje Nederlandsche Fabriek (the Royal Dutch Factory). The introduction of industrial techniques, however, sparked off a debate about the direction of design, influenced by the British **Arts and Crafts Movement**, which led to the founding of the Vereeniging ter Veredeling van het Ambacht (VANK; Society for the Enoblement of the Crafts), an influential body which championed the work of designer craftspeople. However, VANK was out of step with new moves to come to terms with industry and the modern world pioneered by organizations such as the **Deutsche Werkbund** in Germany.

Against this background, the emergence of the **De Stijl** group, the Netherlands' most important contribution to 20th-century design, is rather surprising. This small group of individuals was to make a significant contribution to the **Modern Movement**, with its best-known work coming in the form of the purist **geometrical** paintings of Piet Mondrian and the minimalist structure of Gerrit Rietveld's red–blue chair. De Stijl encouraged a vital Dutch Modernist Movement that affected many areas of design and architecture in the 1930s.

On an international scale, the Netherlands' best-known company is Philips, established in 1891, and boasting its own design studio from the late 1920s. Philips produces consumer products for industry and the home, and it has a reputation for a safe, middle–of–the–road approach to design. However, Dutch design enjoys a strong tradition of clean–cut **Modernist** graphics which continues with Total Design, set up in the 1960s by Wim Crouwel, whose most notable commissions have been for the Dutch Post Office. Studio Dumbar, founded by Gert Dumbar, has a rather different approach in that Dumbar incorporates non-functional, witty or ironic elements in his design.

More recently, these qualities have been expressed by a design cooperative called Droog ('dry' in Dutch), founded in Amsterdam in 1993 by Gijs Bakker and Renny Ramakers, who came to public attention at the Milan Furniture Fair of 1994. Droog experimented with waste materials, **found objects** and playful shapes and imagery which marked a new direction for Dutch design. Leading clients who commissioned Droog work include the ceramic manufacturer Rosenthal and Mandarina Duck, the Italian luggage company. Bakker taught at one of Holland's most important design schools, the **Design Academy Eindhoven**, which became a centre for new directions and research in design. Droog worked collectively and its designers, including Marcel Wanders, showed their work together (inspired by the **Memphis** example of ten years earlier). Hella Jongerius is another Dutch designer with a distinctive vision. Droog manufactured her early designs but she now runs Jongeriuslab, her Rotterdam studio, developing products for manufacturers such as Vitra. The work of these designers has had an enormous influence on approaches to design practice and ensured that a Dutch aesthetic inspires international design directions.

Further reading:

Ramakers, Renny, *Less + More: Droog Design in Context*. Rotterdam: 010, 2002.

ECLECTICISM

A combination of the views and styles of different sources and periods. Applied to design, eclecticism is often used in a disparaging sense, but it originally described the practice of selecting the most desirable elements from **visual culture**. And in the context of 21st-century **Postmodernism** it positively represents the trend towards diversity. Nowadays, a global citizen could wear ethnic clothes, listen to rap music, watch reality television programmes, eat McDonald's for lunch and sushi for supper, and shop for French perfume on the Internet.

During the 19th century, when the West was confronted not only with the panorama of its own art and **design history** but with the magnificence of the East, eclecticism became an important issue. Owen Jones, architect, designer and Orientalist, called for an intelligent and imaginative eclecticism as a response to the vast array of sources from which the contemporary designer could draw inspiration. He, along with Christopher Dresser, E.W. Godwin, Bruce Talbert and Lewis F. Day, borrowed from Islamic, Indian, Chinese and Japanese sources.

Although frowned on by the hardliners of the **Modern Movement**, eclecticism remained a 20th-century theme. Eclectic design affords a freedom of selection and imagery, which has proved very attractive to many contemporary designers. Current taste in **interior design**, for example, often combines antique furniture with aggressive, modernist, **high-tech** materials.

Eclecticism is very close to **historicism**, but the key difference is that the former combines diverse styles in a single product or interior.

Further reading:

Jones, Owen, *The Grammar of Ornament*. London: Dorling Kindersley, 2001 [1856].

ECOCENTRISM

Sustainable and environmental issues have always attracted strong individual thinkers and practitioners, one of whom is the founder of ecocentrism, the Norwegian philosopher Arne Naess (b. 1937). In his role as Professor of Philosophy at the University of Oslo, Naess advocated total commitment to a deeper and more harmonious relationship between place, self, community and the natural world. He was deeply influenced by Rachel Carson's moving testament to the impact of pesticides on the American landscape, *Silent Spring*, and by his own personal commitment to nature. In 1937 he built a cabin on Hallingskarvet Mountain in central Norway, where he developed his work on ecology, thereby putting into practice the 'deep ecology' of his philosophy.

A 1990s movement, ecocentrism perceives humans as part of nature rather than in control of it. An ecocentric attitude favours low–impact technology and is concerned with the environmental impact of large-scale economic growth and industrial development. Emphasis is placed on the value of morally and ecologically sound alternatives. The movement enjoys an international following and produces many websites and publications.

The counter-position, technocentrism, argues that technology is the key driver of human advancement, and the means by which the environment can be managed for the benefit of present and future generations. It is based on an ideology of progress, efficiency and control, and is unwilling to engage in discussions of the wider political, social and ethical dimensions of environmental issues.

Further reading:

Carson, Rachel, *Silent Spring*. Harmondsworth: Penguin, 2000 [1963].
Katz, Eric, Light, Andrew and Rothenberg, David, *Beneath the Surface: Critical Essays in the Philosophy of Deep Ecology*. Cambridge, MA: MIT Press, 2000.

ECODESIGN

The principle of determining which strategy and approach will achieve the most environmentally considered design outcome. Ecodesign is concerned with maximizing the efficiency of a product or system in terms of energy and use of resources. It considers all the environmental impacts of a product throughout its life cycle, alongside standard design criteria such as function, quality and appearance. It also incorporates **green design** practice and places it in the context of a more holistic environmental awareness, seeking to get more utility and value from fewer resources, a principle expressed as **eco-efficiency**. In this sense, ecodesign has been described as being 'greener' than green design, which often focuses on just one part of a product's life cycle.

Ecodesign is closely connected with life-cycle design (LCD) and life-cycle assessment (LCA) which identify points of greatest potential environmental gain in a product's life cycle. The life-cycle principle considers a product's life from the extraction of raw materials, through manufacture, distribution, use, to final disposal, and it is sometimes expressed as a 'cradle-to-grave' approach. More ambitious and holistic is the 'cradle-to-cradle' principle, in which the elements of a product at its end of life become the sources for a new generation of products, perpetuating a closed resource loop which minimizes the need to extract further raw materials. McDonough and Braungart's book discussing this approach is made from waterproof, durable and recyclable plastic, making it ideal for reuse once its lessons have been learned.

Ecodesign tools allow the designer to focus on key points in the life cycle of a product and minimize its environmental impact. Ecodesign strategies include not using hazardous materials, striving for low energy **consumption**, lightweighting, modular construction from uniform elements, and **design for recycling/design for disassembly** (designing for easy dismantling at end of life to allow reuse and recycling of constituent elements). Ecodesign thinks holistically about a product: for example, using fewer components leads to a reduction in total weight, which reduces environmental impact during transportation.

Ecolabels applied to products denote that they meet performance requirements and specific criteria relating to reduced environmental impact and **sustainable** resources. Some of world's strictest ecolabels include Canada's Environmental Choice, Germany's Blue Angel and the US Environmental Protection Agency's Energy Star programme.

Widespread ecodesign practice is being driven by the introduction of takeback legislation which requires producers to collect products at their end of life for disposal, reuse or recycling. The Waste Electrical and Electronic Equipment (WEEE) Directive, for example, will oblige manufacturers to include ecodesign principles in the design of all their new products.

The American manufacturer Herman Miller's modern classic Aeron chair is designed with the life cycle in mind: many of its components have recycled content; it is easily disassembled for refurbishment and repair, extending its life; the design is lightweight; and it is made from a small number of materials, making sorting and recycling easy at end of life.

Further reading:

McDonough, William and Braungart, Michael, *Cradle to Cradle: Remaking the Way We Make Things*. New York: North Point Press, 2002.

ECO-EFFICIENCY

A term used to describe the delivery of goods and services that satisfy human needs and enable high quality of life while minimizing associated environmental impact throughout a product's life cycle. It reflects the basic principles of doing more with less, and that with a more efficient use of resources there is a consequent reduced environmental impact. In addition, eco-efficiency seeks to introduce scientific research methods into **sustainable design** by quantifying, rigorously analysing and testing the amount of utility extracted from each unit of natural resources. While still not an exact science, the aim is to develop a system of measurement to evaluate all new projects and initiatives. The principle of this system expresses the relationship between an output (the utility provided by a product, service or activity) and the input (the environmental impact associated with the provision of the output throughout its life cycle). Maximizing eco-efficiency involves gaining more output per unit of environmental input, and so achieving more with less. Target goals are sometimes set in the form of the 'Factor X' – the improvement in eco-efficiency required to bring a resource's use within the limits of the earth's natural system. A target of Factor Four, for example, denotes extracting twice as much utility or half as much resource.

Technical eco-efficiency is the exploitation of technological advances to reduce the environmental impact associated with an output; and social eco-efficiency aims to increase the level of social quality or quality of life associated with the provision of a particular output.

ECOLE DES BEAUX ARTS

A 19th-century French architectural school famous for developing a method of teaching architecture which is still in use today. In the 19th century the school stood for a rational **historicism**, which could still incorporate a formal, highly monumental approach to planning. The best-known buildings by Beaux Arts graduates are the Paris Opera House of 1868, designed by Charles Gamier, and the great iron and glass Hall of Machines at the Paris Exhibition of 1899, designed by Charles Dutert. Although this building regularly features in Modernist anthologies, it epitomizes Beaux Arts principles in that formal and innovative approaches are explored and exploited.

The school itself was primarily a validating authority. Students were actually taught in ateliers, private architectural schools operated by former students of the institution. The Beaux Arts charged no fees and foreigners were eligible to become students if they could speak adequate French and draw copies of the plaster casts in the Hall of Antique Studies. The most famous foreign student was the American architect Louis Sullivan. In the 1920s, with the rise of the **Modern Movement**, Beaux Arts ideals were largely discredited until finally, after the 1968 Paris student uprising, it was recognized as an anachronism and closed down. Its enduring influence, however, can still be seen in the current trend of architecture and design towards **Classicism**.

EMBODIED ENERGY

A technical term used within **sustainable design**. When research is undertaken to evaluate the environmental impact of a material a key factor is its embodied energy. The term means the sum of the energy required at all stages of production, including the extraction of raw material, its transportation, the energy used in processing, and the transportation of the processed material to the point of use. The fewer steps between origin and use, the lower the embodied energy. Very highly processed materials, such as plastics, have high embodied energy while local materials that do not have to travel far have a lower embodied energy.

EMERGING TECHNOLOGY

Emerging technologies are predicted to make a substantial impact on the design profession in the 21st century. They include biotechnology, **nanotechnology**, smart materials and mobile communications. They are sometimes referred to as GRIN technologies: genomics, **robotics**, informatics and nanotechnology.

ENGINEERING DESIGN

This applies scientific and technological knowledge to design and introduces an analytical approach that allows designers to develop highly imaginative forms and use that would otherwise not be possible. This potential is most evident in the context of architecture, seen in London, for example, in the structural advances of Foster and Partners' Millennium Bridge. The formalization and specialization of the modern engineering profession have led to more accurate and cost-effective designs. An engineer offers specialized knowledge and experience in the sciences and mathematics relating to analysing and designing force-resisting materials and constructions for buildings and other designs. A design engineer therefore establishes the structural design criteria and concepts for the project and communicates this information via drawings and specifications. Close coordination among all members of the design team is essential throughout the design process. Early specialist engineering involvement is especially critical for fast-track and design–build projects, when it is often necessary to issue the structural construction documents well in advance of those prepared by other disciplines. Even in conventional design–bid–build situations the structural system is the first to be constructed, providing the underlying framework for the rest.

Further reading:

Cross, Nigel, *Engineering Design Methods: Strategies for Product Design*. Chichester: Wiley, 2000 [1994].
Laurel, Brenda (ed.), *Design Research: Methods and Perspectives*. Cambridge, MA: MIT Press, 2003.

ERGONOMICS

The study of maximum functional efficiency by observing people in their working environments. The science of ergonomics was particularly developed during the Second World War in order to improve the performance of bomber pilots. Researchers based their studies on similar work in the field, for example anthropometrics, the measurement of the human body and the particular characteristics of different sexes, ages and races. The ergonomists then tested the most comfortable and efficient methods of operating aircraft controls and viewing dials, and tried to apply scientific research to their analysis of human eye range and the strength of the pilots' handgrip. After the war, their findings were also applied to the design of a range of products, from cookers to cars. However, the chair, more than any other designed product, has probably received the most study from ergonomists. Contemporary car seats and office chairs must include ergonomic considerations.

Ergonomics have undoubtedly improved practical considerations of comfort and use, and have been especially important in the development of specialist products for children, the old, the sick and the disabled. Ergonomics, however, is not an exact science, and finding the correct balance of practicality and comfort still requires the intervention of the designer. Ergonomists are trained in psychological and anatomical techniques of information analysis, so they understand the wide differences between people in terms of size and shape, strength, age, experience and background. These user characteristics are taken into account by ergonomic design, whereas **inclusive design** considers the widest range of user needs.

Importantly, in the EU and USA legislation has prioritized ergo-nomics and required its usage in all areas of design. In 2005 in London, for example, the traditional red Routemaster bus was replaced with buses that allow wheelchair and pram access. Ergonomics therefore considers design requirements for the widest use and has become an integral part of the contemporary design process. Most design projects involve multidisciplinary teams, including designers, engineers, market researchers, brand managers and, increasingly, ergonomists. Large manufacturers, such as **Ford**, Philips and Nokia, now routinely employ ergonomists in their in-house design teams.

The UK **Design Council** has identified three categories within ergonomics. Physical ergonomics is concerned with design issues in the workplace, displays, lighting and noise, and focuses on human ana-tomical, anthropometric and physiological characteristics. Psychological ergonomics is concerned with the way mental processes, such as per-ception and memory, are affected by environment. It includes human–computer interaction, human reliability, motivation and work stress. Organizational ergonomics is concerned with staff management, work design, teamwork and quality management.

A well-known example of ergonomics in design practice is the Oxo International Good Grip range of kitchen utensils (1990). This range, designed by Smart Design, aimed to allow great usability while remain-ing stylish. Originally designed to help the CEO's wife, an arthritis sufferer, it has been commercially and critically successful, winning several major design prizes and being included in the Design Collection of New York's Museum of Modern Art. Ergonomic research suggested the use of elliptical shapes and soft, flexible rubber for the handles, and the incorporation of these elements made Good Grips an exemplar of what is known as universal design in the USA (and inclusive design in Europe). By designing ostensibly for a special need regarded as being on the margins of the market, Oxo dramatically expanded the total customer base for ergonomically superior kitchen tools.

See also: **user–centred design**, **inclusive design**

Further reading:

Dul, J. and Weerdmeester, B., *Ergonomics for Beginners: A Quick Reference Guide.* London: Taylor & Francis, 2001 [1993].
Hall, P. and Imrie, R., *Inclusive Design: Designing and Developing Accessible Environments.* London: Spon Press, 2001.
Nemeth, Christopher, *Human Factors: Methods for Design.* London: Routledge, 2004.

EXECUTIVE STYLE

A catch–all term for the lifestyle and trappings of successful managers and high–salary earners. The rise of the executive reflected a new way of thinking about business, a revolution that took place from the late 1950s to the 1970s. The roots of executive style come from New York and the rise of multinational companies. These companies, proud of their size and modernity, encouraged their managers to execute policy decisions, and invented the word 'executive' to describe them. The status of executives was reinforced by such accoutrements as leather briefcases, suits in grey, lightweight fabrics, and Club Class travel. Everything was cool, shiny and new. Executive style always utilized the latest technologies – pagers, computers and car phones – and it was always male. When the style became too bland and too popular, it simply faded away to be replaced in the 1980s by unstructured Calvin Klein suits and Paul Smith accessories, and in the later 20th century by a less aggressive image and a more approachable softer presence in the workplace. Executive style has become a **design history** footnote, but its inspiration can be detected even in the 21st century in the styling of actor Daniel Craig as James Bond.

EXOTICISM

A fashion for all things Eastern, particularly from China and Japan. The interaction between East and West has a long history, starting with the legendary explorer Marco Polo, and ever since Europe has greatly valued imported Oriental objects such as silks and porcelain. It was China which dominated the imagination, but travel there was difficult, so first-hand knowledge of the country was extremely rare. When the craze for chinoiserie reached its height in the 18th century, it was largely inspired by adapting imagery seen on imported and expensive wallpapers and textiles. The designs from Thomas Chippendale's 1754 *Director* indicate the romantic spirit in which all things Chinese were adapted for European tastes. His furniture in the Chinese style can be seen in David Garrick's bedroom, which is reconstructed in the **Victoria and Albert Museum**. One of the very few people to visit China and record a first-hand account at this time was the architect William Chambers (1723–96). In 1757 he spent some time in Canton, and on his return his drawings were published.

The expanding British Empire would soon play a major role in bringing Orientalism to the forefront of public taste. In the late 18th century the East India Company encouraged the study of Indian culture and inspired a vogue for the exotic, seen in the Royal Pavilion at Brighton, built for the Prince Regent. A little later, eminent Victorians began to chart the archaeology and culture of Islamic countries. Edward William Lane (1801–76) was fascinated by Egypt, and in 1836 he published *An Account of the Manners and Customs of Modern Egyptians*. A similar interest was reflected by 19th-century artists as diverse as Delacroix, Hunt and Alma-Tadema. Books such as Lane's precipitated a flood of material on Oriental art and a huge growth in imported goods. Travel, in the form of Thomas Cook's famous tours, and the expansion of the colonies opened up trade and a cross-fertilization of ideas that integrated Oriental ideas with those of the West and vice versa.

A reverence for the East remained a constant theme in the 20th century, reaching a new height in the 1960s with the hippy movement, which identified with the spirituality and craft ethic of Oriental countries. Pop icons such as Jimi Hendrix wore Indian clothes and the Beatles paid homage to the trend by visiting the Maharishi, a Hindu spiritual guide. Over the last decade, long-haul destinations such as India, China and Thailand have become popular travel destinations, allowing increasing numbers of tourists to experience the East for themselves.

Further reading:

Chambers, William, *Designs of Chinese Buildings, Furniture, Dresses, Machines, and Utensils*. New York: Arno Press, 1980 [1757].

Chippendale, Thomas, *The Gentleman and Cabinet Maker's Director: A Reprint of the First Edition*. Leeds: The Chippendale Society, 2005 [1754].

Lane, Edward William, *An Account of the Manners and Customs of the Modern Egyptians*. Cairo: American University in Cairo Press, 2003 [1836].

Said, Edward, *Orientalism*. London: Penguin, 2003 [1978].

EXPERIENCE DESIGN

A new development within design practice which offers enhanced interaction between the product and the consumer. Its objective is to pinpoint the qualities of a brand the manufacturer wants to present to the public. Common terms in experience design are 'brand personality', 'attitude' and the 'emotional response' of the consumer. An example of such an experience is the American Krispy Kreme doughnut chain, which offers customers the opportunity to watch the doughnuts being baked, smell them, see them topped with icing and then packed into distinctive branded boxes. Marketeers now talk about the 'total experience' of the brand, the purpose of which is to develop favourable perceptions of the product, encourage brand loyalty and thereby stimulate sales. In experience design this is not confined solely to the product, but includes the retail experience, **packaging**, staff uniforms and training. Experience design basically revisits one of the great marketing drivers – human emotions, anxieties and insecurities – but it also emphasizes the customer experience to give one product an edge over another.

Companies that have used experience design to engage the customer in a personal way include Nike, with its Nike Town store in Oxford Street, London, and Samsung, with the Samsung Experience in the Time Warner Center in Manhattan, which offers visitors the chance to experience the company's technology in interactive kiosks even though there are no cash registers or points of sales for customers to buy anything they have tried. A fashion retailer using experience design is Topshop, one of the most popular young fashion stores on London's Oxford Street, which offers its shoppers interaction through cafés, radio and TV stations and style advisers to enhance the retail experience. Other retailers are exploring education as an enhancement to the shopping experience, with Sainsbury's supermarket offering maths classes for children while their parents complete the grocery shopping.

Prada in New York's SoHo district, designed by Rem Koolhas, has developed into a tourist destination in its own right.

Further reading:

Bedbury, Scott and Fenichell, Stephen, *A New Brand World: Eight Principles for Achieving Brand Leadership in the 21st Century*. New York: Viking Press, 2002.

Schmitt, Berndt, Rogers, David and Vrotsos, Karen, *There's No Business That's Not Show Business: Marketing in an Experience Culture*. London: *Financial Times*/Prentice Hall, 2003.

Stockmarr, Pernille, 'En Pa Opleveren! Experience Hype!', *Designmatters* 5 (2004): 74–7.

EXPERIENCE ECONOMY

This term describes the emphasis on the perceived need of consumers for experiences and therefore it is connected with **experience design**. Experience economy attempts to categorize the new development in which traditional service industries – for example, air and train companies, insurance firms and banks – are trying to engage customers in something more than their mundane core service. These industries are looking in detail at entertainment models, which first pioneered such techniques in theme parks like Disney Land, and at retail environments. The aspirations of experience design are probably best represented in advertisements. A recent train advertisement portrayed rail travel not as convenient, safe or even cheap but as an opportunity to enjoy fine food, exemplary service, self-discovery and 'the theatre of human life'.

This sector, with its potentially cynical take on human nature, is open to severe criticism. None the less, it is recognized as driving economic change because of the assumption that consumers will be willing to pay more if they are given an experience, rather than simply a service.

EXPRESSIONISM

A dominant movement in art, graphics, architecture and design that begin in the late 19th century. It is characterized by an exaggeration of the materials, colours, outlines or textures of objects in order to heighten the emotional impact. Although historically linked with Northern

Europe, especially Germany and Austria from the 1890s to the 1920s, the themes of Expressionism were revived in paintings of the 1980s, with the depiction of large-scale, heroic themes and the use of tactile surfaces. A well-known exponent of this technique is the American artist Julian Schnabel. Although still evident in the 1990s, Expressionism was largely rejected in that decade in favour of a more restricted range of materials and a more subtle sense of irony.

The major Expressionist groups of the 20th century were Die Brucke (1905–13) and Der Blaue Reiter (1911–14), and German architecture, theatre and film of the 1920s were all profoundly influenced by the movement. Today, Expressionism continues to exert a significant influence on modern graphic design and cinema.

Further reading:

Wolf, Norbert, *Expressionism*. Cologne: Taschen, 2004.

FANZINES

Small-circulation fan magazines sent out on subscription or with membership of a traditional pop fan club. In the late 1970s fanzines became a significant footnote in graphic **design history** with the rise of **Punk**. Taking the message of do-it-yourself to heart, Punk fanzines created a new, alternative graphic design. The best known was *Sniffin' Glue*, first issued in 1977, which was compiled in editor Mark Perry's flat using photocopiers, felt-tipped-pen headlines, badly typed copy and a staple gun. Fanzines challenged the idea that graphic design was the exclusive preserve of trained designers, and thumbed their noses at the formal layouts of mass-circulation magazines.

Terry Jones, former art editor at *Vogue*, brought the fanzine into the mainstream with the launch of *i-D* magazine in 1980. By the mid-1980s, this chronicle of London street style had succeeded in setting graphic design on a new course.

In the 21st century any individualism that would earlier have resulted in fanzines seems to be directed instead towards Internet blogs.

Further reading:

Atton, Chris, *Alternative Media*. London: Sage, 2002.
Sabin, Roger and Triggs, Teal (eds), *Below Critical Radar: Fanzines and Alternative Comics from 1976 to Now*. Hove: Slab-O-Concrete, 2000.

FASCIST DESIGN

This was the result of right-wing political movements in Europe during the 1920s and 1930s. Fascism is an Italian term, first associated with Benito Mussolini, and later with the German Nazi Party and the Spanish Falange. The fascist principles imposed on designers included a reverence for nationalism, a distrust of democracy and a belief in the single-party state. Totalitarian movements promoted particular types of design and architecture. In Germany this was exemplified in the work of architect Albert Speer and in the revival of Gothic type for newspapers and propaganda material.

Further reading:

Golsan, Richard J. (ed.), *Fascism, Aesthetics and Culture*. Hanover, NH: University Press of New England, 1992.
Soucy, Robert, *Fascist Intellectual: Drieu la Rochelle*. Berkeley: University of California Press, 1979.

FAST-MOVING CONSUMER GOODS

An industry term (often abbreviated to FMCGs) to describe those retail goods with a short shelf life, either as a result of high consumer demand or because the product deteriorates rapidly. FMCGs are at the opposite end of the product spectrum from consumer durables – purchases that are made infrequently – for example beds or washing machines.

International companies that specialize in FMCGs include Nestlé, Unilever and Procter & Gamble, which sell such products as soft drinks, shampoo and chocolate bars. Famous FMCG brands include Coca-Cola, Kleenex tissues and Mars chocolate bars. The classic profile of FMCGs is that they have high turnover rate, are bought without a lot of thought by the consumer (impulse buys) and are relatively inexpensive. DVDs, computer games, toothpaste, soap, cosmetics, washing powder and domestic cleaning products are other classic FMCGs.

FEMINISM

A movement advocating equal social and political rights for women which was developed by a group of activists in America in the 1960s and then spread more widely. In terms of a design context it offered the potential of using politics to change design practice. Feminism prompted, for example, art historians to question not only why there had been so few women artists and designers, but how these very words were part of a patriarchal culture and patriarchal control. This questioning has more recently been applied to the younger discipline of **design history**, and a feminist analysis considers the efforts women have to make in order to design, overcoming the limitations imposed by economics and social conventions. For example, feminism brought about a re-examination and a repositioning of the role of Ray Eames, who in the 1970s was largely ignored as the creative partner of Charles Eames. As a result, Ray is now accepted as the creative equal of her husband and practice partner, and she is evaluated in those terms. There is now a widespread recognition of a feminist design history. As in art history, this has resulted in a critical examination of the way design history traditionally emphasized only innovation and an aesthetic **avant-garde**. Now enquiry into an alternative tradition, particularly in such areas as fashion, **popular culture** and ephemera, is encouraged.

While recognizing the importance of documenting women's work, a feminist approach seeks to uncover the historical and cultural conditions in which that work was produced and received in order to challenge the accepted hierarchical and often patriarchal accounts of history. This is particularly evident in the status accorded to **industrial design** and the 'machine aesthetic' over the decorative arts, fashion and popular design.

In the 1980s and early 1990s the feminist emphasis was that there was no one feminist or 'essentialist' approach, just as there is no fixed feminine or masculine experience. **Postmodern** feminist theorists, like **queer** theorists, oppose stereotypes as arcane and irrelevant, arguing that they are determined by society, culture, race and class. Similarly, design historians have begun to consider that women's experiences of the designed world, their role as consumers and the way in which their identities are constructed through such things as **advertising** are not only different from those of men but are of vital importance in the development of a balanced society.

In 1985 Guerrilla Girls was formed by a group of female art activists. They produce humorous posters, stage interventions and publish books. Their activities are illustrated on their website, www.guerrillagirls.com. In spite of the continuing existence of such groups, however, feminism has largely been replaced as an area of research by **gender** studies, which seeks to encompass the experiences of both men and women.

Further reading:

Anscombe, Isabelle, *A Woman's Touch: Women in Design from 1860 to the Present Day*. London: Virago, 1984.

Attfield, Judy and Kirkham, Pat (eds), *A View from the Interior*. London: Women's Press, 1995 [1989].

Gronberg, Tag and Attfield, Judy (eds), *Women Working in Design: A Resource Book*. London: Central School of Art and Design, 1986.

FESTIVAL OF BRITAIN, 1951

In 1948, the Labour government wanted a festival that would suggest a new and optimistic future, and would also provide an international forum on which to promote British manufacturing skills. Its guiding spirit, Sir Gerald Barry, had been a radical journalist and former editor of the *News Chronicle*, and he wanted the festival to symbolize a turning away from the years of austerity. The event was given twenty-seven acres of bomb-damaged land on the Thames's South Bank and a budget of seven million pounds. The finished site included the Dome of Discovery, the world's largest domed structure, and the Skylon, the world's tallest structure, designed by architects Philip Powell and John Moya. The whole area was furnished and decorated in a style known as **Contemporary**. Famous designs included Ernest Race's spindly metal Antelope chairs, Lucienne Day's Calyx fabric, her husband Robin Day's seating for the Festival Hall, and the festival logo by Abraham Games. The event gave many designers, some of whom had gone straight from college into national service, their first opportunity of work.

The festival opened on 3 May and closed in September, having been visited by six million people. Dylan Thomas remembered the influence of 'strong pink . . . rose, strawberry, peach, flesh, blush, lobster, salmon', while the *New Statesman* described it as 'a tonic'. However, a month after the festival closed the Labour government was voted out of office and the incoming Conservatives ordered the demolition of everything on the South Bank, except the Festival Hall.

In 1979 the critic Christopher Brooker suggested that the festival had a lasting influence in showcasing the new town planning that was introduced into so many British cities in the 1950s and 1960s. With the benefit of hindsight, it has also been criticized as marking the point when Britain stopped trying to lead the world and began to revel in nostalgia. The British writer Michael Frayn described it as 'the Britain of the radical middle classes, the do-gooders. In short, the herbivores, or gentle ruminants, who look out from the lush pastures which are their natural station in life with eyes full of sorrow for less fortunate creatures.' Nevertheless, it remains Britain's most important post-war design festival.

Further reading:

Banham, Mary and Hillier, Bevis, *A Tonic to the Nation: The Festival of Britain 1951.* London: Thames & Hudson, 1976.

FOLK ART

Part of a vernacular tradition of design which has long been a source of inspiration for designers. It includes a wide range of objects such as religious figures, decorated barges, woven baskets, ceramic ornaments and cottage furniture. Folk art has slowly evolved through generations of anonymous artisans and has frequently flourished in conditions of adversity amid groups with limited access to materials, such as the early American settlers, or no access to money. That tradition makes documentation difficult, so folk art as an important area of design creativity has been largely neglected. None the less, devotees of the subject exist, with the study of folk art being particularly strong in the USA, where it was 'discovered' in the 1920s and promoted by Gertrude Vanderbilt Whitney, founder of the famous Whitney Museum. Folk art is now recognized as a major American art tradition and a cultural inheritance of fundamental import.

Quite apart from its often high level of aesthetic beauty, folk art is important because of the cultural clues it holds for understanding society's past. The inspiration for folk art is often tied to critical historical moments; it offers a record of the lives of ordinary workers, disadvantaged groups and ethnic minorities. Important collections include decorated household objects, tin ware, weather vanes, toys, tavern signs, painted furniture and hand-stitched quilts. Folk art comprises practical objects such as these but also fantastic examples of human ingenuity and creativity. In the American Folk Art Museum in New York, for example, there is a fragile decorative construction made entirely of chicken bones.

In the 1940s the designers Enid Marx and Margaret Lambert published an important study of British folk art. Nowadays, designers and writers acknowledge their debt to folk art and view it as a serious subject for research as well as an inspiration in terms of style, materials and decoration.

Further reading:

Lambert, Margaret and Marx, Enid, *English Popular Art*. London: Merlin, 1989 [1946].
Maizels, John, *Raw Vision: Outsider Art Sourcebook*. Radlett: Raw Vision, 2002.

FORDISM

Henry Ford (1863–1947) was the creator of the moving assembly line, which revolutionized the structure of the work process and the way 20th-century goods were made and designed. His company was the first to **mass-produce** a cheap, standardized car.

Of Irish Protestant descent, Ford was born in a rural Michigan community but went on to become one of the great industrial giants of the 20th century. He started his career working for the Edison Lighting Company, becoming its chief engineer in 1893. Ten years later he established the Ford Motor Company, which became a phenomenal success, producing some sixteen million Model T cars between 1908 and 1927. The company's moving assembly line, introduced in 1913, became the basis of Fordism and came to represent the ultimate achievement of 20th-century industrial production. It would also have an influence on European **Modernist** architects such as Walter Gropius, who wanted to apply similar methods to their architecture.

However, Ford did not invent the moving assembly line. Something very similar was cited by the Modernist writer Sigfried Giedion – conveyor belts, which were used in Chicago slaughter-houses at the turn of the century. The theories of Frederick Taylor, who proposed new ideas concerning the organization of factories, were equally influential. None the less, Ford has passed into history as the man who turned these experiments and theories into industrial reality. His two famous quotes – 'History is bunk', made in the witness box in 1919 when he sued the *Chicago Tribune*; and 'You can have any colour so long as it's black', about the Model T – support the myth of Ford as the tough 20th-century industrialist reshaping the modern world. His achievement in creating the popular car was imitated in the USA with the establishment of General Motors and in Europe by Fiat and Volkswagen, among many others.

Further reading:

Batchelor, Ray, *Henry Ford: Mass Production, Modernism and Design*. Manchester: Manchester University Press, 1994.

Ford, Henry, *My Life and Work*, London: Heinemann, 1923.

Giedion, Sigfried, *Mechanization Takes Command: A Contribution to Anonymous History*. New York: Norton, 1969 [1948].

Taylor, Frederick Winslow, *The Principles of Scientific Management*. London: Harper & Bros., 1911.

FOUND OBJECT

Otherwise known as *objet trouvé*, this is a natural or synthetic object transferred to an art or design context. Unlike the **ready-made**, it is chosen for its aesthetic or visual appeal and often carries connotations of chance discovery, re-seeing the ordinary and re-evaluating the meanings usually ascribed to objects. Although Kurt Schwitters first introduced the found object (in the form of tram tickets, toy parts and other urban debris) in his 'Mertz' **assemblages** of the late 1910s, it became a central form within **Surrealism** when mixed with other media. Surrealist found objects, celebrated at the 1936 International Surrealist Exhibition in London, included driftwood, pebbles and gnarled branches, with the emphasis on discovery of the 'marvellous' in the ordinary world.

Since the late 1950s, with assemblage, **Pop** and environmental works, the found object has become much used because of its potential to inspire rethinking of the function and meaning of objects in our society, and because it provides a readily accessible source of materials and images. More recently, the found object has become the basis of the Bricolage approach, with the artist as a commentator on the fragmented world.

Further reading:

Waldman, Diane, *Collage, Assemblage, and the Found Object*. London: Phaidon Press, 1992.

FRENCH DESIGN

Always synonymous with style, French products over the centuries, from Sèvres porcelain to Gobelins tapestries and couture fashion, have consistently attracted international admiration. In the early 19th century, France pioneered the trade exhibition, opening the first government-sponsored Exposition de l'Industrie as early as 1798. Napoleon encouraged this trend in 1801, 1802 and 1806, and thereafter no fewer than eleven design exhibitions were held in Paris up to 1849. They were enormously successful, each attracting up to 4,000 manufacturers, and were imitated all over Europe. Indeed, the Paris 1849 Exhibition prompted Prince Albert and Sir Henry Cole to mount the **Great Exhibition** two years later in London. France was subsequently to mount a series of international exhibitions which, in **design history** terms, were the most important of the 19th century. A significant highlight was the exhibition of 1867, notable for showing Japanese design from the Shogun period and reinforcing the 19th-century obsession with the cult of Japan. However, the largest international exhibition was mounted in 1889, with the Eiffel Tower as its centre-piece, a brilliant iron translation of a medieval spire. This exhibition was the first to be illuminated entirely with electricity, while other technological firsts included a demonstration of Alexander Bell's phonograph, which made it possible to hear the Paris Opera with the aid of a stereophonic telephone device. Another section was devoted to primitive villages, including a Javanese kampong, and it was here that the composer Debussy first heard Javanese music.

The Paris 1900 Exhibition saw the climax of **Art Nouveau** design, showing the work of Emile Gallé, Louis Majorelle, Alphonse Mucha and Samuel Bing. After the First World War, the 1925 Exposition des Arts Décoratifs et Industriels marked the height of the **Art Deco** style, which took its name from the exhibition. Again, French designers such as Jacques Ruhlmann, Jean Dunand and René Lalique took the lead in developing a modern **geometric** style using highly skilled craft techniques and rich, exotic materials. In addition, the exhibition provided an international forum for the new **Modern Movement**. Particularly important was Le Corbusier's Pavilion de l'Esprit Nouveau, and the Russian Pavilion, which was the only **Constructivist** building erected outside the Soviet Union. Le Corbusier also built a pavilion for the Paris 1937 Exhibition, but different political priorities by now were influencing design, as was indicated by the German pavilion, dominated by an eagle and a swastika. This exhibition was the last great event of its kind in Paris.

After the war, an organization of architects, decorators and designers calling themselves the Union des Artistes Modernes showed their work in a series of exhibitions called 'Formes Utiles', and in 1955 the French Ministry of Commerce initiated a design awards scheme similar to the Italian Compasso d'Oro. The **CCI** (Centre de Création Industrielle) was launched in 1970, and later moved to the custom-built Pompidou Centre. French design received two more boosts in the early 1980s with the tenure of Jack Lang as Minister of Culture, and the establishment of VIA, an organization set up to promote it. New French design was now epitomized by Grapus, a graphic design practice, and the furniture designers Andrée Putnam, Roland Cecil Sportes and Jean-Michel Wilmotte. However, the most influential and famous French designer remains Philippe Starck, whose prolific work in **industrial design**, lighting, furniture and architecture established him as the first international design superstar.

Further reading:

Design Français 1960–1990: Trois Décennies. Paris: Centre Georges Pompidou, 1988.

FUNCTIONALISM

The theory of functional design. It refers to objects designed solely for practical use, without any ornamentation or decoration. The word itself appears frequently in **Modernism** and one of its basic tenets is the theory that 'form follows function'. Functionalism is therefore part of the rational, ordered Modernist approach to design. Its aims and objectives were clearly expressed by the **Ulm** school of design and the work of its best-known student, Dieter Rams, for Braun. In the 1960s Functionalism was challenged by the new priorities of **Pop**, and later by the diverse approaches of **Postmodernism**. These movements argued that Functionalism was too narrow an approach to design, that it ignored the social meanings individuals give to objects and played down the creative, individualist nature of the designer. In opposition to this, Functionalism is now regarded as not merely a style but a deeply felt commitment to order and progress.

Further reading:

Bloemink, Barbara J., *Design ≠ Art: Functional Objects from Donald Judd to Rachel Whiteread.* London: Merrell, 2004.

FUTURE FORECASTING

Now an established part of the design industry, informing manufacturers and clients about fast-moving trends. It is particularly well developed in the fashion industry but is widely used throughout the creative industries. Typically, advice is offered by a forecasting company which researches a series of trends and presents them to the client to keep them ahead of the game. It is not an exact science but predicts the nature of future markets by researching new social, cultural and technological developments. Its aim is therefore to identify the aspirations of consumer groups to help companies plan their market development.

In 2005 typical forecasting predictions included the following: there would be a growth in consumers wanting an original retail experience; the Viktor & Rolf shop in Milan, with its 'upside-down' interior, would become an iconic model; and people will start to demand that their computer technology is decorated and concealed. Other predicted trends were that those in the thirty–five-plus generation will increasingly be downsizing and opting for a slower pace of life in the country and that there will be continued interest in green lifestyles. A more radical forecast was that pet cloning will be a boom industry of the future.

Future forecasting is also developing as a recognized and serious element of social commentary and a design discipline in its own right.

FUTURISM

A **Modernist** movement based in Italy. It was the creation of Filippo Tomasso Marinetti (1876–1944), a Milanese poet, who published 'The Foundation and Manifesto of Futurism' on the front page of the Paris newspaper *Le Figaro* on 20 February 1909. This article's militant and strident tone announced a new literary and social movement which was designed to free Italy from its 'countless cemeteries' and glorify a 'new form of beauty, the beauty of speed'. The manifesto stressed the youth of its creators ('the oldest among us is thirty'), the rejection of all past values and institutes, and the need for 'courage, audacity and revolt' to embrace the new industrial world of machines, noise, speed, danger and continuous change. Italy at this time was undergoing rapid but late industrialization. The north of the country, especially Milan and Turin, was the centre of this, with the latter being the home of Fiat. Indeed, the motor car, with its speed, its metal and its noise, became one of the chief symbols of Futurism.

After publishing his manifesto, Marinetti gathered around him a group of young artists, poets, musicians and architects committed to his stirring ideas. They included: Umberto Boccioni (1882–1916), painter and sculptor; Carlo Carra (1881–1966), musician and painter; Giaccomo

114

Balla (1871–1958), artist and later interior designer; Gino Severini (1883–1966), a painter based in Paris; Luigi Russolo (1885–1947), musician and creator/performer of 'noise machines'; and Antonio Sant'Elia (1888–1916), architect and designer.

Although best known for such paintings as Boccioni's *The Street Enters the House* (1911) and Balla's *Dynamism of an Automobile* (1912), the movement was also tremendously important and influential for its embracing of urban industrial culture in visual and written forms. Marinetti, a master of propaganda, almost made manifestos essential for any group wishing to reach a large public. He developed Futurist evenings and tours which attracted an even broader audience to multimedia performances of poetry, music, art and design in Italy and the rest of Europe. Unlike many alternative modern movements, Futurism was fiercely nationalistic, with Marinetti seeing it as a resurrection of Italy, as well as a chance to colonize other world centres. Interestingly, though, Futurism was to have its greatest impact in England and Russia, both of which Marinetti visited, and which, for different reasons, had entrenched art traditions.

Strongly influenced by the writings of Nietzsche on the new man (*Thus Spake Zarathustra*, 1883–5), and Henri Bergson's philosophy of matter, time and space (*Matter and Memory*, 1896), the Futurists developed a new language of dynamic lines: lines of force and interpenetrating planes are evident in their paintings, graphics, sculpture and proposed architecture. Although influenced by the Cubists' work, seen in Paris in 1911, their various manifestos on painting, politics, music and sculpture stressed their concern with challenging all accepted values, whether in terms of using new materials like industrial glass, hair and plastics, or the glorification of war and social change (except for women). These manifestos, where the ideas far outstrip those contained in the Futurists' work, had the greatest impact.

During the First World War a Futurist battalion was formed, but following the death of the most innovative members, Sant'Elia and Boccioni, the movement's impetus faded. Marinetti attempted to revive Futurism in 1916 with Balla as the main figure, but as the founder became a more vocal adherent of Mussolini's **Fascism**, the other major figures dispersed.

Further reading:

Martin, Sylvia, *Futurism*. Cologne: Taschen, 2005.
Tisdall, Caroline, *Futurism*. London: Thames & Hudson, 1977.

GENDER AND DESIGN

The concept of gender in this context is assumed to be cultural, and in this way gender differences affect our perception and experience of design. For example, the title of a pioneer study on the impact of gender on the visual appearance of design by Penny Sparke, *As Long as It's Pink*, plays on the cliché of gender colour coding: pink for girls, blue for boys.

Gender studies research has tended to focus more on the arts, and these debates and discourse are not often applied to design practice. However, the findings of gender research are key to our understanding of design production and **consumption**. For example, over the last twenty years gender theory has questioned the assumption that gender is defined from the inherited biology of sex and explored how it might be socially or culturally constructed. The gendering of design into stereotypes – feminine lace, masculine leather, dolls for girls, building bricks for boys – reflects an important aspect of Western culture that has informed the development of design practice. These sets of cultural codes and signs could be exploited or subverted by designers to appeal to consumers. In the 1960s, for example, the birth control pill, which emancipated women, was packaged in pink. Gender theory also explored male and female roles in the design profession. It was suggested that architecture was the masculine and dominant professional activity, interior decoration a female and secondary role. Similarly, **industrial design** is perceived as male, as is **typography**, while textile design is female. Gender studies in design have started to challenge these beliefs and stereotypes.

Whether the differences are rooted in biology or not, gender still remains one of the chief determining factors governing the choice of design career for women. It has been suggested that this reflects the different responsibilities of men and women in the domestic sphere. Women designers are more prevalent in the disciplines of **illustration**, textiles, ceramics and fashion; men within architecture and **engineering design**. Although these divisions are breaking down, even now it would be difficult to find many female art directors in the **advertising** world or car designers in the motor industry. It remains to be seen how changes in the gendering of design professions will develop.

Further reading:

Sparke, Penny, *As Long as It's Pink: The Sexual Politics of Taste*. London: Pandora, 1995.

GEOMETRIC DESIGN

This is design with a rational mathematical or geometric origin. Simple geometric patterns can be found in nearly all prehistoric and primitive societies, but it was the Romans who first produced complex geometric patterns, in their mosaic floors. These Roman forms inspired later Islamic designs, which in turn influenced medieval churches and monasteries in Europe. By the Renaissance, geometric patterns were part of a common language of design, but their importance gained a sharper focus in the 19th century with research into decorative forms appropriate for the new consumer culture of the **Industrial Revolution**. The publication of Owen Jones and Jules Goury's *Plans, Elevations, Sections, and Details from the Alhambra* in mid-century helped to revive a Victorian interest in geometric design. At the same time a number of books were published which tried to explain the phenomenon of pattern repeats, probably as a response to the increasing demands of industrialization. Jules Bourgoin (1838–1907), former Professor of Ornament at the Paris **Ecole des Beaux Arts**, and the British industrial designer Christopher Dresser (1834–1904) explored plant structure as a way of understanding the geometry of the natural world. Another example of this approach can be seen in J. Glaisher's well-illustrated article on snow crystals as sources for designers, which appeared in the *Art Journal* in 1857. These researches influenced the education of young children and student designers alike.

Around this time the educationalist Friedrich Froebel (1782–1852), who believed in the concept of constructive play for children, developed a set of building bricks for this purpose, while Prince Albert had his children instructed in mixing mortar and laying bricks. It is believed that Frank Lloyd Wright played with Froebel bricks in his nursery, and George Ricks, a London school inspector, certainly applied some of Froebel's ideas in the city's schools. Typical of his methods was an 1889 textbook called *Simple Drawing Exercises on Squared Paper*. Ricks believed that exercises in simple geometric design developed hand–eye coordination, even if they did not encourage the imagination.

After the First World War art and **design education** moved towards a more craft-based approach, but geometric exercises reappeared at the **Bauhaus** in the late 1920s. Early abstract artists, such as Piet Mondrian, also experimented with geometric form, but here the relationship is less clear. Fine artists, such as Kenneth Martin, have taken up mathematical approaches to painting, and recent experiments with Japanese computer art suggest that geometric design will continue to exercise a fascination for the creative imagination.

Further reading:

Bourgoin, Jules, *Arabic Geometrical Pattern and Design*. New York: Dover Publications, 1973 [1879].

Dresser, Christopher, *The Art of Decorative Design*. New York: Garland, 1977 [1862].

Jones, Owen and Goury, Jules, *Plans, Elevations, Sections, and Details from the Alhambra*, 2 vols. London: Owen Jones, 1834–45.

GLASGOW STYLE

The Glasgow Four consisted of Charles Rennie Mackintosh, Herbert MacNair and Margaret and Frances MacDonald. Together they launched one of the most influential styles of the late 19th century. Mackintosh, whose work was rediscovered in the 1960s, has since become one of the world's most famous designers, canonized by an international following, and enjoying particularly fanatical support in Japan. He and MacNair both studied at the Glasgow School of Art where they fell under the influence of its remarkable head, Francis H. Newbery. It was Newbery who introduced the pair to the two MacDonald sisters in 1893, and the four eventually married – MacNair to Frances in 1899 and Mackintosh to Margaret in 1900. Although Mackintosh is by far the most famous of the quartet, they were all gifted and versatile designers, and doubtless future research will re-evaluate their individual contributions to the creation of a unique style. What we do know is that by 1892, before they met, Mackintosh had already developed his distinctive **Art Nouveau** decorative style. Later, working as a group, the Four exhibited together at the 1896 **Arts and Crafts** Exhibition and attracted considerable criticism from their more sober English colleagues.

The following year, Mackintosh won the competition to design a new building for the Glasgow School of Art and also started to work on Miss Cranston's series of tea rooms. But these were rare commissions for the Four, so they looked to the Continent for a more sympathetic treatment of their work. Their success was finally secured by a triumph at the Vienna Secession Exhibition of 1900, and the following year the Secessionist magazine *Ver Sacrum* was devoted entirely to the Glasgow School. However, not even this recognition could attract long-term projects for the group, so they continued to rely on commissions from personal friends and a small group of admirers.

By 1914, Mackintosh was embittered and frustrated. He left Glasgow first for Chelsea and finally for France in 1925. By all accounts he was temperamental and not given to making many client concessions. He and his colleagues stepped outside the received Arts and Crafts wisdom of truth to materials and honest construction: much of the furniture they designed is uncomfortable, poorly constructed, painted or stained, all heinous crimes to advocates of the Ernest Gimson school of furniture design. Their best works were formal stage sets, which were beautiful and poetic, with an almost mystical undercurrent seen in the recurring motif of a stylized rose.

There is something tragic about the demise of the Glasgow Four. Frances MacDonald died in 1924, Mackintosh in 1928 (spending the last years of his life painting and virtually unknown) and his wife Margaret in 1933. MacNair stopped designing in 1924, although he lived until 1953. In the post–war period their achievements were known only to the informed few. When Glasgow Council made plans to knock down several key buildings, few people protested as there was little knowledge of this remarkable group. However, the 1960s revival of all things Victorian changed that. Cecil Beaton reworked Mackintosh's style for the sets of *My Fair Lady*, and slowly the work of all of the Glasgow Four developed into a small industry. The Italian company Cassina made reproduction Mackintosh furniture and the group's graphic style became central to the Art Nouveau revival. Their contribution to the visual language of contemporary design is enormous, and Mackintosh's style now brands the city of Glasgow.

Further reading:

Avery, Derek, *Charles Rennie Mackintosh*. London: Chaucer Press, 2004.
Billcliffe, Roger, *Charles Rennie Mackintosh: Textile Designs*. San Francisco: Pomegranate Artbooks, 1993 [1979].

GLOBALIZATION

There is a widespread and shared feeling that we are living in an era of globalization, of multinational business and an increasing homogenization of culture. Globalization is the process by which companies operate on an international level and socioeconomic patterns become adopted on a global scale. High–profile global brands include Coca-Cola, McDonald's, Pepsi-Cola, Nestlé, Mercedes, Disney, Sony, IBM, Toyota and Kodak. This spread of Western companies to new markets, particularly those in developing countries, began in earnest with the worldwide recession of 1979.

'Global' as a term is often interchangeable with 'international'. It is frequently perceived as opposed to regionalization and often associated with the wiping out of regional and national identities. In the last century globalization was seen as the way forward, through increased international trade and the amalgamation of national markets. Since the 1980s, improvements in communication technology and particularly the rise of the Internet have figuratively shrunk the world and broken down borders and barriers, allowing for a free exchange of information and cultures, leading the development of what Marshall McLuhan famously described as the 'global village'. However, a growing coalition of environmentalists, anti-poverty campaigners, trade unionists and anti-capitalist groups see the growth of global companies as creating more problems than it solves. Their dissatisfaction with globalization lies in the fact that it has been of advantage only to the Western world, and that the shifting of production to developing countries has led to the widespread exploitation of those countries in terms of trade and working conditions.

In the 21st century globalization, if not condemned outright, is generally viewed with serious concerns. Many are arguing that differences are disappearing and the consequent uniformity is a major threat to world culture. Whether the consumer is shopping in Shanghai, London or New York, they are now offered the same brands, products and services. Furthermore, unlike old-style multinationals such as Hoover, global companies such as McDonald's and Coca-Cola do not extract and process raw materials locally but simply exploit local markets. Much of the criticism of globalization is levelled at the track records of American multinationals such as these, in the environment and in their working practice ethics, which have allowed them to dominate certain markets by crushing smaller businesses. However, the condemnation has started to have an effect, with some of these companies even allowing webcam access to their factories to allow consumers to judge conditions in the workplace for themselves.

Globalization has led to a great deal of angst about national identity; a fear that the cultures of individual nation-states will be swamped by Westernism; concern that the vulnerable are being exploited; and worry that we will all soon be living in a world of bland product conformity. The expansion of global industries therefore generates complex political and economic questions.

Further reading:

Dicken, Peter, *Global Shift: Reshaping the Global Economic Map in the 21st Century*. London: Sage, 2003 [1986].

Porter, Michael E. (ed.), *Competition in Global Industries*. Boston, MA: Harvard
Business School, 1986.

GOTHIC REVIVAL

From the 1830s the writings of Augustus Welby Northmore Pugin
(1812–52) contained a simple but influential message that the past,
particularly the medieval past, which he called 'Gothic', showed more
understanding of beauty and design than anything the 19th century had
so far achieved. In his *Contrasts*, first published in 1836, Pugin compared
his own materialistic and scientific age unfavourably with the fifteenth
century, when religious faith was transcendent. Not only did this age
produce greater art, he asserted, but society itself was more stable.
Pugin's panacea was the restoration of the Catholic Church. His implied
criticism of every aspect of contemporary society is important in
understanding the psychology of the **Arts and Crafts Movement**.
For Pugin, Gothic, from a moral and visual point of view, was the only
style in which to work. He installed his work at the Medieval Court in
the **Great Exhibition** of 1851, generally acknowledged by his contemporaries to have been a huge success.

This simple idea, of looking to the medieval past as a means of
achieving social reform through design, also underpinned the attitude
of the most important design writer and critic of the 19th century,
John Ruskin (1819–1900). Ruskin, an intense, complex man, self-
preoccupied and famously sexually repressed, helped to shape the taste
and attitudes of his century. He was a precocious child, the son of a
prosperous wine merchant, and in 1837, he went to study at Oxford.
At the age of twenty-four he published his first volume in the series
Modern Painters, a defence of his hero J.H.W. Turner. Six years later, in
1849, he published his powerful polemic *Seven Lamps of Architecture*.
This was followed by *Stones of Venice* (1851–3). Ruskin despised the
industrial world England had pioneered. He was a vocal critic of the
Great Exhibition of 1851 and reserved particular dislike for machine-
made ornamentation. Both *Seven Lamps of Architecture* and *Stones of Venice*
were passionate, monumental defences of the Gothic style, and underlying his research were two important principles: that ornament and
design should be based on stylized natural forms; and that the production
of design had a strong moral dimension. Although the Gothic Revival
tended not to use specific Gothic details in design, the spirit of Gothic
underlay attitudes about vernacular form, truth to materials and the
role of design in society. In his famous notes reviewing Holman

121

Hunt's painting *The Awakening Conscience*, Ruskin attacked the 'fatal newness of the furniture'. Like William **Morris**, he held views that showed a strong social conscience, and his **Guild** of St George was a failed attempt to put his ideas of social reform into practice.

Nevertheless, his writings became sacred texts for the Arts and Crafts Movement. Ruskin and Morris met in 1857 and became allies twenty years later when they worked together for the Society for the Protection of Ancient Buildings. Ruskin was a gifted amateur artist, and although his own attempts at design were largely unsuccessful, his belief that ornament should be based on conventional natural forms proved influential. Indeed, his writings were widely translated abroad, and his attitudes to art, architecture and design inspired Walter Gropius and continued to have a lasting effect well into the 20th century. For instance, Prince Charles's views on design and the revival of rural life (such as his Poundbury village experiment) have their roots in the Arts and Crafts idealism of Ruskin's late nineteenth century.

Further reading:

Pugin, A.W.N., *Contrasts*. Reading: Spire Books Ltd in association with the Pugin Society, 2003 [1836].

Ruskin, John, *Modern Painters*, abridged edn. London: Deutsch, 1987 [1843].

Ruskin, John, *The Seven Lamps of Architecture*. London: Smith, Elder and Co, 1849.

Ruskin, John, *The Stones of Venice*. New York: Dover, 2004 [1879].

GRAFFITI

Words and symbols used to deface public spaces and transport. Deriving from the Italian verb to scratch, graffiti dates back to ancient Egypt, but it has become an interesting subject for artists and designers only since the Second World War, particularly in the 1970s. With the invention of aerosol paint cans, streetwise teenagers from the Bronx, using such names as Fab Five Freddie and Futura 2000, put their marks on the walls and carriages of New York's subway. They signed their work with an individual 'tag', which used a jagged, inflated **typography** and vivid colours that would later influence mainstream graphic design. Opinions as to the significance of 1970s graffiti differ, with some claiming it was a legitimate kind of urban **folk art** while others said it was simply vandalism. Nevertheless, the New York art establishment took up the movement, with Keith Haring becoming the best-known example of a commercially trained artist who exploited the style. Haring's imagery has been widely used in graphic design and incorporated into fashion by designers such as Vivienne Westwood.

More recently, UK artist Banksy (b. 1974) has made a significant impact. He is a prolific graffiti artist from Bristol whose artwork has appeared in London and at other locations around the world. Banksy uses a variety of techniques to communicate a message which is often political and/or humorous. His original street-art form, which combines graffiti with a distinctive stencilling technique, has achieved underground notoriety as well as widespread coverage in the mainstream media. Despite this attention, he has managed to keep his real identity secret.

Further reading:

Banksy, *Wall and Piece*. London: Century, 2005.

Cooper, Martha and Chalfant, Henry, *Subway Art*. London: Thames & Hudson, 1984.

Kolossa, Alexandra, *Keith Haring*. Cologne: Taschen, 2004.

GREAT EXHIBITION, 1851

Proposed by Prince Albert in 1849 and brought to fruition by the artist/designer Sir Henry Cole, the Great Exhibition opened in Hyde Park on 1 May 1851. It was a tremendous success: it attracted millions of visitors, made a profit and the building that was constructed for it became world famous. The architect, Joseph Paxton, built it of glass and iron panels in order to demonstrate the latest industrial techniques and materials. The building was immediately nicknamed the Crystal Palace.

The exhibition itself was a celebration of the new technology and inventions of the **Industrial Revolution**, and it proved extremely influential. It attracted intense newspaper coverage and critics studied the proceedings in some detail. Even allowing for the fact that the manufacturers showed their most elaborate pieces, extravagant **Naturalism** was the order of the day. Popular design was confident, large scale and ornate. Overall, the exhibition is not felt to be Britain's finest design hour, but its importance to design should not be underestimated. Even the project's harshest critics were impressed with Pugin's Medieval Court, which housed **Gothic** furniture and metalwork of his own design.

The Great Exhibition also allowed people to look at the products of other nations, and the Indian section in particular was a revelation. Furthermore, it confirmed that Britain had become the world's most important political and economic power. It therefore marked the beginning of Britain's short-lived but enormously powerful empire.

See also: **British Exhibitions**, **Victoria and Albert Museum**

Further reading:

Hobhouse, Hermione, *The Crystal Palace and the Great Exhibition: Art, Science and Productive Industry: A History of the Royal Commission for the Exhibition of 1851.* London: Athlone Press, 2002.

GREEN DESIGN

Generally the work of someone who supports the protection of the environment, especially a member of one of the political Green parties that have developed all over the world.

The green movement began after the Second World War with the aims of conserving the world's natural resources and preventing industry and its associated pollution from destroying the delicate balance of the world's ecology. It was linked to the postwar American anti-consumer movement, led by Vance Packard (b. 1914), a journalist and key critic of US consumer culture in the 1950s and 1960s. One seminal early green critique of modern society was *Silent Spring*, a poetic and moving book by Rachel Carson describing the devastating impact of the use of agricultural pesticides by American farmers. Similar sentiments also found expression in the growing **alternative design** movement in the 1970s.

These views, however, were felt to be those of an eccentric and slightly quirky minority. They were dismissed as idealistic, hippy ideas that had little relevance to the modern world. The great triumph of green design is that its ideals have gone mainstream. One sign of increasing consumer awareness of green issues was the publication in 1988 of *The Green Consumer Guide*. More importantly, however, green issues have moved on to the legislative agenda. The European Union has introduced a raft of measures to address issues of toxic waste, **packaging** and packaging waste, and recycling. These have impacted not only on Europe but on multinational companies whose products are imported into Europe and so now have to meet EU standards. The EU also intends to introduce an eco-labelling system to help the consumer identify which products are ecologically sound. This is part of a worldwide initiative which has seen the introduction of many new laws to curb the adverse effects of industry. In 1992 at the United Nations Conference on Environment and Development 172 nations signed up to a blueprint for **sustainable** planning, and more recently US legislators made it compulsory for companies to have their waste emissions independently measured. They are now exploring the possibility of banning certain printing inks used for magazines and packaging. And it is not only the politicians who are going green; investors are too. The fastest-growing sector in many of the world's stock markets is ethical investment – in companies with good environmental and social practices.

Green design has now become an industry itself. Among the vanguard are the 02 design group, based in Copenhagen, and Anita Roddick, former owner of the Body Shop, who pioneered recycling and introduced new inks and printing techniques for her products. Furthermore, independent bodies like Friends of the Earth send out information to designers and architects warning them against the use of certain hardwoods because of the effect on precious forest resources. In the past, environmentalists had regarded designers with suspicion, believing them to be people who encouraged **consumerism**. That view has now shifted, and designers are encouraged to get involved with projects at an early stage to help solve key resources issues. They are being asked to consider the long-term implications of their designs and their materials specifications, perhaps by avoiding non-biodegradable plastic or by using recycled products.

Over the past twenty years specific terms have emerged to identify elements in what has traditionally been referenced under the umbrella phrase green design. Eco-, ecological, environmentally friendly, sustainable and green often appear to be interchangeable prefixes, and the fluidity of these terms has led to controversy. Nevertheless, this debate reveals how green design has developed from a specialist interest into a key consideration in design best practice. We can usefully distinguish between green, eco- and sustainable design as a hierarchy of interrelating but distinct terms. Within this hierarchy green design is used to describe single-issue or end-of-life solutions, such as using a recycled material for one element of a product or bolting a catalytic converter on to a petrol engine exhaust to reduce its polluting emissions. These design interventions effectively make a problem less bad, rather then addressing the core issue at a more fundamental level of product, concept or system redesign.

Further reading:

Carson, Rachel, *Silent Spring*. Harmondsworth: Penguin, 2000 [1963].

Elkington, John and Hailes, Julia, *The Green Consumer Guide: From Shampoo to Champagne: High-Street Shopping for a Better Environment*. London: Gollancz, 1988.

McKenzie, Dorothy, *Green Design: Design for the Environment*. London: Laurence King, 1997 [1991].

Packard, Vance, *The Waste Makers*. London: Longmans, 1960.

GUILDS OF DESIGN

The word 'guild' means an association of craftsmen. Guilds developed in the Middle Ages for the purpose of training and protecting their members, and it was this idea of collaboration and mutual support that attracted many 19th-century designers. John Ruskin, for example, founded the Guild of St George in 1878, a doomed attempt to revive the spirit of medieval life. The Art Workers' Guild was founded in 1883 by pupils of the architect Norman Shaw to discuss art and architecture and quickly expanded to include established designers Lewis Day, Walter Crane and William **Morris**. By the 1890s the guild was acting as an important discussion forum for craftsmen and designers. In 1915 its premises were taken over by the newly formed **Design and Industries Association**.

The first commercial design enterprise to choose the name 'guild' was the Century Guild, founded in 1882 by Arthur Mackmurdo with Herbert Home. The purpose of this guild was to 'render all branches of art the sphere no longer of the tradesman but the artist'. It was dissolved in 1888, but the work of its members – especially in graphic design and chair-backs – is remembered as an early example of the **Art Nouveau** whiplash line. The most famous guild, however, founded by Charles Ashbee in 1888, was the Guild of Handicraft. Ashbee, who was inspired by Morris, opened his premises in London's Mile End to train local workers in simple craft techniques. In 1901 he moved 150 workers to Chipping Camden in the Cotswolds to start a social experiment in communal living and design. The Cotswolds had become something of a cult for the **Arts and Crafts Movement**, as a region rich in honey-coloured, vernacular 17th-century architecture and a rural life virtually untouched since the 18th century. Ashbee was part of an advance guard of artists and designers who moved to the region at the turn of the century. His guild advocated self-help, education for all, garden allotments and pageants. It attracted a steady stream of publicity and visitors, and produced simple silverware and jewellery that would inspire more commercial enterprises, such as **Liberty's** department store. In 1907 the guild, never a financial success, finally collapsed. Nevertheless, many of the London East End families stayed on and integrated into Cotswolds life, and the idea of communities of craftsmen and -women continued to find favour in the 20th century across the globe.

Further reading:

Crawford, Alan, *C.R. Ashbee: Architect, Designer and Romantic Socialist*. London: Yale University Press, 2005 [1985].

HABITAT

Established in 1964 by Sir Terence Conran (b. 1931), Habitat was much more than a shop; for a generation of young, middle-class shoppers, it represented a new lifestyle. The first Habitat store, opened in the Fulham Road, London, sold Indian rugs, Polish enamelled mugs, and all manner of lighting and tableware stacked floor to ceiling in warehouse style. For the British shopper, it was a retail revolution. The shops introduced contemporary design at accessible prices, with the interiors laid out in bold colours and featuring in-house graphics. The year 1966 saw another innovation, the launch of the Habitat catalogue. Now acknowledged as a design classic, the catalogue is lavishly laid out, with arty photographs and a simple but striking graphic style. Three years after its inception, it offered Habitat's growing numbers of customers a mail-order service. By 1980, the Habitat group boasted forty-seven stores in Britain, Continental Europe and the USA.

Conran trained at the Central School of Art as a textile designer. After graduation he went on to design furniture, opened a famous restaurant called the Soup Kitchen and launched his **design consultancy**, now called Conran Associates. In the early 1980s he became a driving force behind the retail revolution: in 1981 Habitat merged with Mothercare, a well-known chain of mother-and-baby stores; and in 1983 the company bought Heal's, the famous department store specializing in furniture. The Heal's building, something of a London institution, became the centre of the Conran empire. Conran's expanding business interests also included property development, and he bought an area of London's docklands called Butlers Wharf, which was to play a key role in another of his innovations: the world's first **design**

museum. Since the 1990s, he has also opened a string of high-profile restaurants across London, a venture which has re-established his reputation as a lifestyle design expert.

Further reading:

Phillips, Barty, *Conran and the Habitat Story*. London: Weidenfeld & Nicolson, 1984.

HERITAGE INDUSTRY

Contemporary Britain is sometimes accused of having a fixation with the past. In the 1980s a book by critic Robert Hewison explored the way Britain markets its past. Hewison's thesis was that Britain has an obsession with the past which has undermined the country's ability to cope with the present and the future. While the country faced a massive recession, he argued, a new force was taking over the heritage industry, a movement dedicated to turning Britain into one vast, open-air museum. Hewison is not alone in voicing this disquiet. Tom Wolfe, the American critic, famously described Britain as a huge theme park filled with Elizabethan Beefeaters, Dickensian eccentrics, country cottages and shabby tea rooms.

The commercial possibilities of the heritage industry have, however, been exploited by popular films and television programmes that provide romanticized images of a safe past. In the 21st century heritage occupies a place in the wider context of a mixed economy which enables growth and development of the past alongside the future.

Further reading:

Barnes, Julian, *England, England*. London: Jonathan Cape, 1998.
Hewison, Robert, *The Heritage Industry: Britain in a Climate of Decline*. London: Methuen, 1987.

HIGH TECH

Not a design movement as such but an approach to industrial materials used in new and different contexts. It is sometimes called the 'industrial aesthetic' and as such its origins can be traced back to Paxton's pre-fabricated designs for the Crystal Palace and Eiffel's tower in Paris. It was the **Modern Movement**, however, which developed High Tech in a major way. In 1928 Pierre Chareau designed the Maison de Verre using industrial glass bricks, shop steel ladders and factory shelving. Eight years later the Museum of Modern Art in New York mounted an exhibition that extolled the virtues of, among other items, laboratory glass for the home. Such industrial products appealed to many designers. In 1949 Charles and Ray Eames used a mail-order catalogue to buy off-the-peg factory construction components to build their Santa Monica home. This idea of putting industrial products to other uses continued throughout the 1960s and 1970s and can be seen notably at the **CCI** (Pompidou Centre) in Paris. This controversial building, designed by Richard Rogers and Renzo Piano, made a feature of exposed heating ducts and conduits for such utilities as plumbing and electricity. It was compared to an oil refinery, but a refinery dedicated to culture, painted in primary colours and full of wit and humour. Rogers also designed the Lloyds Building in the City of London, arguably Britain's last great building of the 20th century.

In the 1970s High Tech became fashionable as a style for the home. People began to buy restaurant cutlery and warehouse storage systems. This cult was documented in Joan Kron and Suzanne Slesin's book *High Tech*. The cover photograph showed off the aesthetic with fruit in a concrete bird-bath placed on a tabletop made from deck plate (a material used for the floors of battleship boiler-rooms). Shops selling High Tech style sprang up all over the world. One of the best known in London was Practical Styling, owned and run by Tommy Roberts. High Tech also influenced art, with the term being applied to contemporary art made with sophisticated technology, such as computers, lasers, holograms, photocopiers and even satellite transmissions. In the 21st century the term still connotes a sense of future materials and technology.

Further reading:

Kron, Joan and Slesin, Suzanne, *High-Tech: The Industrial Style and Source Book for the Home*. London: Allen Lane, 1979.

HISTORICISM

Borrowing from the past, a trend which, in recent years, has become associated with the **Postmodernist** Movement. Recently, we have grown used to revivals occurring at ever shorter intervals, such as the reintroduction of the **psychedelic** colours and patterns of the 1960s in the 1990s. Previously, more time would be allowed to pass before old styles were resurrected. For instance, Christopher Wren reworked the medieval past in his Tom Tower at Oxford, while in the 18th century architects and designers borrowed extensively from Egyptian, Greek, Roman and Chinese sources. It was the 19th century, however, that made Historicism its own, and the Victorian era's obsession for the past is reflected in the large number of design source books published on the subject at that time. The most famous of these, and now a standard text that has been endlessly reprinted, is Owen Jones's *Grammar of Ornament* (1856). This book provided manufacturers and designers with a huge range of source material, including Elizabethan, Pompeiian, Moorish and Aztec imagery. All of these styles were tried in designers' attempts to meet the consumer's demand for decoration and ornament. The foremost example of 19th-century Historicism was the **Gothic Revival**, but its architects were at pains to stress that straight copying of imagery was not their aim: rather, they wished to recreate the strength and spirit of the Middle Ages.

With the advent of the **Modern Movement** any attempt at Historicism was frowned on by the **avant-garde**. It was not until the development of post-war **Pop** culture that borrowing from the past became respectable again, but it has now come to play a key role in the pluralist approach to design. The British style magazine *The Face* coined the term 'The Age of Plunder' for this direction, which has played an important role in the inspirational fashion designs of Vivienne Westwood, for instance. She has revived Victorian crinoline, the **Rococo** outdoor fête and imagery from royal pageantry in her anarchic clothes. The term 'plunder' was also applied to graphic design in the 1980s. Peter Saville reworked Roman type, Russian **Constructivism** and 1960s Pop for record sleeves and posters, and thereby reflected a general trend towards what was called the '**appropriation** of images'.

Further reading:

Jones, Owen, *The Grammar of Ornament*. London: Dorling Kindersley, 2001 [1856].
McDermott, Catherine, *Vivienne Westwood*. London: Carlton, 1999.

HOLLYWOOD STYLE

The American film industry was all-powerful in the inter-war years. Its products were the first mass-entertainment and cultural exports of

America to be shown all over the world. The Hollywood film studios comprised a major industry, and a key part of that industry was the army of designers working on sets, props, graphics and fashion. Inevitably, Hollywood was a great source of design ideas. Traditionally, however, design commentators have tended to dismiss its role, rather as traditional European theatre has dismissed its standards of acting and the world of literature has denigrated Hollywood scriptwriters for 'selling out'. These traditional cultural hierarchies have been undermined since the 1960s. Far from being ephemeral, Hollywood films are now seen for what they really were, and in some cases still are: the most important cultural and visual products of the 20th century.

Further reading:

Pickard, Roy, *The Hollywood Studios*. London: Muller, 1978.
Massey, Anne, *Hollywood beyond the Screen: Design and Material Culture*. Oxford: Berg, 2000.

ILLUSTRATION

Before the Second World War illustration was considered to be commercial art, occupying the middle ground between painting and design. In the post-war period it came into its own as a separate creative activity, and illustrators now find work in **advertising**, **packaging**, magazines, poster design and books.

The history of illustration goes back to the earliest printed books, such as the works on architecture by Palladio and Serlio in the 17th century. During the 18th century the trend for illustrated books, trade cards and handbills developed, and the status of illustration was enhanced when the poet William Blake illustrated books of his own poems. As book **consumption** continued to increase in the 19th century, illustrated books proliferated, helped by the development of techniques of colour printing, such as chromolithography, which involved printing from stone blocks (one for each colour), and wood-block printing. These techniques made books particularly attractive to children, and the illustration of children's books quickly became an accepted art form. The best-known practitioners included Walter Crane, Kate Greenaway and Beatrix Potter. Among illustrators of adult books, Aubrey Beardsley took advantage of photographic techniques to reproduce his erotic, brilliant black-and-white illustrations for *The Yellow Book*, a publication devoted to the work of advanced designers. At the same time, well-known artists also worked in the commercial area: Toulouse-Lautrec, for example, produced **Art Nouveau** posters. If his illustration work can be said to occupy one end of the spectrum, the other end was occupied by thousands of jobbing illustrators paid to produce packaging and chocolate-box lids for industry. Their work was little appreciated and their status as creative illustrators was negligible.

More recently, that situation has changed. Contemporary illustrators are well known in their own right and can command huge fees for their work. In the 1960s and 1970s photography looked set to kill off more traditional forms of illustration, but the 1980s saw a tremendous revival of interest in illustration for everything from supermarket packaging to magazines and **advertising**. In the 21st century illustration remains an important design discipline, but its primary success is in contemporary **animation**.

Further reading:

Denny, Norman, *The Yellow Book: A Selection*. London: Bodley Head, 1949.
Wootton, David, *The Illustrators: The British Art of Illustration 1786–2003*. London: Chris Beetles, 2003 [1996].

INCLUSIVE DESIGN

Also known as universal design (especially in the USA) and design for all, and encompassing **user–centred design**, human-centred design, **ergonomics**, usability studies, design for disability (now widely considered an inappropriate term), rehabilitation design, geron-technology and transgenerational design. Inclusive design is about ensuring that environments, products, services and interfaces work for people of all ages and abilities. For instance, rather than specifically targeting disabled people as a minority, design should instead seek the widest possible constituency by ensuring that products appeal to and can be used by everyone. Thankfully, the adoption of this attitude means that products for the disabled are no longer located in specialist shops more like hospital outpatient departments than retail outlets, as they were just a few years ago.

The classic example of inclusive design's new approach is the Oxo Good Grip range of kitchen utensils (see **ergonomics**). This product range proved that there is no need to treat elderly or disabled consumers as special cases; rather, it is more appropriate and useful to integrate them into the mainstream and design with that in mind. This approach benefits not only these groups but the wider community through more thoughtful design of buildings, public spaces, products and services. The adoption of inclusive design has been prompted partly by legislation. In response to a population that is ageing and remaining active for longer (by 2020, half the adult population of the UK will be over fifty years old), the UK government has introduced policies promoting the integration of all groups into mainstream society, in terms of access to work, entertainment and education. The expectation of inclusive design is that it can deliver these new requirements for equality and inclusivity in the future.

Further reading:

Hall, P. and Imrie, R., *Inclusive Design: Designing and Developing Accessible Environments*. London: Spon Press, 2001.

Keates, Simeon and Clarkson, John, *Countering Design Exclusion: An Introduction to Inclusive Design*. London: Springer, 2003.

Preiser, Wolfgang (ed.), *Universal Design Handbook*. London: McGraw-Hill, 2001.

INDEPENDENT GROUP (IG)

A group founded in 1952 by a circle of British architects, writers and artists to explore the world of consumer culture. IG members included Peter and Alison Smithson, James Stirling, Peter Reyner Banham, Richard Hamilton and Eduardo Paolozzi. A major retrospective exhibition of **Pop design** at the Royal Academy in 1991 reinforced the group's position as the founders of Pop.

The IG met at London's Institute of Contemporary Art and developed a shared opposition to the reactionary attitudes of post-war British culture. Soon they organized a now famous series of informal seminars in which they explored all aspects of **popular culture**. Their most original contribution to the analysis of mass-produced design was that they treated it as seriously as high culture. Looking at cars, **advertising** and films, they tried to read them as symbols of the new consumer culture. The group established the idea that artists and architects could explore this world of consumer culture, and its writers, particularly Reyner Banham and Toni del Renzio, published a series of influential articles. The IG's other important contribution to design theory was a reassessment of the **Modern Movement** which challenged its views and authority.

The IG's formal meetings ended in 1955, but it continued to meet and collaborate on an informal basis, working together in the following year on the Whitechapel Gallery exhibition 'This Is Tomorrow'. The group's ideals and aspirations remain an ongoing inspiration for both architecture and design.

Further reading:

Robbins, David (ed.), *The Independent Group: Postwar Britain and the Aesthetics of Plenty*. Cambridge, MA: MIT Press, 1990.

INDUSTRIAL DESIGN

A term covering the products of post-**Industrial Revolution** society. The concept of the industrial designer is therefore relatively new, and his or her role is to adapt the new products of industry to the mass market. Before the Industrial Revolution this did not exist: the task of creating objects for the home was the preserve of artisans and craftsmen. But during the 19th century the three major industrial powers – Britain, the United States and Germany – gradually saw the emergence of industrial designers. The first step towards this was to develop education for designers. Britain set up a School of Design (later the **Royal College of Art**) with the objective of training designers for industry. The best-known graduate from this school was Christopher Dresser, who created designs for **mass production** for companies as diverse as Minton and Elkington's. At the turn of the century in Germany the electrical company AEG appointed Peter Behrens as its industrial designer, and there was a growth in professional organizations such as the **Deutsche Werkbund**, founded in 1907.

It was the USA, however, that saw the real revolution in manufacturing techniques and the role of design. Henry **Ford** developed methods of standardization into twenty-four-hour assembly lines for the production of his Model T car. The USA also produced the first generation of industrial design professionals, including Raymond Loewy, Norman Bel Geddes and Walter Dorwin Teague. Such people were now members of production teams working on the cars, trains, aeroplanes and other hardware of the **Machine Age**. The term 'industrial design' was becoming widely used and was seen as a way of increasing sales and profit.

The status of the profession continued to rise in the post-war years, when designers played a key role in rebuilding devastated Europe. New approaches to educating the industrial designer, begun at the **Bauhaus**, were also developed at **Cranbrook Academy**, the **Royal College of Art** and **Ulm**. Although each industrialized country developed its own national design identity, they all shared a determination to set up professional and government organizations to promote industrial design. Now that the battle to establish industrial design as a legitimate professional activity had been won, a variety of approaches emerged. Manufacturing companies in Japan, for example, tend to regard the industrial designer as an anonymous, although important, member of the production team. In Europe, by contrast, designers like Philippe Starck pioneered the use of their names as marketable brands and became media celebrities.

Further reading:

Buddensieg, Tilmann, *Industriekultur: Peter Behrens and the AEG, 1907–1914*. Cambridge, MA: MIT Press, 1984.

Gorman, Carma (ed.), *The Industrial Design Reader*. New York: Allworth, 2003.

Heskett, John *Industrial Design*. London: Thames & Hudson, 1980.

Read, Herbert, *Art and Industry: The Principles of Industrial Design*. London: Faber and Faber, 1966 [1934].

INDUSTRIAL REVOLUTION

The modern industrial age in which we live and in which design has come to play such an important role is still relatively new. Just over two hundred years ago, the Industrial Revolution laid the foundations for the new industrial age and ushered in the first of many sweeping changes. **Mass production** and mass **consumption** were made possible by the development of new technologies, the introduction of large factories and new patterns of urban living. This 18th-century atmosphere of expansion, intellectual experimentation and exploration opened up a period of change for designers, pioneer industrialists and inventors, including Josiah Wedgwood, Thomas Boulton, Sir Richard Arkwright and James Hargreaves. They reshaped industry and production into the new patterns of the Industrial Revolution.

Towards the end of the 18th century technological change was also beginning to affect traditional industries. In 1759 Wedgwood inherited the family pottery business in Staffordshire and set about reforming it. He introduced steam power, and during the 1760s and 1770s he set ground rules for industrial production that were copied all over the world. He was also one of the first manufacturers to introduce systematic scientific research methods in his factory and he pioneered new methods of marketing and business, being one of the first manufacturers to use newspaper **advertising** and to develop retail display. Even more important were the changes he introduced to the manufacturing process. Wedgwood broke down ceramic production into separate activities, thus creating the fundamental principle of the Industrial Revolution: the division of labour. It was a simple but profound change which overturned the practice of individual workers controlling the whole process of production. Now each worker specialized in a single activity, and the increased use of specialized machines led to the idea that design could be separated from manufacturing. Wedgwood's approach reflected the wider economic theories of his age, particularly those of **Adam Smith**.

Inventions affecting the textile industry provide a model for this industrial change. Spinning was the first area to be mechanized, with the invention of Arkwright's water frame, Crompton's mule and Hargreaves' spinning jenny. This first wave of inventions in the 1770s shifted the production of textiles from small workshops in the home to centralized factory production. The second process to be mechanized was weaving, followed by calico printing, which was revolutionized by the invention of a roller-printing machine in 1783. The rapid expansion of textile production in the Lancashire towns of Manchester, Oldham and Rochdale would change the industrial landscape for ever and make changes to production that impacted across the world.

Further reading:

Chippendale, Thomas, *The Gentleman and Cabinet Maker's Director: A Reprint of the First Edition*. Leeds: The Chippendale Society, 2005 [1754].
Smith, Adam, *The Wealth of Nations*. New York: Random House, 2003 [1776].

INFLATABLE DESIGN

A term applied to inflatable furniture, which was part of 1960s **Pop design**. Designers attempted to make furniture as ephemeral fashion items, with experiments also including paper chairs and tables. Part of the Pop aesthetic was that furniture could be expendable, and the final manifestation of that expendability, made possible by the invention of the welded PVC seam, came with the appearance of 'blow-up' items which could simply be deflated when not needed. Italy led the way with the famous Blow chair, designed by Jonathan de Pas, Donato d'Urbino and Paolo Lomazzi. Britain followed with chairs by Bernard Quention and Roger Dean, while Conran Associates marketed a version for **Habitat** as a 'picnic chair' which came with its own pump and repair kit. The transparent, inflatable chair became *the* accessory for the Pop environment. Later, in the 1980s, Ron Arad experimented with the inflation principle in reverse by designing a chair from which air could be removed by the sitter in order to form an imprint of their body. Inflate is a well-known UK design company that specialized in inflatable objects for home and commercial use, and inflatable furniture still features in leisure consumer products for the swimming pool and beach.

Further reading:

Topham, Sean, *Blowup: Inflatable Art, Architecture and Design*. London: Prestel, 2002.
Williams, Gareth, *Inflate*. Frankfurt: Form, 1998.

INFORMATION DESIGN

A new design discipline that aims to meet the complex information needs of the 21st century, for example by designing airport signage to allow the passengers to locate their departure gates easily and efficiently. It includes **type design**, pictures and text, which can be printed or electronically generated. It also draws on evidence-based research from different fields, such as the psychology of reading and learning, human–computer interaction, usability, **typography**, graphic design, applied linguistics, cognitive psychology, social and political science and computing.

Information design is utilized by industrial companies (for instance, in the publication of instruction manuals), government institutions and pharmaceutical companies. Large organizations and government agencies now rely on it to an extraordinary degree. Indeed, some would argue that usability and ease of understanding are essential elements of modern economic success. Successful information design generates easy-to-navigate websites, tax forms that are clear and easy to return and process, and concise, unambiguous instructions on how to set up machines or dispense medicine. It is therefore the key to consumer safety as well as a profession that instils confidence in service providers.

Essentially interdisciplinary in practice, information design requires the designer to understand how people respond to information, read it, understand it, process it and act upon it. The designer has to understand human interaction with the text, as well as cognitive processing, linguistic theory and psychology. Information design is therefore focused equally on the information provider and the information user. The designer's role is to structure and order the information while considering the location, needs and purpose of the user. He or she therefore serves the needs of both information providers and information users to help us all negotiate the diversity of modern life. Information can be provided and accessed in paper form, over the Internet, on digital TV or mobile phones, so the designer has to make each of these 'channels' as accessible and efficient as possible. Information designers have pioneered clear language and functional writing tools in the form of guidelines and training tailored to particular needs. They use typography and graphic design to organize information with the needs of particular users in mind and transform complex material so that it is easy to understand as well as being attractive.

The order and structure of information are of key importance for large websites and information systems, and this has led to the creation of new roles, including so-called information architects – designers who create the navigation interfaces that allow us to use websites efficiently.

Further reading:

Bhaskaran, Lakshmi, *Size Matters: Effective Graphic Design for Large Amounts of Information*. Hove: RotoVision, 2004.

Mollerup, Per, *Wayshowing: A Guide to Environmental Signage Principles and Practice*. Baden: Lars Muller, 2005.

INNOVATION DESIGN

An integrative approach to innovation that uses creativity and design to develop tools and techniques in order to improve a company's effectiveness. Innovative design can be used in service as well as manufacturing sectors. It is a response to the pressure on companies to be continuously innovative, and supports the development of innovation strategy within the business.

INSTALLATION

A fine-art term used to describe an environment built by an artist. In this context interior designers of the 1980s were attracted to the concept of installations as a way of describing their work. Consequently, the word started to be used in both an art and a design context.

Marcel Duchamp's installation for the first **Surrealist** exhibition in New York in 1942 provided the **prototype** for the fine-art installation and became the basic form for many 1960s movements, such as **Pop** and **Minimalism**. Some artists, including Joseph Beuys and Edward Kienholtz, deliberately used installation's multimedia aspect to break down traditional hierarchical views of art and its function.

The term is now commonly used to describe an artist's or designer's exhibited work, whether it is all of one medium taking up a complete space or a combination of various art forms. The installation has also become a way of displaying important designers' work on commercial premises. An example is Future Systems' incredible exterior for Selfridges' Manchester store in which the form is soft and curvaceous in response to the natural curve of the site, sweeping around the corner and wrapping over the top to form the roof.

Installations have become the perfect form in which to work across the divides of artist, architect and designer, and as such they are in keeping with the fragmented montage effect of **Postmodernism**.

Further reading:

De Oliveira, Nicolas, *Installation Art in the New Millennium: The Empire of the Senses*. London: Thames & Hudson, 2003.
Kachur, Lewis, *Displaying the Marvelous: Marcel Duchamp, Salvador Dali and Surrealist Exhibition Installations*. Cambridge, MA: MIT Press, 2001.

INTERACTION DESIGN

The discipline in which designers examine the interface between people and products or environments. It is the meeting point between design and new technology and it is applied to **product design**. Also known as interface or human–computer interaction (HCI) design, it is a **user-centred** perspective of design and focuses on the convergence of physical and digital technologies. It also explores culture and society, especially the role of technology in people's lives. Although this field has its roots in traditional design practice, it is now largely concerned with products and services that use information technology. Traditionally, the design of mechanical devices such as typewriters, bicycles and washing machines focused on functionality and aesthetics. In products using digital technologies, however, the connections between form, function and usability can be less obvious. Interaction designers therefore use a multidisciplinary approach, drawing on theory as well as practice, to make communication and interaction with computer-based devices as transparent and user-friendly as possible. The aim is to create designs that will enhance ease of use and the exchange of information and so will be successful in the market place.

Interaction design is now a recognized design discipline, with a discourse driven by the human need to interact with technologies. It has also emerged within the last ten years as a field of study in design institutes and universities worldwide. Among the leading centres are the Ivrea Institute in Italy and the **Royal College of Art** in London.

Further reading:

Carroll, John M. (ed.), *Human–Computer Interaction in the New Millennium*. London: Addison Wesley, 2002.
Dawes, Brendan, *Analog in, Digital out: Brendan Dawes on Interaction Design*. Berkeley, CA: New Riders, 1997.

INTERDISCIPLINARY DESIGN

Almost any designed environment demonstrates the fundamental importance of the interdisciplinary team. Electrical engineers, for example, developed the inner workings of the computer, industrial designers the casing, and a graphic designer the screen graphics. Although the principle of teamwork is an old one, the potential of the interdisciplinary team is currently being reassessed, and many of the world's industrial giants, such as IBM and Sony, are exploiting this work method to expand their international markets. For such companies, design teams permit simultaneous input from different perspectives and disciplines, combining the talents of, say, artists, curators, policy-makers, production managers and service personnel. Interdisciplinary teams are expected to take responsibility for the whole project rather than a narrow slice of it. The emphasis on design as a team activity also helps to define the nature of the design profession. The concept of the solitary design genius has become less fashionable. Consequently, the idea of the designer as celebrity could be on the decline, reinforcing the important message that design, unlike fine art, is a shared, mutually dependent activity.

See also: **convergent design**

INTERIOR DESIGN

Also known as spatial design, this relates to the spatial organization, planning, decoration and furnishing of spaces within buildings. Human beings have always created interior spaces for themselves, but the concept of a professional designer manipulating and decorating the interior space of a building is relatively new, truly emerging only in the 20th century. An 18th-century forerunner was the *enseñzblier*, who typically came from an upholstery or furniture background. During the 1760s, for example, Thomas Chippendale, the British cabinet-maker, in effect ran an interior design practice from his shop in St Martin's Lane, London. Clients ordered their furniture there, but they could also purchase carpets and draperies, and hire craftsmen to repaint interior walls. Fontaine and Percier, Napoleon's interior decorators, brought together furniture, textiles and painted decorations within his state living quarters. Similarly, during the 19th and early 20th centuries, furniture retailers such as the London firm of Waring & Gillow would provide reproduction antiques and, if required, create a total environment in keeping with such pieces.

Interior design has historically been overshadowed by the architectural profession. Leading architects of the 20th century, including Charles Rennie Mackintosh, succeeded in creating stunning interiors for the buildings they designed, providing everything from the furniture to floor coverings and light fittings. This approach flourished with the **Modern Movement** of the inter-war ears, when the architect exercised total control over his or her open-plan interiors and created such classics of 20th-century design as Le Corbusier's *Grand confort* chair and Mies van der Rohe's Barcelona chair. After the Second World War, the new profession of interior design acquired greater status with the creation of the British Institute of Interior Design and new, high-level courses on the subject at national art schools. In the early 1950s Sir Hugh Casson and Margaret Casson set up the first postgraduate school of interior design at the **Royal College of Art**. They faced opposition from the Royal Institute of British Architects (RIBA), who still saw interior designers as nothing more than decorators, but gradually opinion changed. Figures such as David Hicks in Britain and Billy Baldwin in the USA became famous as interior designers, and with the founding of specialist journals like *The World of Interiors*, *Interior Design* and *Designers' Journal*, the identity of the profession became more firmly established.

With the retail boom of the 1980s, which was to a certain extent design led, interior design helped to establish new identities for banks, retail shops and building societies. That decade also saw the rise of the powerful interior design practice. Rodney Fitch, for example, was the first to employ over a thousand people. Other practices, such as David Davies, Din Associates, Conran Associates and Ben Kelly Design, ensured that interior design was at last taken seriously as a powerful marketing tool for the retailer.

In the 21st century interior design is now recognized as a design discipline, although spatial design and space planning are increasingly being used as alternative terms for the subject in education and design practice. Very recent trends, such as the decision by the Royal College of Art to close its interior design course, suggest that the future of the discipline is not wholly secure.

Further reading:

Coates, Nigel, *Collidoscope: New Interior Design*. London: Laurence King, 2004.

Conran, Terence and Fraser, Max, *Designers on Design*. London: Conran Octopus, 2004.

McKellar, Susie and Sparke, Penny, *Interior Design and Identity*. Manchester: Manchester University Press, 2004.

INTERNATIONAL STYLE

Another name for the **Modern Movement**. It was 'invented' by Philip Johnson for an exhibition held at the Museum of Modern Art in New York in 1932, but he had borrowed it from a book by Walter Gropius called *Internationale Architektur* (1925). In the 1930s the label stuck and architects in particular began to describe their work as 'international'. 'Modernism' and the 'Modern Movement' are now more commonly used to describe the changes in art and design that occurred in the 1920s and 1930s.

Further reading:

Hitchcock, Henry Russell and Johnson, Philip, *The International Style*. London: Norton, 1966 [1932].

ITALIAN DESIGN

Italy is now synonymous with good design, and Milan is regarded as the undisputed capital of style. But this reputation developed only in the post-war period, and by any standards it is a remarkable achievement. The model Italy offers to emerging design countries in the 21st century is a most important one. As recently as the 1850s Italy was divided into several autonomous principalities and kingdoms: Rome was a papal state, the Bourbons ruled the south and the Austrian Empire controlled the northern territories. Led by popular heroes like Garibaldi, however, there was a gradual movement towards unification called the Risorgimento. However, Italy still had enormous problems: it had been slow to join the **Industrial Revolution** and at the end of the 19th century over 60 per cent of the population still worked on the land, with varying degrees of success. Southern Italy, for example, was one of the poorest areas of Europe. Another major problem was language, because each area spoke its own local dialect. Needless to say, a single, unified national identity proved slow in coming.

None the less, 19th-century Italy was receptive to wider European design ideas. Iron and steel industries developed in the north and the railway system began to spread throughout the country. Some of these changes were reflected at the 1881 National Exhibition, held in Milan. Certainly, the products on display showed off traditional Italian strengths – an impressive workshop craft tradition in marble, glass and ceramics – but in general the designs looked back to Italy's past achievements, rather than forward. More important was the Turin International Exhibition of 1902. Here Italy, with buildings like Raimondo d'Aranco's Rotundo and the furniture of Carlo Bugatti, displayed an original version of **Art Nouveau** called Stile **Liberty**, in honour of the London department store. New confidence and affluence could be seen around the same time in the gallerias of Kings Umberto I (in Naples) and Vittorio Emanuele III (in Milan), both of which were built at the turn of the century. This period also saw the foundation of companies that were later to develop international profiles. These included Fiat, established in 1899 in Turin by a group of ex-cavalry officers; Lancia, set up in 1905; Olivetti, founded in 1908 by Camillo Olivetti; and Alfa-Romeo, established in 1910.

In the early years of the 20th century Italy made its own original contribution to the **Modern Movement** with **Futurism**. This radical movement of artists, architects and poets demanded a complete break with the past, insisted that the museums and libraries should be burned and embraced the glories of new technology. It also inspired a search for a new Italian spirit, which would soon be exploited by the **Fascist** movement, led by Benito Mussolini (1883–1945). Fascism, with its twin values of tradition and modernity, proved an irresistible force, and it was under its auspices in the 1930s that the concept of true Italian design finally emerged. At first, it was dominated by a version of the Modern Movement called **Rationalism**, but this was replaced by the more conservative **Novecento Movement**, inspired by **Classical** sources. Under Mussolini, Italian industry rapidly expanded and the first serious attempts to introduce the new principles of **mass production** were made. Fiat, in particular, introduced the practices of Henry **Ford** to its manufacture of cars such as the 1939 508C. In 1932 Olivetti produced the MP1 typewriter, with a simple body shell that could be made using new production techniques. Indeed, the company was committed to Modernism: former **Bauhaus** staff were responsible for publicity; the innovative Marcello Nizzoli was taken on as chief consultant designer; and between 1939 and 1941 at Ivrea the company built a Modernist steel-and-glass factory. Mussolini also reformed transportation, famously (but erroneously) gaining the reputation that he made the trains run on time. In design terms, trams, trains and ships were among the most aggressively modern objects Italy produced in the inter-war years.

The devastation of post-war Italy prompted the Ricostruzione, a rebuilding programme characterized by remarkable determination. American money from the Marshall Plan helped this effort, but the achievement was Italian. In less than ten years Italy became a modern industrial state that bore comparison with France or Germany. Almost immediately, distinctive Italian goods appeared on the market, including Corradino d'Ascanio's Vespa scooter for Piaggio in 1946, Gio Ponti's 1947 espresso coffee machine for La Pavoni, and Marcello Nizzoli's 1948 Lexicon 80 typewriter for Olivetti. By the end of the 1950s, the distinctive Italian approach to design was established. Moreover, Italian cinema, fashion and literature also attracted international admiration. It was the decade of *la Dolce Vita*, and from here on the status of Italian design only increased. In the 1960s Italy produced some of the best-known icons of **Pop design**: the see-through, **inflatable** Blow chair of 1967; the sag bag or Il Sacco; and the 1965 Brionvega radio by Achille Castiglioni.

In 1972 an exhibition called 'Italy: The New Domestic Landscape' held at the Museum of Modern Art in New York paid tribute to Italy's immense contribution to post-war design and confirmed the dominance of the Italian design ideology. When the massive economic recession of 1973 brought to a close many of the more experimental design groups, Italy consolidated her position with a return to classic design, a move best expressed in the work of Mario Bellini and Vico Magistretti for such companies as Olivetti and Cassina. In response to this Ettore Sottsass and a group of friends started the now legendary

Memphis group. This was a direct attack on the good–taste, conservative aspects of late 1970s design.

In the 21st century Italy has maintained her design reputation and supremacy through the Italian Furniture Fair (Salone Internazionale di Mobile). Here, world–famous Italian manufacturing companies such as Artemide and Cassina commission not only young Italian designers but international stars, for example Philippe Starck, Marc Newson and Jasper Morrison, who help to maintain the Italian reputation for cutting-edge innovation. Held each year in April, it remains the design industry's premier event, attracting buyers, designers and media coverage from around the world. It has developed into a celebration of designer culture that sets the standard for international trends.

Further reading:

Branzi, Andrea, *The Hot House: Italian New Wave Design*. London: Thames & Hudson, 1984.

Sparke, Penny, *Italian Design: 1870 to the Present*. London: Thames & Hudson, 1988.

JAPANESE DESIGN

The profile of Japanese design in the 21st century is identified with new technology, computer graphics, innovative electronic products and **youth culture**. This image represents the tremendous economic and cultural changes that have occurred in the country over the last hundred years.

When the American Navy's Commodore Matthew Perry arrived in Japan in 1854, he ended 250 years of isolation imposed by the ruling Tokugawa shoguns. After a trade agreement was signed between the two countries, the USA presented Japan with a model locomotive, an electric telegraph and a daguerreotype camera. With those gifts the impact of the West's **Industrial Revolution** began. Some twenty years later the English industrial designer Christopher Dresser visited Japan to record what had happened in the interim. He travelled over 2,800 kilometres, visited 68 potteries and published an account of his travels called *Japan: Its Architecture, Art and Art Manufactures* (1882). This book remains a unique account of early Meji Japan and reveals a country on the edge of major transition.

At the end of the 19th century Japan's new trading wealth was used to build up the commercial infrastructure of a modern society, with banks, railways, printing presses, telegraphs, educational institutions and post offices. The Japanese government actively encouraged the estab-lishment of Western-style industry by offering merchants incentives to build factories and importing skilled labour from abroad, while at the same time sending young Japanese to England and the USA to study engineering and science. Many famous Japanese companies were founded at this time. Seiko, for example, was established in 1881, while Toyota has its roots in a company established in 1897. Japanese trade prospered as the late 19th-century European obsession with the country opened up a prosperous export market for luxury products, such as fans, prints, porcelain and lacquerwork. More importantly, European designers began to recognize that Japanese design and culture offered a unique aesthetic approach. Charles Rennie Mackintosh, for example, was inspired by photographs of Shinto temples. Interestingly, in return, the individual style of the **Glasgow School** was copied almost immediately in Tokyo. The Japanese were eager to learn, and books on such diverse topics as **Cubist** theory and architecture appeared in Japanese translation almost as soon as they were printed in Paris or London. Gradually, this East–West exchange increased as ever more designers travelled. The American architect Frank Lloyd Wright was a key player in this exchange. In 1906 he visited Japan and the experience had a profound effect on the development of his work, and in turn on the development of European **Modernism**. In the early 1920s he designed the Imperial Hotel, one of Tokyo's major buildings. Ten years later the Modernist architect Charlotte Perriand also visited and worked in Japan. In these inter-war years European dress and customs were introduced into Japanese life, including American films, jazz music, flapper dresses and **Art Deco advertising**. Japan also shared another widespread, albeit less welcome, development of the 1930s – a build-up of fierce nationalism and massive military investment. Nevertheless, for most Westerners, Japan was still perceived as a 'backward' country. Its status as a significant world power became apparent only with the onset of the Second World War.

That period of Japan's history came to a tragic end in 1945 with the atomic bombing of Hiroshima and Nagasaki. Thereafter, General Douglas MacArthur supervised the American occupying force in the country until 1952. Subsequently, American ideas and help in recon-struction projects were to have enormous effects. By the late 1950s, Japan had developed into a major industrial nation. The new Japanese industries of this time concentrated on producing capital-intensive goods such as cars, motorcycles, radios, television sets, fridges and washing machines. By doing so they created an economic miracle. When still under American control the Japanese set up the Ministry of International Trade and Industry (MITI), which granted the newly founded Sony Corporation permission to buy the manufacturing rights to a new invention, the transistor. It was Japan's mastery of such technology that helped it rise in the late 20th century to become the world's second-largest economy. In 1955 Sony produced its first transistor radio, and four years later it introduced the world's first solid-state television receiver, which had an eighteen-inch screen and weighed only thirteen pounds. Inevitably, Japanese products began to be associated with the latest technological advances, particularly miniaturization. Japanese industry also had a different profile from that of the West. The country's economic boom was reliant on the intense company loyalty of employees and their rigorous work ethic, which was fostered by the guarantee of a job for life for anyone who put in the requisite effort. However, now that dominance in the market place is no longer guaranteed for Japanese products, loyalty of employee to company and vice versa have diminished.

The role of the designer also contrasted with the Western norm. The post-war period saw a rapid expansion in **design education**, but the Western model of lone designer superstars and large design practices was not copied in Japan. Instead, designers joined huge companies and their role was largely anonymous. At the same time, though, Japanese design was reliant on Western ideas, which it freely copied. It was only in the 1970s that a distinctive Japanese quality to design began to emerge. Since then, Japan has retained its unique approach to colour and form but has combined these elements with Western culture and the new technologies that have been developed in the country itself.

Since the 1980s, Japanese fashion has made a strong international impact. Issey Miyake, Kenzo, Yohji Yamamoto, Comme des Garcons and Hanae Mori have all pioneered the use of inventive cuts and monochrome tones, notably the use of black. More recently, Keita Maruyama has become a leading designer; but Japan, like Britain, is now more famous for its street fashion. And the traditional profile of Japanese design is now seen alongside its major creative achievements in computer games, comics and **illustration**.

Further reading:

Davey, Andrew, *Detail: Exceptional Japanese Product Design*. London: Laurence King, 2003.

Dresser, Christopher, *Japan: Its Architecture, Art, and Art Manufactures*. London: Kegan Paul, 2001 [1882].

Sparke, Penny, *Japanese Design*. London: Michael Joseph, 1987.

JUGENDSTIL

The German equivalent of **Art Nouveau**. It comes from the title of a magazine launched in Munich in 1896 which, although not exclusively a design magazine, acted as a showcase for the Art Nouveau style.

KITSCH

From the German verb *verkitschen* (to make cheap), Kitsch has had various meanings since the term was first coined. Originally it referred to objects of no real use, such as knick-knacks, souvenirs, non-functional tableware, glass ornaments and novelties. In 1939, however, the American art critic Clement Greenberg used it to describe jazz, **advertising** and trash novels – broadly speaking, the areas we now define as **popular culture**. In the 1960s it became an umbrella term for items of bad taste and vulgarity that were nevertheless embraced by people of sophisticated sensibilities. This continued into the following decade, when young, middle-class couples 'ironically' decorated their homes with plaster flying ducks and carefully selected 'witty' and 'amusing' items. Placed in the context of an affluent home, Kitsch could be safely enjoyed and admired. It was also an area appropriated by admirers of **Camp**. The 1980s saw a fashion for the florid religious imagery of Southern Europe and South America, typified by 3D **illustrations** of the Madonna and the Sacred Heart.

Kitsch is a sensitive area because enjoyment of it relies on a sense of knowing superiority, which is not far removed from condescension or arrogance. To put it simply, an object that enjoys the status of Kitsch in a smart city drawing room may at the same time be on display as an object of reverence in another home. Several mainstream critics object to Kitsch because in their opinion it dupes the weak and poor. Greenberg felt that it betrayed the consumer because it is ultimately undemanding and unsatisfying. Eradication of the cheap, tacky and tasteless is still a driving force in the design establishment. None the less, playing with the boundaries between conventional good taste and Kitsch has enriched the language of contemporary design.

Further reading:

Dorfles, Gillo, *Kitsch: An Anthology of Bad Taste*. London: Studio Vista, 1969.
Gillilan, Lesley, *Kitsch Deluxe*. London: Mitchell Beazley, 2003.
Greenberg, Clement, *Art and Culture: Critical Essays*. Boston, MA: Beacon Press, 1961.

KOREAN DESIGN

Due to its geographical location between China and Japan, Korea shares cultural and design traditions with both of those countries. However, until the 20th century, it was an independent country for four thousand years. That ended with Japanese annexation in 1910. After the Korean War of 1950–3, the country was divided along the 38th parallel by the United Nations into two zones, North and South Korea. South Korea developed into a modern capitalist democracy while the North became a closed communist country cut off from the outside world and with limited economic development.

After 1953, design initiatives moved slowly, with South Korean manufacturers tending to focus on sourcing products from around the world in order to produce a local version with small modifications. Since the early 1970s, however, South Korea has become a major player in the global economy. Design has helped to drive this success through three government-sponsored five-year 'National Design Strategies'. The Korean Institute of Design Promotion (KIDP), established in 1970 by the government, has played a key role by establishing national design identities and characteristics, organizing an ambitious programme of funding for the design industry, and staging international exhibitions and conferences. Recently, three regional design centres in Gwangju, Busan and Daegu have been founded to promote a better use of design and strengthen the design industry at the regional level.

Design education is also well supported in Korea. Every year approximately 38,000 design students graduate from college, university or graduate school. Among a number of renowned design schools are the design department at Seoul National University, which is famous for its **design research**; Hongik University, which is more art-oriented; and Kookmin University, whose reputation is strongly based on **product** and **automotive design**. Two emerging centres are the design departments at KAIST (the Korean Advanced Institute of Science and Technology), which enjoys strong government support for IT and media research, and at Handong University.

Korea's design image has changed from that of imitator to innovator. Unlike China, it has succeeded in establishing international brands, such as Samsung, LG and Hyundai. Samsung can be seen as a model for all Korean industry as it has deliberately shifted its brand image away from engineering and towards design. It is now one of the world's most important electronics brands, and its example has energized the country's design industry.

Korea is now a world leader in product design but it is also growing in strength in film, **illustration**, **communication design** and fashion. It has even started exporting design services to foreign countries in recent years. China is one of its biggest customer countries, and there is ever increasing cooperation in design between the two countries. The Korean design studios Design Blue, Dadam Design Associates, Design Mall, Design Wow and MI Design are particularly strong in the Chinese market.

South Korea has not developed a designer star system like that of Europe. As in Japan, most of the best designers work anonymously for the country's large corporations. However, KIDP launched a programme in 2004 to award prizes to around twenty-five young Korean designers to promote their work both nationally and internationally.

Further reading:

Korean Art and Design: The Samsung Gallery of Korean Art. London: Victoria & Albert Museum, 1992.

Korea Institute of Design Promotion. See: <http://www.designdb.com/english/kidp/index.asp>.

LANDSCAPE DESIGN

This evolved into a profession in the mid- to late 19th century. The American Society of Landscape Architects (ASLA), for example, was founded in 1899. Landscape design was developed to meet the new challenges of industrialization, urbanization and the growth of cities. One of the founders of the practice was Frederick Law Oimstead (1822–1903), best known for his design of Central Park in New York City. Landscape design now focuses on the development of land and its resources, and includes land design, management and **conservation**. It seeks to understand the landforms, climate and geology that shape a landscape and the social and cultural forces that then change that landscape as communities develop. Landscape designers might work on residential developments, parks, public spaces, historic preservation or restoration. The key to its success as a design activity is the recognition that landscape design is an interdisciplinary activity and must be integrated into the whole design process. Landscape design as a design process seeks to balance stewardship of the land with the needs of the community by minimizing the use of resources, conserving ecosystems, and utilizing renewable resources, recycling and recovery. In the 21st century landscape designers are members of interdisciplinary teams for serious planning projects and are not brought in as an afterthought but are integral components of the development proposal.

Further reading:

Bell, Simon, *Elements of Visual Design in the Landscape*. London: Spon Press, 2004 [1993].

Reed, Peter S., *Groundswell: Constructing the Contemporary Landscape*. New York: Museum of Modern Art, 2005.

Rogers, Elizabeth Barlow, *Landscape Design: A Cultural and Architectural History*. New York: Harry N. Abrams, 2001.

LIBERTY'S DEPARTMENT STORE

Liberty's in London is much more than a shop. Since it was founded in 1875, it has pioneered innovative retail trends, helping to shape contemporary taste. Indeed, by the end of the 19th century, the Italians were calling the new **Art Nouveau** Movement the '*Stile Liberty*'. The shop's founder, Arthur Lasenby Liberty (1843–1917), started his career as an importer and helped to create the vogue for all things Japanese. James McNeill Whistler and Oscar Wilde shopped at Liberty's, and for the Gilbert and Sullivan musical *The Mikado* the store sent buyers to Japan to source exactly the right costumes. In 1884 a costume department opened, headed by the architect E.W. Godwin, which sold children's clothes in the Kate Greenaway style and unstructured gowns for women. Liberty's employed leading **Arts and Crafts** designers, of whom Archibald Knox is perhaps the best known. He was responsible for a range of silver and pewter inspired by Celtic forms. The other important area Liberty's pioneered was textile design, commissioning George Walton, Charles Voysey, Lindsay Butterfield and Arthur Silver. The quality of these designs has led to many remaining in continuous production ever since. Liberty's remains an iconic store, notably in the fields of fashion, accessories and furniture.

Further reading:

Adburgham, Alison, *Liberty's: A Biography of a Shop*. London: Allen and Unwin, 1975.

Calloway, Stephen (ed.), *The House of Liberty: Masters of Style and Decoration*. London: Thames & Hudson, 1992.

LIFESTYLE

A fundamental concept for design. Lifestyle may be defined as both an aspiration concept used to persuade consumers to buy a range of products; and the mode of living of a particular group that can be studied in order to develop new products, such as the lifestyles of the growing elderly population.

LIGHTING DESIGN

Candles, fire, oil lamps and then gas have all provided lighting. But the use of electricity introduced lighting as an integral design type for the modern world. By 1900, electric lighting had spread to such an extent that a growing industry had developed to provide lighting design and light fittings. Electric lighting design has always been closely related to the development of bulb technology. The old-style tungsten bulbs still used in many homes are virtually identical to those Edison and Swan invented in 1879, using a coiled tungsten filament as light source, surrounded by a mixture of gases that slow the process of oxidization that eventually ends a bulb's life. Tungsten lights can be coloured or clear, and they are cheap and flexible, but they are not energy efficient, with only 6 per cent of their energy emitted as light and the remainder wasted as heat.

An early innovator in lighting design was the British designer William Arthur Smith Benson (1854–1924), who set up a metal design factory in Chiswick for **Morris & Co**. He was arguably the first designer of modern light fittings for the home. In the early 1900s, when the German critic Hermann Muthesius published *Das Englishe Haus*, his study of **avant-garde** British design, the final few pages were devoted to images of Benson's electric lights. More conventional were the table lights designed by **Tiffany** and Co. to shade direct light. Industrial lighting was more experimental, including tungsten strip lighting for factories and hospitals. The Dutch designer Gerrit Rietveld famously exploited this technology for his **geometric** hanging light designed for a doctor's clinic and later used it for the office of **Bauhaus** director Walter Gropius.

The 1920s saw the evolution of a new type of lighting design which concentrated on the quality of light rather than simply designing around the bulb. Interesting here is the work of Paol Henningsen, whose light fittings for the Danish company Louis Poulsend received several prizes at the 1925 **Art Deco** Exhibition and remain modern classics.

Henningsen combined reflectors of different sizes that give off direct and indirect light without any glare, which has ensured their enduring popularity as dining-table lights. The search for a modern aesthetic in lighting also led to a range of **mass-produced**, functional lighting for both the home and the office. The British designer George Cawardine's 1932 anglepoise lamp is such an example, based on the physiology of the human arm. But the most famous light of the 20th century was made by a female designer, Marianne Brandt, whose Kandem table light was designed as a bedroom side-light. Its push-button switch made switching it on and off when one is half awake easier, and this feature, along with its small and adjustable shade, has influenced the design of lamps ever since.

Later lighting design responded to the **Pop** aesthetic of the 1960s. The Boalum lamp by Artemide (1970) used light bulbs in industrial translucent tubing to give off a soft and gentle glow. Technology developed for use in car reflector bulbs was also adapted for domestic lighting design at this time, including the Parentesi lamp (1970), the Flos, designed by Achille Castiglioni, and Richard Sapper's Tizio lamp (1972), which used a halogen lamp which offered a concentrated light source. One of the most original lighting designers of the 1980s was the German Ingo Maurer, who exploited the development of halogen bulbs and fluorescent lights. Maurer produced a series of sculptural, low-voltage lighting **installations** that the consumer could touch and move freely.

Lighting technology is now extremely sophisticated, using computer systems to allow maximum control of effects, and exploring energy-saving solutions.

Further reading:

Bowers, Brian, *Lengthening the Day: A History of Lighting Technology*. Oxford: Oxford University Press, 1998.
Muthesius, Hermann, *The English House*. London: BSP Professional Books, 1987 [1904].
Pavitt, Jane, *Brilliant: Lighting Design*. London: V&A, 2004.

MACHINE AGE DESIGN

A popular description of products from the inter-war period, parti-cularly those from the USA. The Machine Age was marked by a belief in new technology that was not shaken by the Depression years of the 1930s. The US public, influenced by designers such as Raymond

Loewy, Buckminster Fuller and Norman Bel Geddes, saw an image of 20th-century America take shape, an image that reflected the visual appearance of the machine. Automobiles became as sleek as spaceships, while trains, ships and even buses acquired the new **streamlined** look. The same shapes were used for domestic appliances, such as fridges, radios, televisions and washing machines. Artists Alexander Calder and Joseph Stella, photographer Margaret Bourke White, and filmmakers, manufacturers and engineers all celebrated the new, machine-dominated world. Their work and that of the other important innovators, such as the architects of skyscrapers, factories, service stations and bridges, shaped new attitudes and a new culture.

Machine Age design was not a single style, but took on board **Art Deco**, **Modernism**, streamlining, **Constructivism** and **Functionalism**, creating a powerful group of images and objects whose influence continues to impact on contemporary design.

Further reading:

Banham, Peter Reyner, *Theory and Design in the First Machine Age*. Cambridge, MA: MIT Press, 1980 [1960].

Bel Geddes, Norman, *Horizons*. New York: Dover, 1977 [1932].

Teague, Walter Dorwin, *Design This Day: The Technique of Order in the Machine Age*. London: Studio Publications, 1947 [1940].

Wilson, R.G., Pilgrim, D.H., Tashjian, D., *The Machine Age in America, 1918–1941*. New York: Brooklyn Museum, in association with Abrams, 1986.

MARS

The Modern Architecture Research group (MARS) was a short-lived British organization to promote the ideas of the **Modern Movement**. Formed in April 1933 by British architects as a response to the French **CIAM** group, its members included Wells Coates and the historian Sir John Summerson, and its first exhibition was held in the Burlington Galleries early in 1938. The group published plans for the radical redevelopment of London, which were largely ignored, and in 1957 it disbanded.

Further reading:

Jackson, Anthony, *The Politics of Architecture: A History of Modern Architecture in Britain*. London: Architectural Press, 1970.

MARXISM

A theory of political economy and history developed by Karl Marx in the 19th century in response to the **capitalist** industrialization of production. The theory, which went on to be applied to many areas of intellectual life, including design, divided society into two antagonistic classes – the bourgeoisie and the proletariat. Either you owned the means of production or you were exploited by those who did. Marx placed the profit motive at the centre of capitalist production. The proletariat, a class of wage labourers, sold their labour for a fixed sum, while the capitalists pocketed the difference between the price of that labour and the price of the product. Marx argued that this means of production, and the economic base on which it relied, became the foundation for the whole of society, including legal and political structures, and forms of social consciousness and ideology. He saw history as the history of class struggle – ancient, feudal and modern bourgeois – but believed that capitalism, in using the proletariat as its labour force, was sowing the seeds of its own destruction. This analysis of capitalism was complemented by his political theories, as shown in *The Communist Manifesto*, which he co-wrote with Friedrich Engels. Marxism became a tool of analysis used in many areas of intellectual life and a theory for social change, most notably put into practice by the Russian Revolution in 1917.

Many designers, artists and architects have subscribed to Marxist beliefs. William **Morris**, while not strictly a conventional Marxist, certainly held revolutionary socialist beliefs, and other designers sought to create individual, utopian, often rural social experiments. In the late 1960s Italian designers such as Ettore Sottsass and later Gruppo Strum became famous for their espousal of Marxist ideas, but the capacity of the designer to change society has always been severely limited.

Further reading:

Marx, Karl and Engels, Friedrich, *The Communist Manifesto*. London: Penguin, 2003 [1848].

MASS PRODUCTION

The production of the largest number of standardized goods for the most competitive price. It requires huge factories and a large labour force of semi-skilled workers trained for specifically designed and

155

repetitive tasks, which have to be completed in a specified time. An early example of mass production was devised by Marc Isambard Brunel in 1769 for the Portsmouth Block Mills to manufacture pulleys for sailing ships. Nowadays, the process is generally thought of in terms of conveyor belts that deliver component parts to factory workers – assembly lines using specially designed machinery. The **Ford** Motor Car Company in Detroit famously developed this system at the beginning of the 20th century. Ford researched modern methods of production, including the work of Frederick **Taylor**, who developed early time-and-motion tests to increase production and worker efficiency. In 1908 it took fourteen hours to assemble a Model T, but after the introduction of mass-production techniques this was slashed to ninety-three minutes. Ford was also able to lower the price of a car from $1,000 to $360. Unsurprisingly, in light of such benefits to the company, mass production became the factory standard for the 20th century.

Today, electronic processes have often replaced the assembly-line operatives, and huge workforces are becoming a thing of the past. Sometimes called Post-Fordism, there has been a move away from single-site production towards multiple sites, introducing the concept of the global assembly line. This is reflected in the UK economic model, which has seen the decline of heavy industries, the emergence of the service sector and a move towards an **experience economy**.

See also: **Fordism**

Further reading:

Batchelor, Ray, *Henry Ford: Mass Production, Modernism and Design.* Manchester: Manchester University Press, 1994.

MATERIAL CULTURE

An academic discipline with a wide historical scope that is of interest to design because it focuses on the object more than the text. It is interdisciplinary, drawing upon historical studies, design studies, museology history, human geography, anthropology and archaeology. It is based on the concept that, because historians rely on texts, they have overlooked objects, or material culture, as an important source of evidence, and have therefore failed to develop a methodological framework for its study. This is in marked contrast to such disciplines as archaeology, anthropology, art history and folklore, in which objects are paramount in **cultural analysis**. Material culture therefore attempts to explore the relationships between artefacts and society within their historical context, and researches into the links between society and the production and use of culture. Everything from ancient Egyptian artefacts to modern domestic appliances, ephemera and clothing are analysed to provide insights into past and present cultures that would be impossible to glean through documentary sources alone.

Further reading:

Journal of Material Culture. See: <http://mcu.sagepub.com/>.

MEMPHIS

A radical new design group launched in 1981 by the Italian architect Ettore Sottsass. The name combined references to American pop music and to the ancient Egyptian capital, epitomizing the kind of irony and ambiguity that Sottsass enjoyed in his design practice. He started Memphis with the help of a group of collaborators, employees and friends, among them Michele de Lucchi, George Sowden, Martine Bedin, Hans Hollein, Michael Graves, Arata Isozaki, Nathalie du Pasquier, Marco Zanini and Matheo Thun. The group launched its collection in a showroom in Milan to coincide with the September 1981 Furniture Fair. It was an overnight sensation. The objects and furniture shown resembled children's toys: they were playful and used a bright palette of colours. Decoration was given a new importance, mixing together different patterned laminates appropriated from 1950s Milanese coffee bars. And the furniture challenged basic assumptions. Why, for example, should the legs of a table be identical?

From the beginning the media gave Memphis extensive coverage, with photographs appearing on the pages of the international press from New York to Tokyo, and in return the group delivered exciting, newsworthy collections. However, Memphis was not without its critics. Some felt it was elitist and had turned its back on the **Modernist** tradition of design. Leading curators at the **Victoria and Albert Museum** and at the Museum of Modern Art in New York viewed the group as an exclusive **avant–garde** whose work was going down a cul-de-sac and would have no influence on mainstream design. They were to be proved totally wrong. The group was formally wound up in 1988, but not before it had earned an important position in the history of design. Memphis objects inspired a whole generation of designers, with their influence obvious in the quirky details on Ikea furniture and the work of the **Dutch** design collective Droog. Leading museums all over the world now collect the originals, and exhibitions reassessing the contribution the group made to contemporary design have been organized by the **Design Museum** in London.

Further reading:

Radice, Barbara, *Memphis: Research, Experiences, Results, Failures and Successes of New Design*. London: Thames & Hudson, 1985.
Watson, Anne, *Mod to Memphis: Design in Colour 1960s–1980s*. Sydney: Powerhouse Publishing, 2003.

MILAN TRIENNALE

During the 1950s, the Milan Triennale became the main showplace for modern Italian design. The tradition of Italian exhibitions had begun in 1923 in Monza, leading to the first triennale in 1933, held at Milan's Palazzo d'Arte, which showed the work of Italian **Futurists** alongside other exponents of the **Modern Movement**. In 1957 the theme was Europe, in 1961 compulsory schooling, and in 1964 leisure. These triennales reflected vigorous Italian debates concerning the nature and direction of design, and they attracted international press attention. More recently, Milan's annual furniture fairs have replaced the triennales as the main arenas for displaying Italy's continuing dominance in design.

MILITARY DESIGN

Many civilian products and systems exploit the results of the research and development invested in military technology and warfare. For instance, laminated plywood developed for use in British fighter places was converted into the sculptural shapes of furniture in the 1950s. In the same decade other designers were working on the space programme, which for Russia and the USA was dominated by military and sur-veillance considerations. Both sides allocated enormous resources to this and other areas of military design. In fact, in the Soviet Union the space/military programme was virtually the only area in which a designer could work with the same resources and prestige given to Western industrial designers of consumer products.

The influence of military products on design styling is easy to recognize. During the 1950s and 1960s atomic motifs were on everything from cars to coffee tables. The space race sparked off futuristic visions of the kitchen and also led to spacesuit mini-dresses and visors. Alternative groups like the hippies, who combined combat jackets with long hair and beads, also appropriated military uniforms and accessories. The 1970s saw a trend towards radio and hi-fi styling that evoked the utilitarian field equipment in the Vietnam War. In the 21st century such military allusions are part of the wide repertoire of visual references the designer can plunder. However, there remains a divide between real military and civilian design, with the former subject to tight security measures.

MINIMALISM

In its broadest sense, this term applies to the art and design of the 1960s that either reduced the 'art work' involved in the production of an object or used a limited range of materials and expression. More specifically, it denotes a primarily American movement that deliberately avoided references to the meaning or content of works in order to emphasize the 'object quality' of art: the fact that it existed like any other object, without needing grand metaphysical statements. This was in part a reaction to previous soul-revealing paintings of the 1950s by such artists as Willem de Kooning and Jackson Pollock, but it was also a rejection of the hallowed status of art itself. Influential on design were the sculptors Donald Judd and Carl André (infamous for his 'pile of bricks' at the Tate Gallery), who often chose to work with mass-produced, easily accessible materials, such as stainless steel, prefabricated sheet metal and copper floor tiles. Frequently arranged in predetermined mathematical designs, unworked on by the artist except for placement, these artworks challenged the convention of the hand-crafted, beautiful art object. Variously named primary structures, serial art, ABC art and simply 'good design', Minimalism can be seen as a rejection of artifice and therefore part of an earlier, anti-illusionist modern tradition.

Minimalist objects were often shown as **installations**, the concern with surface detail suppressed in favour of a broader awareness of the object–spectator relationship in space and time. Influenced by Gestalt theories, questions of perception and experience became important and were applied to writing, dance and theatre, as well as to art and design.

Minimalism as a term that implies reduction to a fundamental level of function and beauty has had a continuing role in design, from early Greek ceramics to the work of the 19th-century **Shaker** community. It has also influenced design as a wider cultural expression. For example, the refined interiors and products of classic Japanese culture inspired the revolutionary ideas of **Modern Movement** designers. Mies van der Rohe's assertion that 'Less is more' reflects the enduring power of Minimalism.

In the 21st century, the work of many designers across a range of disciplines is associated with an exploration of Minimalist values. They include John Pawson's **interior design**, Bruce Mau's graphics, Jasper Morrison's **product designs**, Rei Kawakubo's fashion and the buildings of the Japanese architect Tado Ando.

Further reading:

Baker, Kenneth, *Minimalism: Art of Circumstance*. London: Abbeville Press, 1988.

Meyer, James, *Minimalism: Art and Politics in the Sixties*. London: Yale University Press, 2001.

MODERN MOVEMENT

A group of architects and designers who set about creating a new aesthetic for the 20th century, an aesthetic that for most of its practitioners was not just a style but an article of faith. This spirit of change and innovation was a worldwide trend and led to the movement also being described as the **International Style**. The key features of Modernism were rationalism and objectivity that provided a sharp contrast with the 19th century and its obsessions with style revivals and decoration. Modernism, unlike the **Arts and Crafts Movement**, believed in the city as the future for all, made possible by the new inventions and products of the **Machine Age**. 'Form follows function' is a Modernist slogan that reflects the movement's rational, ordered approach to design.

Modern Movement designers also expressed the belief that **mass production** led inevitably to pure **geometric** form, and so they totally rejected decoration. Two more slogans of the Modernists – Mies van der Rohe's 'Less is more' and Le Corbusier's description of the house as 'a machine for living in' – have underpinned attitudes and approaches to design throughout the 20th century. This purist approach was not, however, the whole story, and Modernism during the 1920s and 1930s was never a single, homogeneous movement. That image was largely constructed in the post-war years by carefully editing out the individual, **Expressionist** contributions to 20th-century design made during those years. An interesting case in point is the **Bauhaus**, the most famous design school of the period, which saw hardline Modernism developing alongside the diversity of Expressionist decorative work. Similar diversity can also be seen in the very different styles of Modernism that developed around the world: **De Stijl** in Holland; **Constructivism** in Russia; Le Corbusier in France; **Futurism** in Italy; and Scandinavian and American variants. While there are common links between these there is also complexity and diversity. De Stijl, for instance, promoted a rigorous aesthetic using primary colours, as well as white, grey and black, which restricted design to flat planes and strong geometric shapes. Members of the movement were also inspired by theosophy, whose strict, puritanical element reflected the prevailing Dutch Calvinist culture. The Soviets, on the other hand, had a different ideology in that their work provided practical products for the Revolution, such as clothes, workers' cafés and housing. Meanwhile, the Italian Futurists hoped to create a new, modern country free of the past and ready to engage with the industrial culture of cars, machines and aeroplanes and allied themselves not to socialism but to right-wing **Fascist** ideology.

More individual was the work of Le Corbusier in France. His approach to architecture and design represents the embodiment of the pure Modernist spirit. In his famous book *Towards a New Architecture* he advocates a universal and timeless geometry using simplicity and pure form. In this respect his work has a direct relationship to classical antiquity, but he also believed that mass-produced products could share these timeless qualities and be integrated into a new architecture appropriate for his time, which afforded comfort, sunlight, order and harmony. In practice this meant open internal spaces and dramatic white concrete outlines in his most famous buildings, including the Villa Savoye.

The Scandinavians and the British adopted a less extreme approach. For instance, in general they preferred to use natural materials and design less extreme geometric forms. American industrial designers Raymond Loewy, Walter Dorwin Teague and Norman Bel Geddes applied the styling of the Machine Age to trains, fridges, vacuum cleaners and cars at the 1939 **New York World Fair**, which took as its theme 'a vision of the future'.

The Modern Movement, then, never produced a single manifesto, although it did come near to it with the Congrès Internationaux d'Architecture Moderne (**CIAM**), a campaigning body of architects, writers and designers who met and debated the movement's ideas in the 1930s. However, two important Modernist design writers did emerge. The first was the CIAM's secretary, Sigfried Giedion. His 1948 publication *Mechanization Takes Command* is a key **design history** text and the first book to argue that the anonymous, technical aspects of the subject are just as important as the history of creative individuals. The second was Nikolaus Pevsner, whose *Pioneers of Modern Design* has now been standard reading for every design student for seventy years. This book had a single and powerful ideology: that the history of design in the 19th century prepared the ground for the inevitable rise of Modernism. Pevsner helped to create a popular perception of design being practised by a series of male heroes, and at the same time virtually invented the history of the subject as an area worthy of serious academic study.

Modernism affected other disciplines, including economics. The theories of John Maynard Keynes (1883–1946) epitomized scientific rationalism and provided an interesting parallel with the design philosophy of the Modern Movement. Keynes's view was that enlightened intervention of liberally minded intellectuals at the state level could improve the economy. His ideas were written up in *The General Theory of Employment, Interest and Money* (1936), set against the background of Roosevelt's New Deal, which created employment for artists, designers and architects in Depression-hit America. After the Second World War many of Keynes's ideas were put into practice when the Labour government in the UK supported the idea that design and designers could help regenerate the economy. In fact, in the post-war period, governments throughout Europe and in the United States applied many Modernist ideas to massive rebuilding programmes. The disappointing legacies of these reconstruction programmes have proved so profound that they go a long way to explaining the loss of confidence in the Modernist vision.

Its assumptions and values were first effectively challenged by **Pop design** in the 1960s and then by **Postmodernism** in the 1970s. Modernism was exposed to some major critical re-evaluation, and its critics were loud and forceful. It was argued that its rules on material and form were dictatorial, that it was too narrow an approach to design, and that its reverence for the machine diminished the creative, imaginative nature of the human spirit. Equally, it was said that it ignored the complex meanings and emotional functions individuals can give to objects.

Nevertheless, the Modern Movement has always had a claim to the moral high ground because of the importance it placed on the mass-produced object for all, and on the relationship between design and social function. For these reasons, it is generally linked with the left-wing values of the inter-war period. However, its great achievements were not restricted to that time. After 1950, it found expression in the distinguished **industrial design** work of Dieter Rams, and in the ordered and rational approach of the so-called Swiss School of **Typography**. In the late 20th century architects such as Norman Foster and Richard Rogers reinterpreted the aspirations of the Modern Movement for the contemporary era with a series of buildings, including the Millennium Dome. These two men joined a long list of the century's great pioneers in architecture, design and art theory who were, in one form or another, dedicated Modernists. From the perspective of the 21st century, however, it is inevitable that the movement's history is interwoven with a legacy of hero-worship, conflicting facts and mythology that continue to fuel debate and argument.

Further reading:

Giedion, Sigfried, *Mechanization Takes Command: A Contribution to Anonymous History*. New York: Norton, 1969 [1948].

Keynes, John Maynard, *The General Theory of Employment, Interest and Money*. London: Macmillan, 1936.

Le Corbusier, *Towards a New Architecture*. London: Butterworth Architecture, 1989 [1927].

McDermott, Catherine, *Design Museum: 20th Century Design*. New York: Overlook Press, 2000.

Pevsner, Nikolaus, *Pioneers of Modern Design: From William Morris to Walter Gropius*. London: Yale University Press, 2005 [1936].

Powers, Alan, *Modern: The Modern Movement in Britain*. London: Merrell, 2005.

MORRIS & CO.

Brainchild of William Morris (1834–96), writer, designer, craftsman and political activist, the 'Firm', as it was to become known affectionately by those associated with it, was originally called Morris, Marshall, Faulkner & Co. Founded in 1861, the original partners included Edward Burne-Jones (1833–98), Dante Gabriel Rossetti (1828–82), and Ford Madox Brown (1821–93), all painters, and the architect Philip Webb (1831–1915), who had designed the Red House at Bexleyheath for Morris and his wife Jane in 1859. Peter Paul Marshall (1830–1900) was a surveyor, and Charles L. Faulkner (1834–92), who was to become business manager, was a mathematics don at Oxford.

The Firm began as an informal working agreement among close friends 'who were also artists'. They described themselves as 'Fine Art Workmen in Painting, Carving, Furniture and Metals', which, given their inexperience, was somewhat optimistic. Nevertheless, they advertised the following services:

I   Mural decoration . . . in dwelling-houses, churches, or public buildings.
II   Carving generally, as applied to architecture.
III   Stained glass, especially with reference to its harmony with mural decoration.
IV   Metal work.
V   Furniture either depending for its beauty on its own design . . . or its conjunction with figure and pattern painting. Under this head is included embroidery . . . besides every article for domestic use.

Morris, Marshall, Faulkner & Co. first attracted public attention at the South Kensington International Exhibition of 1862, and the Firm had its greatest early success with stained glass, which displayed a distinctly Pre-Raphaelite influence. Excellent examples of it can be seen at the **Victoria and Albert Museum**'s Green Dining Room (1866), still in use as a café, but the majority of the company's stained glass was ecclesiastical. Many of the wallpapers and textiles produced by the Firm, widely imitated by other late 19th-century designers such as Lindsay Butterfield, are still in production, some in the original colour ways.

In 1875 the partnership of Morris, Marshall and Faulkner was dissolved and Morris became the sole proprietor of the Firm, now called Morris & Co. The company's showrooms were at 449 Oxford Street, close to the centre of London's luxury furniture trade. In the main it enjoyed commercial success after weathering the recession of the early 1880s, which drove a number of its leading competitors into bankruptcy. Fortunately, much archival material relating to its history has been preserved, together with many of the wooden blocks used for printing wallpapers. The Firm's clients were generally prosperous members of the middle-class intelligentsia, which had burgeoned in the 1870s and 1880s. Nevertheless, Morris sometimes complained of having to work for the 'swinish rich'. He and his Firm undoubtedly exercised a great influence on British **interior design** in the last three decades of the 19th century, and during the 1890s, through such journals as *The Studio*, their work became well known in Europe. The Firm's business example was emulated by A.H. Mackmurdo's Century **Guild**, W.A.S. Benson's Bond Street shop, C.R. Ashbee's **Guild** of Handicraft, and in Europe by the Belgian architect Henri van de Velde and Josef Hoffmann, the Viennese architect who became associated with the **Wiener Werkstätte**, a cooperative of artists and craft workers.

In spite of its success and wide influence, however, Morris & Co. was wound up at the outbreak of the Second World War in 1939.

Further reading:

Naylor, Gillian, *The Arts and Crafts Movement: A Study of its Sources, Ideals and Influences on Design Theory*. London: Trefoil, 1990 [1971].
——— *William Morris by Himself: Designs and Writings*. London: Time Warner, 2004 [1988].
Ruskin, John, *The Seven Lamps of Architecture*. London: Smith, Elder and Co., 1849.
——— *The Stones of Venice*. New York: Dover, 2004 [1879].
Todd, Pamela, *The Arts and Crafts Companion*. London: Thames & Hudson, 2004.

NANOTECHNOLOGY

An umbrella term that covers a wide range of scientific activities carried out at the microscopic or even molecular level. A nanometre is a billionth of a metre, about an 80,000th the diameter of a human hair. Nanotechnology is thus the science of the very small ('nano' is Greek for 'dwarf'). There are two current approaches to nanotechnology: 'top down' and 'bottom up'. Top down refers to making nano-scale structures by machining and etching techniques, whereas bottom up (or molecular) nanotechnology refers to building organic and inorganic structures atom by atom or molecule by molecule. The nanotechnology that is practised today is generally at the less sophisticated top-down stage.

Commentators believe that nanotechnology can, in principle, be applied to virtually any sector, so it could affect every sphere of our lives, including healthcare, computers, consumer gadgets, energy, defence and food. The cosmetics giant L'Oréal is already marketing a range of skin treatments containing tiny particles, despite concerns about their possible long-term effects on the human body. The electronics giant Philips is conducting research into applications of technology at the nano scale, including high-resolution printed displays and miniature nano-LEDs in which the colour of emitted light can be precisely tuned. Chemists at Italy's University of Bologna, UCLA and the California NanoSystems Institute have designed and constructed a nano-motor that is powered by sunlight. It can work continuously without any external interference, and operates without consuming any fuel or generating any waste. There is also the potential for anti-cancer drugs to be delivered direct to the tumour by tiny nano-bots (robots of microscopic proportions), for computers the size of sugar cubes, and for smart bullets that never miss their target. Nanotechnology therefore seems certain to be hugely important in future **product design** and manufacture, promising myriad design applications at potentially low cost.

Foresight is a think-tank and public-interest institute in Palo Alto that is dedicated to educating society about the benefits and risks of nanotechnology, and supporting nanotechnologies that may contribute to solving the critical challenges faced by humanity. These challenges include meeting energy needs with clean solutions, providing abundant clean water globally, increasing health and life expectancy, and maximizing the productivity of agriculture. Obviously, if nanotechnology can help in these fields that is to be welcomed, but many argue that an international regulatory body must be set up immediately to oversee this new science and approve its products before they are released on to the market.

Further reading:

Foresight. See: <http://www.foresight.org>.

NARRATIVE DESIGN

A relatively new term within design practice describing the use of storytelling techniques to enhance creativity. Designers, indeed all creatives, have always explored narrative techniques to engage the consumer with their products and services, and this is reflected in the processes of **experience** and **interactive design**.

Storytelling and understanding a sequence of events to market a product and make an impact have been used by the **advertising** industry for nearly a century, but these techniques are now also of interest to product designers. Narrative design tries to use storytelling to engage the user by 'writing a script for a product', and the design process is becoming more complex as designers attempt to understand the consumer and the market.

NATURALISM

In 1550 Giorgio Vasari described nature as 'the beautiful fabric of the world' and the most important source of inspiration for the creative artist. That was certainly true in the Gothic period and the Renaissance, when artists borrowed freely from nature's inexhaustible supply of decorative shapes and forms. Naturalism, then, was part of the prevalent belief in a world of beauty made by God, but an alternative view of nature also had an important impact on design. The scientific analysis of nature was a secular approach, and one which designers were to exploit more and more. The painters William Dyce (1806–64) and Richard Redgrave (1804–88) developed this approach for **design education**. Redgrave saw nature as a resource which should be investigated by scientific methods and its principles applied to design for **mass production**, a viewpoint that was widely accepted and expanded in the 19th century, although critics like John Ruskin viewed the idea as barbaric. Nature, he argued, was not a machine. Other Victorians took up the application of science to design with more enthusiasm, however, as is shown by Christopher Dresser's important botanical work on plant structure.

The **Great Exhibition** of 1851 saw the proliferation of literal, exact Naturalism, which some design reformists felt went too far. Redgrave's *Supplementary Report on Design* (1852) strongly objected to what he saw as the improper adaptation of natural forms: a gas jet, for example, coming from a holder shaped like a flower. Nevertheless, the **Arts and Crafts Movement** advocated nature as a source for design, and William **Morris** and **Art Nouveau** designers were equally committed to Naturalism. In the 20th century, however, Naturalism was not at the forefront of design innovations. **Art Deco** developed a stylized approach to natural forms, while 1950s design was inspired by atomic and crystal structures. The 1960s saw the revival of Victorian patterns, but later an imaginative Naturalism developed, epitomized in the design of H.R. Giger's creature for the 1979 film *Alien*. In the 21st century Naturalism as a style trend can be seen in the revival of certain wallpapers and decorated tablewares, and in computer graphics looking to nature for more user-friendly alternatives to **High Tech** on screen.

Further reading:

Carlson, Allen, *Aesthetics and the Environment: The Appreciation of Nature, Art and Architecture*. London: Routledge, 2000.

Dresser, Christopher, *The Art of Decorative Design*. New York: Garland, 1977 [1862].

Hobhouse, Hermione, *The Crystal Palace and the Great Exhibition: Art, Science and Productive Industry: A History of the Royal Commission for the Exhibition of 1851*. London: Athlone Press, 2002.

Pointon, Marcia, *William Dyce, 1806–1864: A Critical Biography*. Oxford: Clarendon Press, 1979.

Ruskin, John, *The Stones of Venice*. New York: Dover, 2004 [1879].

Vasari, Giorgio, *The Lives of the Most Excellent Painters, Sculptors, and Architects*. New York: Modern Library, 2002 [1550].

Wornum, Ralph, *Analysis of Ornament: The Characteristics of Styles: An Introduction to the Study of the History of Ornamental Art*. London: Chapman & Hall, 1856.

NEW AGE

A term used to describe a sector of 1990s society which rejected the high-profile consumerist values of the previous decade in favour of an emphasis on spirituality, organic food, alternative medicine, yoga and meditation. New Age suggests a return to social concerns, a rejection of hard-edged materialism, interest in ecology and a more sympathetic examination of 1960s issues such as **alternative lifestyles**. New Agers chose organic cotton clothes and washable nappies, but generally continued to be consumers in modern **capitalist** society. *Absolutely Fabulous*, a popular British comedy programme about a PR consultant starring Joanna Lumley and Jennifer Saunders, caught the element of irony that has always been associated with the term.

NEW JOURNALISM

The design writing of the 1960s, which sought to describe the influence of **popular culture**. During the 1950s, the British **Independent Group** had encouraged critics and writers to develop a creative approach to writing that would give it a place alongside the new **Pop Art** movement. Important in this context is Peter Reyner Banham. New Journalism, like Pop Art, challenged tradition, in the form of serious academic writing, which used its own language and addressed a small and exclusive audience. A number of critics now wanted to look at, and treat seriously, areas of popular culture which previously had been ignored or denigrated – subjects such as soap operas, pop stars, customized cars, pulp fiction and Las Vegas. While all of this now seems perfectly ordinary, it was then revelatory to a new generation of readers and writers. The most important American exponent of New Journalism was Tom Wolfe, who established a writing style that was a Pop form in its own right, a combination of creative writing and reportage. There are very few contemporary writers on design who have not been influenced by New Journalism.

Further reading:

Banham, Peter Reyner, *Theory and Design in the First Machine Age*. Cambridge, MA: MIT Press, 1980 [1960].
Wolfe, Tom, *The New Journalism*. London: Pan, 1975.

NEW LOOK

The extravagant post-war clothes designed by Christian Dior. Wartime shortages had led to governments laying down fashion rules in order to conserve precious resources. Clothing tended to be austere, almost military in appearance, and colourful fabrics were in short supply. So it is not hard to see why designers and women turned to more romantic, feminine styles once the war ended. What was surprising was that Christian Dior managed to launch his New Look collection so quickly – on 12 February 1947. In opulent contrast to wartime austerity, he produced narrow shoulders, padded hips and extremely full, ankle-length skirts. The New Look caused a sensation. In Britain questions were asked in the House of Commons about the ethics of a style that used up to fifty metres of fabric per dress. But royal approval of the New Look came when Princess Margaret wore a full skirt, and almost immediately mass-produced copies, albeit using less fabric, appeared in chain stores everywhere. The New Look was an international success and re-established Paris as the fashion capital of the world. Dior died in 1957, but the fashion house which bears his name is still one of the world's top couture houses.

Further reading:

Cawthorne, Nigel, *The New Look: The Dior Revolution*. London: Hamlyn, 1996.
Jackson, Lesley, *The New Look: Design in the Fifties*. London: Thames & Hudson, 1991.
Rethy, Esmeralda de and Perreau, Jean-Louis, *Christian Dior: The Early Years 1947–1957*. London: Thames & Hudson, 2001.

NEW YORK WORLD FAIR, 1939

The largest international exposition ever held. Sixty foreign nations and hundreds of American exhibitors celebrated 'The World of Tomorrow'.

The exhibition's futuristic theme, **streamlined** architecture and displays of the most advanced scientific and technological gadgetry pointed the way forward.

The origins of the New York World Fair were in business and financial interests, the aim being to stimulate trade and develop the city as a tourist centre. Its timing, on the eve of Second World War, meant that it reflected the design, architecture and cultural themes that dominated the USA in the mid-20th century. The theme of a technological future was perfect for the pioneering industrial designer Walter Dorwin Teague, who was given the job of overseeing the project. Teague commissioned the great designers of the period, including Donald Deskey, Raymond Loewy, Russell Wright, Norman Bel Geddes and Egmond Aren. In this respect the project was the United States' last great statement of the streamlined style which dominated the country in the 1930s and 1940s, and found expression in the fair's two centre-pieces: the 610-foot Trylon and the huge, domed Perisphere. The fair's cultural theme was expressed in its commitment to functional architecture, the planning of the site as an overall piece of landscape design and the relationship between technology and new forms of artistic expression. Teague was particularly committed to the idea of showing Americans a vision of the future in education, the home and family, transportation and urban planning. Indeed, the fair presented a confident view of every aspect of the American way of life. Later in 1939, however, the outbreak of war in Europe brought with it rather different priorities and concerns.

Further reading:

Blackburn, Sara (ed.), *Dawn of a New Day: The New York World's Fair 1939/40*. New York: New York University Press, 1980.

NICHE MARKETING

A fast-developing selling strategy for products and services that is making an impact on design. It refers to the practice of recognizing a gap in the market and targeting the consumer with a single, specialized product. Niche marketing is generally used by smaller companies concentrating on establishing a strong brand and market position, classically with luxury products. Rolls-Royce, for example, specializes in the luxury car niche. Over the last twenty years pioneer retail examples of successful niche marketing include Tie Rack and the Sock Shop chains. Now the term is more widely seen as the division of a company's products into a number of ranges which can then be targeted at specific customers, thereby maximizing profit.

Further reading:

Dalgic, Tevfik (ed.), *Handbook of Niche Marketing: Principles and Practice*. New York: Haworth Press, 2006.

NOVECENTO MOVEMENT

The distinctive architectural style of the Italian **Fascist** Party of the late 1930s. Mussolini did not share Hitler's personal interest in architecture and design, but he was passionate about promoting Italian nationalism and unity. Novecento reworked references to the glories of Rome through a modern idiom, and Mussolini ordered Italian new towns to be built in the style. The most impressive of these was Sabaudia, named after the ancient kings of Italy, in the province of Latina.

Because of their association with Fascism, Novecento and its exponents were not widely popular, but the movement did encourage Italian industry to employ important architects such as Gio Ponti, Carlo Scarpa and Pietro Chiese to design new products. One of the classic products from this period of Italian design was the faceted coffee-maker designed by Alfonso and Renato Bialetti in 1930.

After 1945 Novecento indirectly continued to have an important effect on post-war Italian design. For Italians, design had important ideological and political connotations that were not present in, say, Britain or America. The implications of design were therefore deeply serious and encouraged a tradition of debate and criticism which has enriched the development of Italian design and helped to make it unique.

OMEGA WORKSHOPS

A British group of painters, writers and designers associated with the Bloomsbury Group. The art critic Roger Fry organized Omega, which opened in July 1913 at 33 Fitzroy Square in London, with the idea of encouraging artists to design furniture, carpets, pottery and textiles. The designers included Fry himself, Duncan Grant and his wife Vanessa Bell, Frederick Etchells and Nina Hammett. It was always rather an amateur organization, devoted to bright colours and a painterly technique that owed something to **Cubism** and Fauvism. Some have suggested its success during this period came about only because wealthy clients did not have access to Paris because of the war and so used Omega's work as a substitute.

The Omega workshop was liquidated in 1921, but its work lives on in a Sussex farmhouse called Charleston, where Grant and Bell lived. Recently restored, the house is full of decorative murals, painted furniture and fireplaces, a style which was out of step with 1920s and 1930s **Modernism**. The Courtauld Institute Galleries also have a good collection of Omega-type objects. Opinion about Omega and Charleston is divided between those who think it self-indulgent and amateurish, and those who admire its energy and use of colour and decoration. But the Omega group continues to inspire with repro- duction textiles and wallpapers as well as a revival of painted decoration for the interior.

Further reading:

Anscombe, Isabelle, *Omega and after: Bloomsbury and the Decorative Arts*. London: Thames & Hudson, 1981.

OP-ART

An abstract painting style of the mid–1960s which was recycled almost immediately by textile and graphic designers. Op did not derive from **Pop**, but was an abbreviation of 'optical illusion'. The best-known exponent of the style was Bridget Riley, and her paintings of wavy black lines set against a white background were copied directly as fabric designs for miniskirts and jumpsuits, and for mural decorations in trendy city apartments. Op-Art techniques were also widely copied on 1960s record sleeves and **Psychedelic** posters, and it retains a strong influence on contemporary pattern design.

Further reading:

Follin, Frances, *Embodied Visions: Bridget Riley, Op Art and the Sixties*. London: Thames & Hudson, 2004.

ORGANIC DESIGN

A loose term for any form of design which derives from natural forms, whether animal, plant or crystalline. Nature was traditionally considered by artists, architects and designers to be the supreme source of inspiration for both decorative motifs and structural form. Greek and **Gothic** architecture was conventionally thought to be based upon imitations of nature, and in the 20th century the historian of ideas Arthur J. Lovejoy (1873–1962) classified this dependence upon nature for inspiration as 'nature as aesthetic norm'. Such inspiration was widespread in the publishing boom of the 19th and early 20th centuries. In 1904 Ernst Haeckel (1834–1919), the leading European exponent of Darwinism and the most prominent marine biologist of his age, began publishing *Kunstformen der Natur* (*Art Forms of Nature*) – a series of beautiful coloured plates illustrating microscopic undersea organisms, radiolaria and other sea creatures, such as jellyfish – which had a wide international circulation. Earlier, German **Art Nouveau** (or **Jugendstil**) designers – like August Endell (1871–1925), Hermann Obrist (1862–1927) and Bernard Pankok (1872–1943) – had been inspired by the magnificent **illustrations** in Haeckel's previous scientific publications. In France, the architect René Binet (1866–1911), designer of the Paris department store Au Printemps – published *Esquisses Décoratives* (1903), which demonstrated how Haeckel's illustrations could be transformed into jewellery, metalwork, or pattern. Hector Guimard (1867–1942), designer of many of the Paris Métro station entrances, is another important French designer whose work falls comfortably into the category of organic. Other important French designers who based their work upon natural forms include: Eugène Grasset (1845–1917), Mathurin Méheut (1882–1958) and Eugène Maurice Pillard Verneuil (1869–1942). In Britain Christopher Dresser (1834–1904), a successful botanist who became a leading designer for industry, made great use of organic forms – especially plants – in his work.

Nature was also a tremendous inspiration for the **Modern Movement**. Le Corbusier, who assiduously studied nature as a boy in Switzerland, developed an organic system of measurement based upon the proportions of the human body, which he published as *Le Modulor* (1948). Frank Lloyd Wright (1867–1959), the most prominent 20th-century American architect, practised what he described as 'organic architecture'. He did not advocate that architects should borrow natural forms, but rather that in wooded areas they should employ wood, while in areas where rock predominated (Los Angeles, for example) they should use cinder blocks. His desert houses had meandering plants – appropriate to the plentiful space available – and were built of stone. In other words, Wright's conception of 'organic' meant simply collaboration with nature. In Scandinavian design, the work of Alvar Aalto was especially notable. His Savoy vase, for instance, was based on the natural forms of Finnish lakes. Organic forms also inspired much of the work of 1960s **Pop** designers, memorably pieces by Luigi Colani, which evoked human sexual organs.

Organic forms in furniture became popular again in the 1990s with such items as Matthew Hilton's *Balzac chair* and Marc Nelson's aluminium *lounge chairs*. The use of natural forms and nature itself has also been used as a counterpoint to technology, to soften and humanize developments in that area. At a simple level, the most popular computer screen savers in the 21st century are images of fish, animals and nature.

Further reading:

Haeckel, Ernst, *Art Forms in Nature*. Munich: Prestel, 1998 [1904].

ORNAMENT

An immense variety of ornament has been produced throughout the ages, which has created a rich heritage on which designers may draw. From the **Industrial Revolution** onwards, ornament and decoration have generated intense design debates. Is ornament appropriate? How much and when should it be used? Nevertheless, ornament was central to 19th-century design, and many Victorians attempted to raise it to an authentic art form in its own right. Owen Jones's *Grammar of Ornament* (1856) still provides the best account of the subject. In the 20th century the **Modern Movement** was generally opposed to ornament, but it is difficult to understand this attitude. Viennese architect Adolf Loos set the ball rolling with his famous 1908 essay 'Ornament und Verbrechen' ('Ornament and Crime'), but this was intended to be ironic and not necessarily an ideological opposition to ornament. Loos himself favoured classical ornament on many of his buildings, while his personal taste in furnishings tended towards such items as Oriental carpets. There is really nothing in the ethos of the Modern Movement which precludes ornament, even though Le Corbusier ridiculed decoration in many of his writings, including *L'Art decorative d'aujourd'hui* (1925), which attacked **Art Nouveau** details that refused to die. One explanation for why so many in the Modern Movement felt uneasy about ornament can be found in the new design teaching established at the **Bauhaus**, which emphasized individual creativity through a basic design course that excluded ornament. Teaching ornament was viewed as retrogressive, harking back to outmoded 19th-century design schools. (Art schools in the 1960s went through something similar when they attempted to abolish traditional life-drawing techniques.)

None the less, pattern books of traditional decoration, such as Seguy's **Art Deco** designs, continue to be produced. Ornament and decoration became key issues for 1960s **Pop design**, and in 1966 Robert Venturi's *Complexity and Contradiction in Architecture* argued for a reconsideration of ornament. With the rise of the **Postmodern Movement** he was soon joined by many other writers and critics, including Charles Jencks, Robert Jensen and Tom Wolfe. The Postmodernist campaign in defence of decorative pattern was largely successful, and put it back on the design agenda.

Further reading:

Brolin, Brent C., *Architectural Ornament: Banishment and Return*. New York: Norton, 2000.

Durant, Stuart, *Ornament: A Survey of Decoration since 1830*. London: Macdonald, 1986.

Jones, Owen, *The Grammar of Ornament*. London: Dorling Kindersley, 2001 [1856].

Le Corbusier, *The Decorative Art of Today*. London: Architectural Press, 1987 [1925].

Loos, Adolf, *Ornament and Crime: Selected Essays*. Riverside, CA: Ariadne Press, 1998 [1908].

Venturi, Robert, *Complexity and Contradiction in Architecture*. London: Architectural Press, 1977 [1966].

PACKAGING DESIGN

Packaging design has a clear functional purpose but also a creative element, and it can be crucial in increasing sales. In addition, it performs an extremely important social role: packaging of gifts is a means to express love and affection and mark important formal moments. In this respect it provides key social and status indicators and forms part of a code of behaviour.

The history of modern packaging can be traced back to the end of the 18th century. France led the way in preserving meat, vegetables and fruit in airtight glass containers. Then, during the early 1800s, an industrial process was developed to can food for Napoleon's army, and later this was introduced into a number of civilian food industries. The US fishing industry led the way, followed by meat and vegetables producers. Manufacturers quickly learned that such products enjoyed increased sales if they were attractively branded and packaged. International brands such as Kellogg's corn flakes, Campbell soups and Colman mustard were launched in this period, and they all had packs that were so closely identified with the product that they came to represent the food itself. The point of such packs then, as now, was to make the product distinctive and recognizable to the consumer. Simple rules quickly emerged: the vital role of colour and a strong brand image. For example, the early use of a Quaker figure for oats expressed fairness and good value, while the distinctive use of the Kellogg signature acted as a guarantee of quality.

New packaging techniques were soon developed, including the airtight circular tin in the late 19th century. This was used for everything from scouring powders to biscuits and tobacco. In the 20th century plastic was introduced, and this had a profound impact on packaging design. Its versatility meant that it came to be used more than any other packaging material. For example, its plasticity made it ideal for squeezable toothpaste tubes. Other plastic innovations include the polymer PET bottle that revolutionized the fizzy-drinks market in the 1970s. The ubiquitous Tetra Pak was developed by a Swedish company in the 1950s, constructed from a paper tube which can be pinched to create a pyramid shape. Other packaging developments included aluminium foil for snack products; and modified atmosphere packaging, in which fresh food is placed in a plastic film bag with high nitrogen and low oxygen content. Manufacturers have also differentiated their brands by unique and innovative packaging shapes, such as the Johnson Wax Toilet Duck cleaner and the 1998 Sapporo beer can, which was designed to perform like a traditional beer glass. This use of distinctive shapes in packaging design is especially marked in the fiercely competitive and lucrative perfume market.

Recently, packaging has responded to changing demographics and consumer needs. In the West, for example, the growing number of people living on their own has led to the development of single-portion ready-meals. The ecology lobby has reacted angrily to these developments, pointing out the unsustainable levels of waste that such packaging generates. Increasingly, decades-old packaging systems are being reassessed and seen as the most suitable solutions. For example, the pressed paperboard egg box, a low-tech solution to transporting eggs, has never been bettered. And British households still enjoy one of the world's most successful recycling schemes – the doorstop delivery of milk. The milk is delivered first thing in the morning and the previous day's empty bottles are picked up, washed and reused. Refillable detergent packs are now more common and more accepted. New technology has also contributed to **sustainability** in packaging. For example, flow pack film for chocolate bars reduces the total amount of packaging and is completely recyclable.

Further reading:

Calver, Giles, *What is Packaging Design?* Hove: RotoVision, 2004.
Myerson, Jeremy and Vickers, Graham (eds), *Rewind: Forty Years of Design and Advertising*. London: Phaidon Press, 2003.

PLANNED OBSOLESCENCE

A marketing strategy pioneered in the USA that deliberately limits the lifespan of consumer products. Durability and lifelong service were qualities people traditionally prioritized when selecting furniture and products for the home. That situation subtly changed in the 1950s, when companies started to make products which had a limited life and would therefore need to be replaced when other, supposedly better models came on to the market. There was nothing new about this as a marketing strategy: the fashion business had been doing it for years. But the extent to which it was adopted by manufacturing industry was extraordinary.

Design reformers like Vance Packard swiftly voiced protest. Packard wrote *The Waste Makers* in 1960 as a direct attack on obsolescence, which he saw as a social evil, an attempt by manufacturers to exploit the gullible and the vulnerable. On the other hand, industrialists and industrial designers saw it as a wonderful opportunity to provide choice, to stimulate the economy and to create objects of design wonder. In this context, the classic American car of the 1950s is an excellent example.

Interestingly, the issue of obsolescence was diverted in the 1960s by **Pop design**, which actively embraced the principle of the throwaway object as a liberating lifestyle concept. In the 21st century, with environmental concerns about waste at the forefront of contemporary design thinking, planned obsolescence is itself becoming an obsolete term.

Further reading:

Packard, Vance, *The Waste Makers*. London: Longmans, 1960.
Slade, Giles, *Made to Break: Technology and Obsolescence in America*. Cambridge, MA: Harvard University Press, 2006.

POP DESIGN

A design movement that flourished between 1963 and 1971, beginning in London and eventually influencing design throughout Europe and the USA. The essence of Pop design lies in its challenge to the traditions of Modernism, which had dominated international design during the post-war years. In **design education** leading Modernist designers and design theorists of the 1930s had a tremendous influence over burgeoning design professionals. Led by the ideology of the **Modern Movement**, design had to function well, be austere, and be made to last. But this older generation of designers and theorists, including Herbert Read in Britain and Walter Gropius in the USA, were now to be challenged by a younger generation of design theorists and practitioners.

Beginning with Peter Reyner Banham and the **Independent Group**, who met informally at the ICA from 1952 to 1955, this younger generation evaluated the legacy of the Modern Movement and proposed a new aesthetic criterion for interpreting design which was based less on functional qualities than on the desires and needs of the consumer. The Independent Group argued that design values need not be universal and everlasting, but could legitimately be ephemeral. This new pluralist approach laid down the critical foundations for Pop design in the 1960s.

As a result of higher standards of living, particularly among the sixteen–twenty-four age group, there was an increased demand for consumer goods, which distinguished the younger people from their elders. This had first made an impact during the 1950s, and it was one of the main catalysts for Pop design in the 1960s. As the Beatles reached number one in the charts in 1963, so young consumers sought out design artefacts to express a shared **youth culture** and identity. Fun furniture, for example, was created in a variety of ephemeral materials: in 1964 Peter Murdoch designed a paper chair constructed out of five-layer laminate and printed with bright polka dots that could be stored flat, bought cheaply by the young consumer and easily replaced. There were similar developments in fashion, such as the disposable paper dress. Typically, surface patterns from the 1960s included flags, bull's-eyes, stripes and other Pop and **Op** motifs borrowed from painters like Jasper Johns, Bridget Riley and Andy Warhol. Designers favoured surface pattern rather than three-dimensional forms, and they explored themes which emphasized a new optimism in the power of youth culture and innovation. Typical of this new mood were the miniskirt and the space-age outfits of André Courrèges, which incorporated plastic ankle boots and white-visored helmets. Pop design, particularly in graphics, was also characterized by a revival of Victorian and Edwardian forms. A series of exhibitions and books on the decorative arts of those periods provided an important inspiration, as did the desire to challenge the dominance of neat, clean Swiss **typography**. The swirling lines and decadence of Aubrey Beardsley seemed ideally suited to the hedonistic atmosphere of 1960s youth culture.

Banham continued to attack outdated Modernism and to support Pop design in his writings for *New Society* throughout the 1960s. Soon, however, the witty, ephemeral and often superficial aspects of Pop design no longer seemed relevant, especially when environmental issues and the oil crisis of 1973 took hold. In that year Charles Jencks, a student of Banham, developed the Independent Group's approach into a more sophisticated **Postmodernism** with his book *Modern Movements in Architecture*. Unfortunately, the sharp wit of Pop design became submerged in the 1970s by **Postmodernist** theory, which was found largely in architecture and developed into a new concern for **Classicism**. However, there has recently been a strong revival of interest in Pop, particularly in fashion design. The artefacts of the 1960s are now eagerly collected and designers have revisited the optimism and confidence achieved in that era.

Further reading:

Jencks, Charles, *Modern Movements in Architecture*. Harmondsworth: Penguin, 1985 [1973].

Whiteley, Nigel, *Pop Design: Modernism to Mod*. London: Design Council, 1987.

POPULAR CULTURE

The urban folk culture that exists in an industrially developed society. It has energized design and the design profession for over a century. It is usually defined as commercial culture derived from a set of industries linked to entertainment, such as sport, book publishing, electronic media and **advertising**. As such, it has been viewed as the antithesis to high culture, which is usually represented by opera, theatre and the ballet.

Popular culture's growth is linked to the **Industrial Revolution** of the 19th century, and the urban population's demand for entertainment. In this sense, it is a specifically modern, urban phenomenon that replaced **folk art** (a rural and individual art form) as the principal **visual**

culture of working-class people, who in the 19th century had more leisure time and money than ever before. Popular culture was represented in a wide variety of new entertainment forms, including illustrated newspapers, serialized novels, funfairs, films, music halls, professional football, comics and, later, radio and television. For much of the 20th century none of this received much in the way of formal attention from museums or academic researchers.

Artists and designers, however, were fascinated by the scope and vigour of popular culture and found inspiration in its vitality and modernity. This appreciation of popular culture grew enormously in the 1960s with the emergence of **Pop Art**, and the relationship between design and popular culture went from strength to strength. The motifs, forms and cultural references of popular culture are now integrated into our understanding of contemporary fashion, graphics and advertising. In the **Postmodernist** period academic hostility to popular culture has been replaced by appreciation of it as a major source of inspiration for contemporary design and visual culture.

Further reading:

Harrington, C.L. and Bielby, D.D. (eds), *Popular Culture: Production and Consumption*. Oxford: Blackwell, 2001.
Journal of Popular Culture. See: <http://www.msu.edu/~tjpc/>.

POST-COLONIALISM

The period after the end of European colonial rule, and in design terms the style that has developed in this era as a consequence of the colonial experience. The history of colonialism is one of brutal exploitation whose after-effects are still being experienced across the globe. Countries such as the Congo (colonized by Belgium), Mozambique (Portugal) and Algeria (France) all experienced the full cultural impact of colonial rule. However, such countries also influenced the cultures of the colonizing powers.

Orientalism, by the influential writer and critic Edward Said, shaped the academic discipline of Post-colonial Studies and could even be viewed as its founding work. Post-colonialism, with its complex experiences and diverse cultural interaction, has moulded national identities, cultures and styles. In cultural terms this can clearly be identified in literature and films, including the work of directors Gurinder Chadha, Shekhar Kapoor, Farida Ben Lyazid, Deepa Mehta and Mira Nair.

Design cannot claim to lead post-colonial theory, but it is immersed in interpreting and representing the creativity of diverse cultures. Indeed, London, the creative capital of the world, has achieved this status partly because it is so culturally diverse. British design is as likely to come from individuals born in Asia, South America or Africa as from indigenous Britons. Perhaps more than that of any other country, British design reflects the complexities and richness of a variety of communities and cultures. As a result, diversity is perhaps now the most important single element in the UK design profession.

Further reading:

Fusco, Coco, *The Bodies that Were Not Ours and Other Writings*. London: Routledge, 2001.
Said, Edward, *Orientalism*. London: Penguin, 2003 [1978].

POSTMODERNISM

A term widely used to describe major cultural developments in the late 20th century as well as a design style. It has become the prevailing cultural paradigm. In this period there has been a profound and funda-mental social and technological change, including the development of new communication technologies, **globalization** and the growth of the mass media. More than anything else, the free circulation of information through the Internet epitomizes the cultural ambitions of Postmodernity, as a decentralized and non-hierarchical structuring of society. However, the meanings and influence of Postmodernism are not fixed. It remains a contentious and imprecise term whose meaning has been devalued to such an extent that it is now used to describe virtually anything new or novel in design. Broadly speaking, it is a response to, and a reaction against, the absolutes implicit in **Modernist** theory and practice. Some theorists have interpreted Postmodernism as a split from Modernism while others have suggested it is a continuation of the earlier movement, but there is agreement that it marks a crisis of faith in the Modernist utopian dream of inevitable progress based on human reason. It signalled the late 20th-century age of uncertainly and cynicism, which suggests that the very nature of Postmodernity defies definition.

As a term, 'Postmodernism' was first used to describe new archi-tecture and design in the 1940s and then the **Pop** aesthetic of the 1960s. However, it is most closely associated with Robert Venturi's groundbreaking book of 1966, *Complexity and Contradiction in Architecture*, in which he introduced an innovative new concept – 'the messy vitality of the city' – and through a series of clever examples from history changed our understanding of the city. Eleven years later, this revolution was documented in a bestselling book by the American architectural historian Charles Jencks called *The Language of Post-modern Architecture*. For Jencks and other like-minded critics, the use of the term 'Postmodernism' implied a critical position against formal Modernist principles and values.

Building on this momentum and the ideas of the 1960s, Postmodernist designers revived a series of ideas, materials and imagery which had been rejected by the Modernists. One of the best-known examples of Postmodernist design came from Italy in the work of Ettore Sottsass and Michele de Lucchi for **Memphis**. Their furniture used mixed materials, combining plastic laminates with expensive wood finishes, and overturned such formal conventions as table legs should be identical and shelves horizontal. The French designer Philippe Starck also developed the stylistic **eclecticism**, wit and irony which defined Postmodernism. This can be seen especially in his furniture for a series of seminal New York hotels in the 1990s in collaboration with the hotelier Ian Schrager.

The freedom Postmodernism offered was similarly liberating for other design disciplines. Textile designers experimented with scale and mixing patterns, often combining diverse imagery on the same design in the manner of a chaotic collage. Graphic design, previously heavily influenced by the fixed and purist rules of Swiss **typography**, began to mix typefaces, play around with printing conventions and **appropriate** imagery from innumerable sources. These changes had the important effect of making the traditional dividing lines between art and design less distinct and less clearly defined. Postmodernism has also changed the processes and conventions of art and design commissioning, exhibiting and selling work.

Postmodernism signalled a new emphasis on interdisciplinary work that crossed over anthropology, philosophy, sociology and science, and brought these methologies into design and **design education**. Likewise, the rich **visual culture** of consumer products provided academics with important case studies. The most important Postmodernist theorists have all been French: Roland Barthes, Jean-François Lyotard, Michel Foucault and Jean Baudrillard. Barthes (1915–80), a literary scholar and critic, has had an especially significant influence on designers. His book *Mythologies* contains a number of essays on consumer culture, such as toys, **advertising** and the Citroën DS car.

Originally published in 1957, it was not translated into English until 1972, but since then it has come to enjoy a near-legendary status. Barthes found **popular culture** interesting not from a visual design point of view but because it reveals the secrets of contemporary society. From the world of design, he attempted to extract the meanings, or in his words 'the mythologies', of imagery and form. He sought to understand the framework that governs society, and in this sense he represents a **Structuralist**'s viewpoint. This concept of design as a series of cultural signs that can be formally analysed became part of the new discipline of **semiotics** and signalled a wider move in design practice away from merely practical, problem-solving activities to a larger world of intellectual ideas.

Change was imposed on design by technologies that dismantled old, established disciplines, such as typography and graphic design. The idea of things being fixed and part of a shared view of the world was gone. Postmodernists had lost confidence in such certainties which Lyotard famously called the 'grand narratives' – the work of Darwin, Marx or Freud and Einstein. For design, the Postmodernist principle of cultural pluralism had important and immediate effects on the way design looked, the way designers thought about themselves and the way in which the design debate was framed and discussed. With the decline of Modernist ideals a different design ethos began to emerge, a move towards style and appearance over content and function. This is famously exemplified by Philippe Starke's lemon squeezer for Alessi.

However, it is important not to overstate the influence of Post-modernist theory on design practice. In the late 20th century Postmodernism can be read as a design style identified by the revival of historical detail, bright colour and ornament on products ranging from Zanussi fridges and Alessi kettles by Venturi to Japanese transistor radios. Design writers have attempted to identify as features of Postmodern style irony, wit, nostalgia, revivalism, quotation, pastiche and parody. Finally, Postmodernist design contrasts with Modernism in its focus on the individual, rather than on society as a collective. This Postmodern emphasis on personal identity is also understood as lifestyle, with its concept and value positioned in the image construction of the individual and their surroundings as an extension of identity. In 21st-century design culture, fluidity and ephemerality have replaced permanence.

Further reading:

Barthes, Roland, *Mythologies*. London: Vintage, 1993 [1957].
Butler, Christopher, *Postmodernism*. Oxford: Oxford University Press, 2002.

Jencks, Charles, *The Language of Post-modern Architecture*. London: Academy Editions, 1991 [1977].

—— *The New Paradigm in Architecture: The Language of Post-modernism*. New Haven, CT: Yale University Press, 2002.

Muggleton, David, *Inside Subculture: The Postmodern Meaning of Style*. Oxford: Berg, 2000.

Venturi, Robert, *Complexity and Contradiction in Architecture*. London: Architectural Press, 1977 [1966].

POSTSTRUCTURALISM

A theory that developed in the 1970s as a critique of **Structuralism** and posed a new challenge to the **Modernist** fixed canon of beliefs. The connections between philosophical thought and architecture could be seen in the writings of Jacques Derrida (b. 1930) and were also demonstrated in his personal collaborations with such architects as Bernard Tschumi and Peter Eisenman, famously for the Parc la Villete in Paris. Eisenman described his Poststructuralist approach to architecture 'as independent discourse, free of any values classical or any other'.

Further reading:

Kipnis, Jeffrey and Leeser, Thomas, *Chora L Works/Jacques Derrida and Peter Eisenman*. New York: Monacelli Press, 1997.

Tschumi, Bernard, *Cinégramme Folie: Le Parc de la Villette*. Sevenoaks: Butterworth Architecture, 1987.

PRIMITIVE

A term denoting art and design produced without access to modern technology. Historically, the word related to long-held prejudices about so-called 'primitive' cultures that were 'fixed' in an evolutionary time warp. There is now a more informed assessment of the important role such cultures have played in the development of Western art and design. An interesting example of this is Aboriginal culture, which is now seen as full of sophisticated skills that Westerners have been too ignorant to understand. The novel *The Songlines* (1987) by Bruce Chatwin draws on this theme, as does the American film *Dances with Wolves* (1990), which also attempts to reverse a historical view of Native Americans as 'savages'.

The Victorians tended to view primitive objects as curiosities, and while they admired them as natural, unfettered by artifice or European 'corruption', they could be championed only in terms of Rousseau's idea of the 'noble savage'. Thorough research into such objects and the cultures that created them was thin on the ground, restricted to the likes of Henry Balfour's Pitt Rivers Museum, the anthropology collection at Oxford, and exhibitions such as the 1886 Colonial and Indian Exhibition in London, which showcased elaborate African objects from the Gold Coast.

There were very few attempts to apply primitive decoration and form to 19th-century design, although Owen Jones and Christopher Dresser championed Aztec art, and Dresser copied simple ceramic shapes for the Linthorpe Pottery. A more powerful effect can be seen on painting. For many artists, primitive culture came to represent something untainted, powerful and anti-academic. The romantic myth of escape began, the best example being provided by Paul Gauguin's retreat to Tahiti. Primitive art also helped to trigger one of the most important revolutions in 20th-century art – the development of **Cubism**. Both Picasso and Braque collected and drew African masks in their quest to develop non-representational art.

Such minority tastes have since become mainstream interests. Television and the rise of global travel have brought remote cultures much closer; and now that it has been integrated into the vocabulary of international design, the primitive has lost much of its iconic power.

Further reading:

Chatwin, Bruce, *The Songlines*, London: Vintage, 2003 [1987].
Flam, J. and Deutch, M., *Primitivism and Twentieth-century Art: A Documentary History*. Berkeley: University of California Press, 2003.

PRODUCT DESIGN

A modern alternative to the term '**industrial design**'. Product design is the process of developing new products for volume production. The global market is a very competitive environment, and for a manufacturer the design of a product is a key factor in business success. It affects every aspect of a manufacturing business, from production to marketing and customer services, and increasingly designers are asked to contribute to the overall strategy for a product, to provide direction and validation. This element of **convergence**, connecting product design to every part of the development process, is typically represented by Jonathan Ives's product designs for Apple. The classic case study for integrating the processes of design, marketing, **advertising** and customer services is the Apple iPod.

Dick Powell, director of the product **design consultancy** Seymour Powell, usefully described product design for the **Design Council**. The process starts with the brief, which combines research from marketing about consumer need, specifications for manufacturing and finally sales planning and profit potential. Ideas for the new product then follow initially as drawings or simple models – a stage called **concept design** – after which the process of concept development will test the product. At the subsequent design development stage the designer works with a team including experts in sales and marketing. This team produces the final model for manufacture.

Product design is now widely applied to any number of products, ranging from hospital equipment to transport systems to consumer durables for the home.

Further reading:

McDermott, Catherine (ed.), *The Product Book*. Hove: British Design & Art Direction, in collaboration with RotoVision, 1999.

PRODUCTION DESIGN

The work of production designers, also known as set decorators or film architects, deals with the physical space in the creation of a filmed environment. Production design results in spaces that allow interplay between the camera and the performers and so it influences the action and creates the cinematic atmosphere. German cinema can claim to have pioneered this design area in the inter-war years, famously in such films as *The Cabinet of Dr Caligari* (1919) and *The Blue Angel* (1933), but America came to dominate international film production standards with the creation of distinctive contemporary looks in everything from musicals of the 1930s to cult films of the 1990s.

Production design is integral to understanding moving-image text, with the emergence of themes, motifs and colours offering clues that help to unravel plot, character and underlying concepts. The production designer works closely with the producer and director to create a design style or concept that will visually interpret and communicate a story, script or environment appropriate to the production content and action. This process is driven by the need to create an illusion that will aid the viewers' suspension of disbelief. It is an enhancement of the script through the visual element whether in a historical, contemporary or futuristic setting. The means of achieving this is an interdisciplinary process involving architectural structures, scenic elements, sculptural forms, lighting and technology (such as LCD panels), props and project management. Production design plays an important role in the success of any movie, play or programme as it provides the audience with a visual context that enhances the production content.

Further reading:

Barnwell, Jane, *Production Design: Architects of the Screen*. London: Wallflower, 2004.

PROTOTYPE

A model of a potential design replicating what the final manufactured object will be like before it is put into production. As ideas and concepts develop, the purpose of prototypes is to help the design team develop the proposed design for testing and evaluation. They can be paper sketches, computer-generated models or fully functional scale models. Rapid prototyping has been used since the 1980s when a product is close to the market. Also known as solid freeform fabrication, this is the construction of physical objects with 3D printers, stereolithography machines or selective laser sintering systems. RP is therefore a type of computer-aided manufacturing (CAM) and is one of the components of rapid manufacturing. Designers are often not involved at the prototyping stage, when interdisciplinary teams, including engineers and **sustainability** experts, are brought in to take the product to production.

Further reading:

Mills, Criss, *Designing with Models: A Studio Guide to Making and Using Architectural Design Models*. New York: Wiley, 2005.

Pham, D.T. and Dimov, S.S., *Rapid Manufacturing: The Technologies and Applications of Rapid Prototyping and Rapid Tooling*. London: Springer-Verlag, 2001.

PSYCHEDELIC DESIGN

A design style based on the images and colours associated with the hallucinogenic drugs that were popular during the late 1960s. These drugs, especially LSD, were used to explore the subconscious and stimulate the imagination, much as Ecstasy was used to reduce inhibitions in the Acid House movement of the late 1980s. The release in 1967 of the *Sgt. Pepper's Lonely Hearts Club Band* album by the Beatles, with a cover designed by the **Pop** artist Peter Blake, is generally credited with launching **Psychedelia** as a style.

In the late 1960s Psychedelia had its biggest impact on graphic design. In 1967, the poster designer Michael English formed a partnership with Nigel Weymouth called Hapdash and the Coloured Coat, and their work epitomized the style, using fluorescent colours that conjured up the images of an LSD 'trip'. The emphasis was on free-floating, flowing forms, many of which were borrowed from **Art Nouveau** images. The intense sexual imagery of Aubrey Beardsley was especially important, combined with the posters of French artists Alphonse Mucha and Henri Toulouse-Lautrec. Another important graphic designer was Martin Sharp, who worked for Jimi Hendrix and Bob Dylan. For designers, Psychedelia was a liberating exercise in creativity, which stressed the importance of the individual through improvisation, free-form composition and technical innovation. The pop poster was the perfect expression of the new drug culture because it was a mass medium, it was cheap and accessible, and it communicated the new consciousness. Also important was the graphic style of *Oz* magazine, launched in 1967 by editor Richard Neville. The magazine's layout was a pure Psychedelic vision, combining hallucinatory lettering, favourite shades of turquoise and magenta, and illegibility, which was achieved through super-impositions and out-of-focus images.

The influence of Psychedelia soon spread, being used to decorate the outsides of buildings, such as English and Weymouth's Red Indian façade for Granny Takes a Trip and the Beatles' Apple **boutique**. The Psychedelic fashion that these shops stocked was produced by, among others, The Fool. This group was committed to visual **eclecticism**, drawing on medieval ideas and ethnic influences from gypsy culture and India, all in bright, clashing colours.

Psychedelic design's influence continues to be felt in the multimedia worlds of **advertising**, film, fashion and **retail design**.

Further reading:

Bussmann, Jane, *Once in a Lifetime: The Crazy Days of Acid House and afterwards.* London: Virgin, 1998.

Grunenberg, Christoph and Harris, Jonathan (eds), *Summer of Love: Art of the Psychedelic Era.* London: Tate, 2005.

Vaizey, Marina, *Peter Blake.* London: Weidenfeld & Nicolson, 1986.

PUNK

The name used to describe a British youth cult of the late 1970s notable for aggressive make-up, shaved heads, safety pins worn as body decoration and ripped clothes. It was partly a reaction to a massive economic recession which undermined the confidence and optimism of the previous decade. The values of the 1960s, especially those associated with hippy culture, were despised by the teen generation of the 1970s. Punk inspired a new, raw form of music, produced by such bands as the Buzzcocks, the Clash and, most notoriously, the Sex Pistols. Managed by Malcolm McLaren, the latter enjoyed a high media profile, with Jamie Reid designing their record sleeves and Vivienne Westwood their clothes. Although Punk was popularly seen as the product of working-class urban and essentially deprived youth, the involvement of Reid, McLaren and Westwood is interesting in that they were not young (all three were in their thirties) and they had all trained at art college. McLaren and Reid especially were typical art college products, and this link between Punk and art colleges is important. Radical performance art, as well as Dada events, influenced both Punk and the student political attitudes of the 1960s. Many famous Punk slogans – for example, 'Never trust a hippy' and 'Anarchy is the key, **do-it-yourself** the melody' – were inspired by Situationist writings of the 1960s. So Punk had a rich intellectual background, but at the time this was ignored in favour of the media view of it as emerging from the council flats of Brixton, Manchester and Liverpool.

None the less, British youth developed a unique style seen in the rich club and music scene which flourished in the late 1970s and early 1980s. It also proved to be an important influence on British fashion, graphics and furniture in the late 20th century. As a strand of anarchy and rebellion, Punk has come to represent the individuality of British design, becoming something of a national tradition, a visible icon that is as recognizably British as black taxis and red buses.

Further reading:

McDermott, Catherine, *Vivienne Westwood*. London: Carlton, 1999.
Marcus, Greil, *Lipstick Traces: A Secret History of the Twentieth Century*. London: Picador, 1997 [1989].
Savage, Jon, *England's Dreaming: Sex Pistols and Punk Rock*. London: Faber and Faber 1991.

QUEEN ANNE REVIVAL

An architectural style which used red brick and details from Dutch vernacular architecture. Philip Webb's Red House, built for William **Morris**, pioneered the revival of red brick, together with the use of terracotta decorative panels, elements which formed the basis of the style called Queen Anne Rival. The best-known exponent of the style was Richard Norman Shaw (1831–1912), who designed Swan House on the Chelsea Embankment. The façade played with picturesque fenestration details, especially the revival of paned glass windows, and the building had Dutch-inspired gable roofs and dormer attic windows.

QUEER THEORY

'Homosexual' is a 19th-century term that was largely superseded in the 1960s and 1970s by the terms 'gay' and 'lesbian', words which denoted a new pride and confidence. In the 1990s, however, the term 'queer' was introduced as a more inclusive description that also encompasses bisexual and transsexual people. The aim was to open up discussion and debate about sexuality and not restrict it to one group.

The French philosopher Michel Foucault is acknowledged as the pioneer of queer theory, arguing that sex is not a stable facet of identity. For example, women who lived alone in the early 20th century could be defined by society as respectable spinsters, but in the early 21st century they might equally be seen as repressed lesbians. Queer theory therefore became a key aspect of cultural politics.

Its impact on design is connected to a shift of perceptions about gay taste. From the late 1980s, in design terms, homosexuality came to represent positive consumer values – humour, pleasure and sophistica-tion – and the idea developed that gay taste was superior to that of heterosexuals. This concept was later brought to the mainstream by the award-winning American comedy *Will and Grace*. Queer theory allowed the expression of a more brash and outspoken element to emerge alongside the concept of gay taste, which gave the issues a new currency and edge.

Further reading:

Morland, Iain and Willox, Annabelle (eds), *Queer Theory*. Basingstoke: Palgrave Macmillan, 2005.

RADICAL CHIC

A term of ridicule invented by Tom Wolfe to describe the rather cynical trend adopted by the rich and famous in the 1970s of flirting with revolutionary groups. John Lennon and Yoko Ono, for example, took up with black activist Malcolm X, while Leonard Bernstein hosted a party for the notorious Black Panthers. This fad was short-lived, but the term survived and is now used to denigrate the work of designers who **appropriate** ideas and cultural influences in their work while having no real commitment to their source.

Further reading:

Wolfe, Tom, *Radical Chic; Mau-mauing the Flak Catchers; The Painted Word*. London: Picador, 2002 [1971].

RATIONALISM

Italy's version of the **Modern Movement** in architecture and design emerged in 1926 in the form of a manifesto written by a group of young architects called the Gruppo Sette (Group of Seven). Its members were Sebastiano Larco, Guido Frette, Carlo Enrico Rava, Luigi Figini, Gino Pollini, Giuseppe Terragni and Adalberto Libera. Their work was well received in the early 1930s and featured in *Domus* magazine. In Como Terragni built the famous Casa del Fascio from 1933–6 for the **Fascist** Party while Figini and Pollina built a radical steel-and-glass factory for Olivetti at Ivrea. Mussolini himself appeared sympathetic and supportive of the group's aims. For a brief period, their work reflected the revolutionary and socialist aspects of the early Italian **Fascist** Party. However, the influence of Rationalism was short-lived as it was perceived to be too international and too radical. By the mid-1930s, it was clear that the Fascist Party no longer subscribed to socialist ideals, having become a party of middle-class values. Mussolini now preferred the more conservative **Novecento** style, which used refined **classical** and therefore Italian sources. Rationalism, however, did not die completely. Its values and vision proved an inspiration for the new generation of Italian designers that emerged after 1945, including Vico Magistretti, and did much to stimulate the vitality of the late 20th-century Italian design.

Further reading:

Schumacher, Thomas L., *Surface and Symbol: Giuseppe Terragni and the Architecture of Italian Rationalism.* New York: Princeton Architectural Press, 1991.

READY-MADE

Objects or images removed from their normal environment and function and re-presented in an art or design context. The iconoclastic Marcel Duchamp, with his bicycle-wheel exhibit, introduced the concept of ready-made in 1913. The practice challenged existing concepts of art, such as the supremacy of the original, hand-crafted object, as well as giving new form to the object by placing it in a gallery. For Duchamp, the ready-made supposedly possessed no aesthetic qualities and was one of many indistinguishable, mass-produced objects; unlike the **found object**, which was chosen for its uniqueness.

The concept of **appropriating** an already-made object or image was also part of the late 1950s neo-Dada revival and would be crucial to **Pop** imagery. In more recent years, with the development of **semiotics** and **feminism**, the ready-made has become a way of revealing, confronting and deconstructing the tenets of contemporary **capitalist** culture across all the arts. Duchamp became a hero for many young designers educated in the late 1960s and 1970s, particularly those who wanted to introduce art practice into the discipline of design. Key exponents of this were Daniel Weil, in his **industrial design** for Pentagram, and the interior designer Ben Kelly. The use of the ready-made continues in design in the work of Dutch designers Droog, Tom Dixon and Toord Boonjte.

Further reading:

Duve, Thierry de, *Pictorial Nominalism: On Marcel Duchamp's Passage from Painting to the Readymade.* Minneapolis: University of Minnesota Press, 2005.

Ramakers, Renny, *Less + More: Droog Design in Context*. Rotterdam: 010, 2002.

READY-TO-WEAR

A development that revolutionized the clothing industry. Until the late 19th century, if you wanted new clothes, you either made them yourself or you employed a dressmaker to do so. The concept of buying 'off-the-peg' therefore took some time to develop. It was partly driven by the Victorian need with formal mourning clothes; indeed, there were shops which specialized in mourning attire and could supply everything that was needed for a sudden bereavement. Ready-to-wear was also stimulated by women's growing taste for tailored clothes, inspired by the cutting skills of the male tailor rather than the traditional drapery skills of the female dressmaker. The 1860s saw some important technological breakthroughs, including the development by a Leeds menswear company of a band saw capable of cutting through many layers of cloth at once. Triggered by the demand from women for comfortable travel clothes, this technology was applied to women's serge walking suits, and ready-to-wear took off. Its development led to a boom in **retailing**, the growth of department stores and the emergence of mail order.

Further reading:

Waddell, Gavin, *How Fashion Works: Couture, Ready-to-Wear and Mass Production*. Oxford: Blackwell Science, 2004.

RECYCLED DESIGN

An area of creative design with a long history. Reusing materials is a key element of human creativity driven by resourcefulness and necessity. Young boys in the African country of Burundi use footballs made of plastic bags held together with elastic bands because that is all they have. The Powerhouse Museum in Sydney exhibits 19th-century furniture carefully and lovingly made from old packing cases by early colonial settlers who had to reuse every scrap of material they could find. **Design for Recycling**, on the other hand, is a technical **sustainable** design process.

Recycling discarded industrial scrap is not a new design idea, but in the 1980s it became very fashionable. It was a strong British design theme, particularly in furniture, practised by a group of young designer/makers, most notably Ron Arad and Tom Dixon. Arad used old leather car seats for his Rover chair, and off-the-shelf car aerials for domestic lights. Dixon coined the term '**Creative Salvage**' to describe the trend. (It was also sometimes known as 'Junk Aesthetic'.) Young fashion designers made hats decorated with cigarette packets and the foil caps from champagne bottles. Also interesting in this context is the Mutoid Waste Company, a group of young artists who used junk to create **installations** in derelict London warehouses, and the Crucial Gallery in Notting Hill Gate, which specialized in selling furniture and artwork by such makers. The same spirit can also be seen in British **interior design**, with **found objects** integrated in the work of Nigel Coates and Ben Kelly. The latter's famous Hacienda nightclub in Manchester incorporated traffic bollards into the design scheme, while Coates shipped an Edwardian revolving door to Japan for the entrance to his Tokyo Metropole restaurant, and a section of an aeroplane hung as a sculpture in his Café Bongo in the same city. In the later 20th century the Junk Aesthetic became an element in a wider agenda of sustainable design concerns.

More recently, recycled design has explored the problem of consumer waste, most of which, including clothing, **packaging** material, metal, paper, glass and plastics, is simply thrown away and transported to landfill sites. In 1995, the RPC-2 chair by UK designer Jane Hatfield was one of the first products to be made of recycled material. To make the chair, various plastic bottles were heated and compressed to form sheets which had flecks of brilliant colour and even in some places sections of printed text. These sheets were then moulded into the chair shape. Smile Plastics UK also produce sheets of multicoloured plastic from discarded bottles. These have become very fashionable in upmarket design shops. More recently, the company has branched out and now also makes sheets from crisp packets, vending cups, yoghurt pots, crushed CDs (sourced from pirate copies seized by UK Trading Standards officers), toothbrushes and even banknotes.

In the 21st century recycling continues to be a strong design theme. The Brazilian brothers Fernando and Humberto Campano designed their Favela chair from hundreds of pieces of recycled wood, while their Sushi sofa, manufactured by the leading Italian furniture company Edra, used offcuts of carpet, felt, rubber and plastic. European design examples of recycling include the work of Jurgen Bey of the Dutch design group Droog. His outdoor garden furniture is made from compressed garden waste, so at the end of its life it can be broken up and returned to the compost heap.

Other innovative ideas for recycling include converting green glass, which accounts for 80 per cent of the discarded glass in the UK, into glass sand for golf-course bunkers, which is easy to maintain and drains well. In America, Patagonia, a Californian outdoor clothing company, has pioneered the production of fleeces made from plastic bottles as well as the use of environmentally friendly hemp and recycled polyester. It is also exploring ways in which the consumer can return garments to the factory for recycling. Meanwhile, in Africa, there are abundant examples of the creative use of reclaimed waste products. One well-known project by Olu Amoda at Yaba College of Technology, Nigeria's premier art school, uses trash found on the streets of Lagos. And the Mozambican artist Kester has famously transformed assault rifles and automatic pistols into furniture, thereby delivering a message about both recycling and conflict resolution. In 2005 his 'Tree of Life' installation became the centrepiece of the British Museum's new Africa Gallery.

Further reading:

Addis, William, *Building with Reclaimed Components and Materials: A Design Handbook for Reuse and Recycling.* London: Earthscan, 2006.
Reclaimed: Recycling in Contemporary British Craft and Design. London: British Council, 1999.
Walker, Stuart, *Sustainable by Design: Explorations in Theory and Practice.* London: Earthscan, 2006.

RETAIL DESIGN

All aspects of the design of a store: frontage, signage, display, lighting and point of sale. The history of retail design can be traced back to the great department stores of the 19th and early 20th centuries. In Paris there were the Bon Marché (1852) and Printemps stores, followed by Marshall Fields in Chicago, Selfridges in London and Macy's in New York. These enormous emporia provided an affluent, middle-class market with new places to shop. The next retail design innovation, aimed at a working-class market, swiftly followed: the chain store. Frank Winfield Woolworth opened his first shop at the turn of the century, and by 1919 he had over 100 more across the USA. Chain stores were cheap and cheerful, but they did establish an important retail design trend: the idea of a strong shop identity using bold company logos. In Britain during the 1930s chain stores such as Boots the chemist appeared on many more high streets.

The post-war period saw the next important retail design change with the development of the shopping centre. The United States pioneered the out-of-town shopping centre, which catered for families and had generous parking facilities. Meanwhile, Europe pioneered the city-centre shopping precinct. Rebuilding bomb-damaged cities provided an opportunity for new urban planning ideas, and the shopping centre, with a traffic-free zone and light, airy shops, made its first appearance in Rotterdam in the early 1950s. In contrast to these early shopping centres, the 1960s saw the rise of the individual retailer-designer, such as Barbara Hulanicki, who founded the Biba **boutique**, and Sir Terence Conran, who pioneered a new approach to shop design in his **Habitat** stores.

During the last twenty years the developed world has seen important social and cultural changes affect patterns of shopping. In the UK, for example, consumer spending is now the dominant force in the economy. It has become a leisure activity, with the shopper expecting constantly changing, high-quality shopping environments complete with cinemas, cafés, restaurants and other facilities. This has led to an important shift in retail design. During the 1980s, for example, the massive expansion of British design was led by the retail sector. Rasshied Din defined retail design's role as to 'link instinct, art and commerce', and it has been estimated that approximately 70 per cent of British multiple retailers had their shops completely redesigned during this period. In addition, the design of expensive, one-off designer shops, representing the couture end of **retailing**, attracted massive media attention. Examples include Sir Norman Foster's shop in London for fashion designer Katherine Hamnett and Eva Jiricna's work for the influential British retailer Joseph. Such new retail concepts mean that the retail experience has a key role to play in terms of brand enhancement. The retail space is now understood to have as important an effect on sales as the goods themselves. Retail designers therefore aim to produce individual retail experiences for their clients.

In the late 20th century, however, consumer shopping habits shifted again with the rise of Internet retailing. Retail design is now seen as imperative in enticing shoppers back on to the high street. Retailers from all sectors have followed this lead, with even estate agents and banks realizing the need to use retail design to create an appealing environment. It is therefore seen as a tool to reshape and regenerate urban centres all over the world.

Further reading:

Barreneche, Raul A., *New Retail*. London: Phaidon Press, 2005.

Din, Rasshied, *New Retail*. London: Conran Octopus, 2000.

Fitch, Rodney and Knobel, Lance, *Retail Design*. New York: Whitney Library of Design, 1990.

RETAILING

The last 200 years have seen the introduction of new methods of retailing and marketing design, which include the development of chain stores, supermarkets, shopping malls and mail-order services. Mail order needed the establishment of efficient postal services to flourish, but ordering from catalogues has a longer history. In the 1760s it was possible to visit Thomas Chippendale's studio on St Martin's Lane in London and select furniture designs from his catalogue, the *Director*. Meanwhile, Josiah Wedgwood equipped his travelling salesmen with a sample case and a catalogue to take orders from customers over a wide area of the country. However, posting orders direct to a company was a 19th-century retailing development, devised in the USA to help overcome the problems of shopping at a distance. The first to offer the service was Montgomery Ward, founded in 1872, followed in the 1890s by Sears, Roebuck and Company. These were the first distinctive mail-order companies. By 1900, Sears was receiving and dispatching over 100,000 orders a day, and to cope with this demand it pioneered new methods of dispatch and customer service.

In Britain mail order tended to be an extension of the service well-known department stores offered to their customers. For example, Fortnum & Mason mailed out food hampers, while the Army & Navy department store catered for the needs of the Empire, shipping clothes and goods to distant British colonial families. In the recession years of the 1920s and 1930s catalogue companies essentially became credit brokers for families with limited means. They offered extended credit terms and relied on a local agent to organize the collection of money and to distribute the ordered goods.

This link between mail order and poor sections of the community is one that the companies have tried to shake off. The best-known attempt was the Next mail-order catalogue, launched in 1987 by the influential retailer George Davies. The catalogue was produced as a designer item in itself, with a hardback cover, smart photography and slick graphics. No longer did orders have to be made through a local agent; it was now possible to phone the company direct, and delivery was promised within forty-eight hours. However, in spite of such updates, mail-order sales declined in the 1990s with the rise of Internet shopping.

Other key retail developments include chain stores and supermarkets, which have their origins in the late 19th century. The first chain-store group was Woolworths, founded in the 1880s. It was followed by the A&P Company, which grew from 585 stores in 1913 to 11,500 during the 1920s. The earliest English chain stores, such as Sainsbury's, operated like traditional grocery shops, with a shopkeeper and assistants serving behind a counter. This changed with the rise of supermarkets. Early in the 20th century the USA introduced the concept of cash-and-carry stores. In the recession of the 1920s and 1930s the low overheads of these outlets, reflected in lower mark-ups on the stock, made them very popular. In 1916 Clarence Saunders had introduced a turnstile and the idea of self-service at a store in Memphis called Piggly Wiggly. This was the beginning of an international revolution in retailing. The development of huge supermarkets led to the closure of small stores and markets and brought to an end the era of personal service.

Further reading:

Chippendale, Thomas, *The Gentleman and Cabinet Maker's Director: A Reprint of the First Edition*. Leeds: The Chippendale Society, 2005 [1754].

ROBOTICS

The development of machines which resemble human beings and are designed to perform routine tasks. Currently, Japan leads the world in the science of robotics.

The word 'robot' was first used by the Czech playwright Karel Capek in the 1920s, but clockwork mechanisms for mechanical dolls were developed back in the 16th century. By the 18th century, these mechanisms had become very sophisticated: some dolls could play the harpsichord while others could write or draw pictures. This tradition of mechanical toys and gadgets remained popular well into the 20th century. From the 1950s, however, progress in computer technology led to advanced automated machines and eventually to the building of industrial robots. The first experimental models were introduced in the 1960s in Japan. These early robots performed single tasks, such as spot welding or paint spraying. In Japan today robots can make sushi or perform sophisticated factory assembly tasks.

However, an authentically 'human' machine has not yet been created. Robots need wheels or crawlers to 'walk', and their movement is currently far from smooth. Most of the robots in use simply reproduce a sequence of pre-set movements or respond to sensors which can detect changes in temperature, pressure and texture. The most critical research, in the area of **artificial intelligence**, is far from completion, but it will eventually make robots capable of making decisions. This means that future robots will not be limited to working in factories: they will be able to do dangerous work in nuclear power stations, engage in rescue operations and space travel, and care for the special needs of handicapped and old people. Eventually, they will be commonplace both at work and in the home.

Further reading:

Schodt, Frederick L., *Inside the Robot Kingdom*. Tokyo: Kodansha, 1988.

ROCOCO REVIVAL

Rococo was an 18th-century European decorative style characterized by curving, asymmetrical ornament based on nature, with three-dimensional scrolls, shells, cartouches and waterfalls. In the 1820s the style enjoyed its first revival, and in the early 20th century it reappeared as an international design trend in **interior design**.

Elements of this highly decorative style can now be seen not only in wallpapers and prints but in furniture and lighting. The revival of the chandelier for the 21st-century home allowed a touch of Rococo to emerge yet again, as did theatrical, high-style pieces of furniture. One well-known example was the gold Rococo-style chair used in the popular TV series *Big Brother* in 2006.

ROYAL COLLEGE OF ART

A postgraduate university in London with an international reputation in design. Its roots go back to the 19th century, when in 1835 the government, concerned that standards of British design needed to be improved, ordered the appointment of a Select Committee on Arts and Manufactures. Education was seen as the most important way of improving standards of design in industry, so there was a recommendation for the establishment of a series of design schools. The project expanded quickly to eighty schools by 1860, and the student body rose from 3,000 to 85,000. But there were conflicting views about what and how design students should be taught. Controversies raged about the syllabus, which reflected deep divisions concerning the role of design in society, a debate that continues to this day. One important school of thought believed that design students needed direct contact with industry, but more controversial was the curriculum content. The key arguments focused on style of ornament design, its appropriateness, production, quantity and method of manufacture, and these debates generated publications and much discussion. Ornament was central to 19th-century design, so much so that an attempt was made to raise it to the status of an authentic art form in its own right. Research into the common language of design gave way to research into decorative forms appropriate for the new consumer products of the **Industrial Revolution**.

The Royal College of Art started its life as the Government School of Design at Somerset House in 1837. The first director, the architect and designer J.B. Papworth (1775–1847), lasted only a year, to be replaced by the painter William Dyce (1806–64). Dyce had been sent to France and Germany to study European methods of **design education**, and he returned home with several firm ideas, including a conviction that design students needed direct contact with industry alongside life-drawing classes. His guiding principle for the School of Design, however, was that ornament should have a **geometrical** basis, and in 1842 he published a teaching manual called *Drawing Book* which put forward this approach.

In 1853 the small School of Design became the National Art Training School and moved to South Kensington. During the 1850s and 1860s, the school, now run by Henry Cole (1808–82) and Richard Redgrave (1804–88), enjoyed tremendous success. Famous teachers of that period included Owen Jones, Gottfried Semper, and Christopher Dresser, a former pupil who published design books and provided designers and manufacturers with source material on designs as diverse as Aztec, Elizabethan, Roman and Islamic. From this body of research important theories and approaches to ornament and design were developed. Designers were required to meet public demand for pattern repeats on virtually all consumer goods, and the school's curriculum reflected this in a series of exercises and projects designed to facilitate the production of repeat pattern-making. Sources such as Islamic art were important in this context because they provided examples of abstract pattern-making which avoided the pitfalls of extreme **naturalism**, a trend that had attracted much adverse criticism at the **Great Exhibition**.

Towards the end of the century, however, the school moved away from radical design education and towards the education of fine artists, a direction that was confirmed in 1896 when Queen Victoria granted it the title Royal College of Art. By the 1930s, though, it was recognized that a shake-up at the school was long overdue. This finally came after the war with the appointment in 1948 of Robin Darwin as principal, and he revived the college's international profile in design. Under its current director, Christopher Frayling, the Royal College of Art is now enjoying a renewed period of influence. In 2007 its annual degree show will fill not only the College buildings but a large tent in Kensington Gardens, reflecting the increasing influence and prestige of the institution.

Further reading:

Frayling, Christopher and Catterall, Claire, *Design of the Times: One Hundred Years of the Royal College of Art*. Shepton Beauchamp: Richard Dennis, 1996.

Great Britain, Department of Art and Science, *The Introduction to the Drawing Book of the School of Design Published in the Years 1842–3 under the Direction of W. Dyce*. London: Chapman & Hall, 1854.

MacDonald, Stuart, *A Century of Art and Design Education: From Arts and Crafts to Conceptual Art*. London: Lutterworth Press, 2005.

RUSSIAN DESIGN

Before 1900 there were two contrasting strands to Russian design: a strong peasant craft tradition combining religious imagery with pottery and textiles; and a luxury, high-end style identified with aristocrats and the family of the Tsar. However, a vibrant **avant-garde** also made a contribution in the early years of the 20th century. For example, Léon (Leonid) Bakst (1866–1924) was the most influential designer for Diaghilev's Ballets Russes. His designs, based upon Russian folk and Central Asian traditions, were widely emulated by **Art Deco** designers. Another important figure in the Ballets Russes during the years 1909–24 was Alexander Benois (1870–1960), the designer for Stravinsky's revolutionary *Petrushka*. There was also Erté – Romain de Tirtoff (1892–1990) – a costume and stage designer.

For most of the 20th century, though, Russia and Russian design were dominated by the **Marxist** regime of the Soviet Union. The rise of Josef Stalin after 1925 led to authoritarian, bureaucratic rule and centralized planning. This command economy excluded the producers from the decision-making process, and although the system enabled the Soviet Union to industrialize at a rapid rate, the costs were enormous, not least for the millions who died from famine as farming was forcibly collectivized. The producers, having no role in the planning of production, lost interest in the process, while the planners, lacking any democratic input, made decisions based on arbitrary quotas rather than real needs. As centralization became less efficient and more corrupt, there was economic stagnation, a loss of quality and a decline in innovation, especially in consumer goods. Stalin also imposed Soviet Socialist Realism across the whole of cultural production, including design. This was regarded as the only style appropriate to the working class, but in reality it corresponded to the needs of the state. Any elements of the avant-garde and the innovative style of **Constructivism** were replaced with a narrative realism based on the art and literature of the 19th century. It was in this atmosphere that post-war designers had to train. After graduation, they were assigned to a factory or later to one of the Vniite state design practices. (Vniite, the All-Union Scientific Research Institute of Industrial Design, was founded in Moscow in 1962 in a bid to make Soviet design competitive with that of the West.) Opportunities for personal creative development were therefore strictly limited. Some relief came in the early 1960s under Nikita Khrushchev, but long-term hopes for change in the 1970s were dashed.

Wholesale change finally came with the introduction of *perestroika* (restructuring) and *glasnost* (openness) under Mikhail Gorbachev. Western companies and designers looked forward eagerly to the opportunities an open Russian market would offer, but changes within design did not match those in the rest of Russian society. In 1990 Kingston University organized 'Soviet Design in the West' at the **Victoria and Albert Museum**. This conference, the first of its kind, provided a fascinating but depressing insight into Russia at the time. The country's manufacturing industry was dilapidated and under-resourced, and there was little focus on design as a strategy to achieve a broad-based economy.

However, since the collapse of the Soviet Union in 1991 there has been some interesting work in product design, graphics and fashion, although Russian brands have had little impact on the global market. The sectors of the economy that have developed fastest are those that are closely connected with consumers, such as **packaging** and **interior design**. **Industrial design** falls into two sectors: one-off objects; and specialized products, such as Russia's best-known export, the Kalashnikov submachine-gun. However, the profession of industrial designer is being developed through such organizations as the Union of Designers, which in 2005 boasted about 3,000 members.

See also: **Marxism**, **Constructivism**

Further reading:

Gray, Camilla, *The Great Experiment: Russian Art, 1863–1922*. London: Thames & Hudson, 1982 [1962].

SATELLITE TOWN

A post-war term coined to give the outer suburbs of large cities their own identities. Croydon, outside London, is an example. 'Satellite town' is sometimes interchangeable with 'new town', a name given to such places as Harlow and Peterlee, which were parts of the expansion programme of post-war Britain.

Further reading:

Hall, Peter, *Cities of Tomorrow: An Intellectual History of Urban Planning and Design in the Twentieth Century*. Oxford: Blackwell, 2002 [1988].

SCANDINAVIAN DESIGN

The products of Denmark, Finland, Sweden and Norway share common design features, such as a love of natural materials, particularly wood, and a commitment to rational form, which have created a look that is both stylish and adaptable. In the post-war period there was a deliberate attempt to market the designs of these countries as a single movement. They appeared at the **Milan Triennales**, for example, and at exhibitions in the USA and Europe, including Formes Scandinaves at the Louvre in 1958. During the 1950s and 1960s Scandinavian designers came into their own, and the range and virtuosity of their work in glass, ceramics, textiles and furniture made Scandinavian design *the* domestic style of the period.

This design tradition has its roots in the late 19th century, when all the Scandinavian countries practised their own versions of the **Arts and Crafts Movement**, being essentially craft-based. There were, however, attempts to come to terms with industrial change. In 1915 the Svenska Sjlodforeningen was set up in Sweden, modelled on the **Deutsche Werkbund**. The result was the first sign of a new 20th-century Swedish style, illustrated in the work of Wilhelm Kage (1889–1960) for the famous ceramic factory Gustavsberg, and Edward Hald (1883–1981) for Orrefors glass. The 1930 Stockholm Exhibition showed off the new Swedish design, and its combination of the traditional and a new rational aesthetic was seen in the furniture of Bruno Mathsson (1907–88) and Josef Frank (1885–1967), as well as in the architecture of Gunnar Asplund (1885–1940). The exhibition made an enormous impression on the rest of the world, with the work admired for being rational and moderate, qualities that Sweden continued to exemplify through to the post-war period.

During this time Denmark was also gaining an industrial reputation for the design of furniture. The first important Danish name is Kaare Klint (1888–1954), who ran the Copenhagen Cabinet Makers' Guild in the 1930s. In the post-war period Finn Juhl (b. 1912), inspired by modern sculpture, pushed wood to its limits in a series of chairs, using loosely woven textiles with natural polished surfaces. Meanwhile, Arne Jacobsen (b. 1902) is best known for his plywood stacking chairs, Egg and Swan, from the early 1950s. More recently, Verner Panton (b. 1926) has continued this tradition of innovative Danish furniture. Also important is the Danish family company that Georg Jensen inherited in 1936 from his father, a famous **Art Nouveau** silversmith. The Jensen Company produced modern tableware and jewellery that was **minimal**, practical and tremendously influential.

Finland moved into the international design spotlight rather later. Before the Second World War the country's most important designer, the architect Alvar Aalto (1898–1976), became famous for his plywood furniture designs, which remain in production as classics. In the post-war period, however, Finnish designers were considered the most radical in Scandinavia, with the work of Tapio Wirkkala (1915–85) and Timo Sarpaneva (b. 1926) for the glass company Iittala, and Kaj Franck (b. 1911), who designed ceramics for Arabia. Textiles were another strong area, with the Marimekko Company (founded in 1951) and Vuokko Oy (in 1964) achieving an international reputation for their bold, striped fabrics and simple dress designs.

Of the Scandinavian countries, only Norway failed to make a significant contribution to **interior design** in the 1950s. This was partly because it had a small population and did not enjoy the economic expansion of the other Scandinavian countries.

Scandinavian design dominated world taste in the late 1950s and early 1960s, when no contemporary interior was complete without a Danish chair or a Swedish rug. Shops with names like Dansk and Svensk appeared in cities all over the world. More recently, a new generation of young designers, including Snowcrash, have reacted against the Scandinavian tradition. Snowcrash first came to public attention in 1999 with an **installation** at the Milan Furniture Fair and then went on to develop furniture for Artek and Cappellini. They work in industrial materials sourced from shipbuilding and the transport industry. More traditional Scandinavian companies have also updated their products. In recent years, Marimekko has successfully relaunched interior design products that utilize Maija Isola's bold floral fabrics of the 1960s; Iittala has commissioned international designers for its new product range; and Fiskars has developed an award-winning series of garden tools. Another significant contribution to global design has come from the Finnish company Nokia, now the world leader in mobile telephone and communications technology. It is a global brand known for its investment in design and its advanced features and services.

However, all of these companies are dwarfed by Scandinavia's most famous design export, Ikea, a furniture company with over 250 stores worldwide, a global brand and an international lifestyle phenomenon, Uniquely, in this sector, it is successful in Asia as well as Europe. The *Forbes* Rich List recorded the company's annual turnover in 2004 as $16.4 billion and its founder, Ingvar Kamprad (b. 1926), as one of the richest men in the world. Kamprad named the company by using his initials alongside 'E' (from Elmtaryd, the family farm) and 'A' (in recognition of his hometown, Agunnaryd). He is famously frugal, and promotes that ethos throughout the company. For instance, Ikea furniture is not manufactured in Sweden: the company uses factories in developing countries to keep down costs. This has attracted media criticism of workers' conditions and pay. Furthermore, while the company actively promotes its green credentials, many critics point out that Ikea encourages frequent, wasteful refurbishment, famously highlighted in a UK television advertisement that urged consumers to 'Chuck out your chintz'. This commercial reinforced the idea that Ikea promotes a throwaway culture at odds with **sustainable** principles.

Kamprad founded Ikea in Almhult, southern Sweden, in 1947 to produce flat-pack furniture, and opened the first Ikea branded store in 1958. International expansion saw the first US store open in 1976, the first in the UK in 1987, the first in China in 1998 and the first in Russia in 2000. Each store sells products from a large warehouse that requires customers to plot a circuitous route to find what they desire. Other common complaints relate to few sales staff being on duty, poor after-sales service and long queues. Nevertheless, the stores, catalogue and website are all extremely popular. There are distribution centres all over the world but Almhult remains the company headquarters, with an 180,000-cubic-metre warehouse and sophisticated automatic distribution systems that are envied worldwide as models of efficiency.

The Ikea design approach retains a strong Scandinavian identity, seen in the use of natural wood, **minimalist** shapes, high technology, new materials and strong colours. The company has extended the image of 20th-century Scandinavian **Modernism** and ensured that it has become an immensely widespread domestic living style. Its relationship with design, however, is complex. Ikea supports **design education** in Sweden and promotes the work of named designers, but it also ruthlessly copies high-profile, successful designs from outside the company.

Further reading:

Cabra, Raul and Nelson, Katherine (eds), *New Scandinavian Design*. San Francisco, CA: Chronicle, 2004.

Fiell, Charlotte J. and Fiell, Peter, *Scandinavian Design*. Köln: Taschen, 2005.

Helgeson, Susanne, *Swedish Design: The Best in Swedish Design Today*. London: Mitchell Beazley, 2002.

McFadden, David R. (ed.), *Scandinavian Modern Design: 1880–1980*. New York: Abrams, 1982.

SCIENTIFIC MATERIALISM

A theory developed in the 19th century which claimed that the world could be explained in scientific and technical terms without the agency of divine intervention. Charles Darwin's *On the Origin of Species* (1859), which presented his theory of evolution, is the leading example of this movement. This had an impact on design by encouraging designers to see the discipline as an evolutionary process. The concept that certain rational designs deserved to survive by virtue of their efficiency and function was particularly important in the 19th century, when designs were often mindlessly historicist.

In the 20th century the heritage of scientific materialism was reflected in the work of Raymond Loewy, whose design charts showed the evolution of the train and the motor car. Another indirect consequence of this 19th-century school of thought is the concept of the design classic, the survival of an object which embodies enduring qualities of form, function and appearance: the survival of the fittest design.

Strong opposition to scientific materialism came from design critics such as John Ruskin, who stressed the spiritual nature of creativity. Ruskin's position on the human versus the scientific continues to polarize debate in the 21st century.

Further reading:

Loewy, Raymond, *Industrial Design*. London: Fourth Estate, 1988 [1979].

SCREEN DESIGN

The selection and placement of objects on a screen. The development of the digital media industries has led to several new design disciplines, and screen design, for example, has become a high-profile and widely demanded process which helps to satisfy a great variety of communication needs. It involves the concept, design, direction and production of motion graphic sequences for television, cinema, **advertising**, exhibitions, performance and corporate events. Screen designers develop storyboarding and presentation skills, digital editing and effects. The key elements of screen design are organization and visual interest, and it involves what to use – text, images or video – and where to place them on the screen.

Further reading:

Goux, Melanie and Houff, James A., <*On Screen*> in *Time: Transitions in Motion Graphic Design for Film, Television and New Media*. Hove: RotoVision, 2003.

Mullet, Kevin and Sano, Darrell, *Designing Visual Interfaces: Communication Oriented Techniques*. Mountain View, CA: Prentice-Hall, 1995.

SEMIOTICS

The science of signs, and a methodology which explores the structures that help to reveal layers of meaning either in a cultural activity or in a design object. By the 1960s, designers had begun to recognize the value of semiotics as a way of understanding the visual world, how language can be made meaningful and how design might communicate that meaning to the consumer. In terms of design, therefore, semiotics could help in the understanding of cultural values and therefore desires.

Language is arguably the most universal system of signs, and in the early 20th century the Austrian philosopher Ludwig Wittgenstein and the Swiss linguist Ferdinand de Saussure carried out key studies of it. This pioneering research did not analyse the concepts on which ideas were based but the language in which they were expressed, in search of an underlying bias that might be expressed in terms of race, class or gender. Signs, as Saussure famously commented, have a 'life in society'. He suggested that a sign has three characteristics: it must have a physical form, an image, a photograph or a sound; it must refer to something other than itself; and it must be used a within a shared cultural code. The interest for designers in this is that the meaning of a sign is entirely cultural. Take, for example, the shared cultural language of flowers in Victorian England. Red roses are a sign: for Saussure, they signified love. They are also a domesticated garden flower. It is easy to see how cultural signs within semiotics could add layers of meaning to design, to the language of **advertising**, for example, which could play with juxtapositions and overturn social conventions and meanings.

Umberto Eco used Saussure's theory as an analytical tool to assess architecture. And Roland Barthes developed semiotic methodology for designers through his analysis of the complexity of signs within the consumer's experience of design. His *Mythologies* (1957) was the first attempt to develop a semiological analysis of design, for which he suggested three levels: the denotative – for example 'this is a car'; the connotative – 'cars enable modern life'; and the mythical – cars 'symbolize sexual freedom'. In terms of design, Bathes famously used the example of photography to demonstrate such layers of meaning. A photograph of the fashion model Kate Moss records her face but its styling and location can denote supermodel, mother or (in 2005) criminal drug-user, depending on the image location – in a newspaper or on an advertising billboard.

The advertising industry in particular relies on mythical interpretations of semiotics to sell cars. This sector of the industry has exploited shared male cultural values about sex, speed and freedom, and the meanings generated in these adverts are culturally specific to gender, age and class. Semiotics focuses on the culture within which the signs operate, and meaning is dependent upon shared structures of understanding. Recognizing that meaning was dependent on, for instance, shared cultural codes (which are also understood to be historically located and subject to change) meant that audiences could no longer simply be thought of as passive receivers. Semiotics gave them 'something to do', made them active in the meaning-making process, and they bring with them cultural experiences, discourses and ideologies for the process of making sense.

Semiotics was a good technique for design to make a spontaneous, instinctive activity more self-reflective and critical. Most writings on semiotics, however, have concentrated on the theoretical issues of the subject, and designers have not consistently applied these theories to the practice of design. Semiotics had more effect on design writing and criticism in the late 20th century, resulting in a new tradition of cultural, film and media studies. A pioneer study was completed in 1978 by Judith Williamson, whose book *Decoding Advertisements: Ideology and Meaning in Advertising*, applied the methods of semiotics and post-Freudian analysis to graphic design and suggested an approach within design discourse, rather than practice, that employed semiotics to good effect.

Further reading:

Barthes, Roland, *Mythologies*. London: Vintage, 1993 [1957].
Baudrillard, Jean, *Selected Writings*. Oxford: Polity Press, 2001 [1988].
Eco, Umberto, *Semiotics and the Philosophy of Language*. London: Macmillan, 1984.
Sanders, Carol (ed.), *The Cambridge Companion to Saussure*. Cambridge: Cambridge University Press, 2004.
Saussure, Ferdinand de, *Course in General Linguistics*. London: Duckworth, 1983 [1916].
Williamson, Judith, *Decoding Advertisements: Ideology and Meaning in Advertising*. London: Marion Boyars, 1978.

SERVICE DESIGN

Responses to the needs of the service industries, including health and transport facilities. Service design attempts to offer greater efficiency, profits and ease of customer use to such industries through design techniques, and recognizes that their users – be they commuters, shoppers or hospital patients – are now looking for a 'totality' of service of very high quality. In industrialized nations across the world the service sector has been growing at the expense of manufacturing industry, and this trend looks set to continue. Business and management professionals are beginning to understand that the design of services is therefore a key component for economic growth and development.

The challenge for the designers of services is that there are more customers to be considered than in manufacturing, and they have more complex needs which must be understood and addressed. Innovation in the service industries is generally easier, however, because customers tend to be willing to accept changes in those industries. Another issue facing this design practice is that services cannot be patented, and intellectual property is more difficult to protect. Copying of competitors' practices is therefore an easy and cheap option for some businesses.

Further reading:

Hollins, Gillian and Hollins, Bill, *Total Design: Managing the Design Process in the Service Sector*. London: Pitman, 1991.

SHAKER DESIGN

The Shakers were originally an English nonconformist community, established by Ann Lee in Manchester in the 18th century. In 1774 she and a small group of followers emigrated to the USA and founded a series of communities on the East Coast, some of which survived until the 1960s. After initially settling near Albany, in 1786 the Shakers founded their main base at New Lebanon, New York. This became an independent, communal society where they could live, work and worship without persecution. The Shakers were distinguished from other communal groups by the strict religious tenets that guided every aspect of life, including sexual abstinence. Purity of mind, harmony and order were the most esteemed Shaker virtues. Their lasting achievement was to translate these beliefs into a series of refined, austere buildings and furniture which have now become part of the vocabulary of modern design. Shaker carpenters and craftsmen took the metaphor of moral perfection straight, upright and foursquare and translated it into a series of simple ladder-back chairs, tables, boxes and cupboards that owed something of their inspiration to the tradition of the English 18th-century vernacular furniture. One distinctive feature of their rooms was a high wooden rail from which pegs protruded at regular intervals. On these were hung chairs and clothes. Shaker design abhorred any decoration and used plain, natural wood.

Although quirky and extremely idiosyncratic, it is not hard to see why this anonymous, elegant and rational furniture has attracted many devotees. Shaker furniture used the language of form to express spiritual beliefs, with the communities believing that work, by teaching a sense of order, benefited the individual. 'Put your hands to work, and your hearts to God' was a favourite maxim. The communities acted for the benefit of all but at the same time valued the skill and talent of the individual. Soon their furniture was widely admired by contemporaries in the 'outside' world, and the Shakers developed many familiar items for the home and the workshop, including the flat broom, the wooden clothespin and packaged garden seeds.

Their furniture was always highly regarded, but the closing of their chair factory at New Lebanon in the early 1940s marked the end of Shaker furniture-making. However, from the 1970s Shaker repro-duction designs became internationally popular, selling through a series of retail outlets. The term 'Shaker style' is now widely applied as a marketing device to kitchen utensils or brands of paint to connect and associate them with this strong tradition.

Further reading:

Larkin, David, Rocheleau, Paul and Sprigg, June, *Shaker Built: The Form and Function of Shaker Architecture*. London: Thames & Hudson, 1994.

Sprigg, June, *By Shaker Hands*. Hanover, NH: University Press of New England, 1990.

SMITH, ADAM

Adam Smith (1722–90) was a Scots economist, whose major work on economics, *An Inquiry into the Nature and Causes of the Wealth of Nations*, was the first analysis of the wider implications of the **Industrial Revolution**. He was the first to recognize that manufacturing industry had overtaken agriculture as the most important area of production, and his theories were to be extremely influential on economic theory in the 19th century, and subsequently on design and industry. To illustrate his argument on the division of labour, Smith used the now famous example of a worker manufacturing pins. If, he pointed out, the worker were responsible for all the manufacturing operations, his output was small, but if the worker concentrated on a single aspect of production, output increased dramatically, perhaps as much as a hundredfold. It was the beginning of a production process that would finally lead in the early 20th century to the American car assembly lines of Henry **Ford**. Smith also pointed out that increased production on its own was not enough for economic success. Marketing and, although Adam did not identify it as such, design were also crucial factors on which the success of the new industries of the Industrial Revolution would depend.

Further reading:

McLean, Iain, *Adam Smith: Radical and Egalitarian*. Edinburgh: Edinburgh University Press, 2006.

Smith, Adam, *The Wealth of Nations*. New York: Random House, 2003 [1776].

STREAMLINING

A design process developed in the USA during the 1920s and 1930s by designers such as Raymond Loewy and Walter Dorwin Teague. Streamlining promoted smooth, aerodynamic shapes for industrial products ranging from cars, ships and airplanes to simple pencil sharpeners. The designers claimed a scientific rationale for these shapes, citing natural forms such as ice floes and wind-tunnel experiments in the car industry. However, while there was some substance to these claims, the reality was that streamlining simply evoked the period's romance with technology and the machine. The European **Modern Movement** tended to dismiss streamlining as a mere style and claimed it was not a serious contribution to the development of 20th-century design. Nowadays, the products of the American designers involved in streamlining have come to evoke a heroic age of confidence in design.

Further reading:

Hanks, D.A. and Hoy, A.H., *American Streamlined Design: The World of Tomorrow*. Paris: Flammarion, 2005.

Loewy, Raymond, *Industrial Design*. London: Fourth Estate, 1988 [1979].

Teague, Walter Dorwin, *Design This Day: The Technique of Order in the Machine Age*. London: Studio Publications, 1947 [1940].

Wilson, R.G., Pilgrim, D.H. and Tashjian, D. *The Machine Age in America, 1918–1941*. New York: Brooklyn Museum, in association with Abrams, 1986.

STRUCTURALISM

An interdisciplinary approach developed in the 1960s and 1970s whose most important idea in design terms was that cultural forms could be understood through language. It became popular with academics concerned with analysing language, culture, anthropology, sociology, linguistics and design and society. These include Michel Foucault (1926–84), Roland Barthes (1915–80), Jean Baudrillard (1929–2007) and the anthropologist Claude Lévi-Strauss (b. 1908). Foucault provided a major critique of conventional approaches to sociology and history, including influential studies of asylums and prisons. Although his writings are not concerned with objects, his theories, it is argued, should be part of the contextual study of design and its role in society in a broader cultural debate. For example, Foucault's theories of family structure could inform a designer commissioned to produce children's toys. These theories of social structure, however, do not analyse or account for the random, irrational quality of human creativity, which is arguably an essential element in design.

Further reading:

Lévi-Strauss, Claude, *Structural Anthropology*. New York: Basic Books, 1999 [1973].
Smart, Barry, *Michel Foucault*. London: Routledge, 2002 [1985].

STYLING

An area that has undergone considerable changes of meaning in the last hundred years. For the pioneers of the **Modern Movement** in the 1930s styling was a pejorative term for mere surface decoration, which was a façade. It was seen as the opposite to an understanding of form and function. Members of the emerging American design profession in the same period were accused of being 'mere' stylists because Raymond Loewy, for example, would typically take an existing product, famously the duplicating machine, and simply design a new external casing for it. But Loewy understood that through styling a designer could create a distinctive visual image for a product or a company.

Nowadays, the term 'styling' is not widely used in design, and stylist has been further relegated to a description of hairdressers and personal shoppers. 'Style', however, does still connote fashionable status and flair.

Further reading:

Loewy, Raymond, *Industrial Design*. London: Fourth Estate, 1988 [1979].

SUBCULTURE

A group with shared interests and social practices. However, subcultural groups are diverse and difficult to define. For example, there are gay and religious subcultures, but the word also has wider applications. In the UK there have been many white, working-class youth subcultures, including Teddy Boys, **Punks** and Skinheads, all highly visible because of their focus on fashion, style and image.

Typically, as was the case with these three groups, a subculture is a reaction against mainstream culture. One important characteristic of **Postmodern** theory was its new focus on those social groups that were marginalized by modernity, which usually meant anyone other than a white, heterosexual male. In terms of design, the emergence of identifiable subcultural groups has allowed fashion, style and taste to develop

– for example, through the influence of a gay sensibility. As subcultural groups have sought to define themselves in terms of fashion, music and products, their original styles and creative energy have had a significant impact on mainstream design, **advertising** and the media.

Further reading:

Hebdige, Dick, *Subculture: The Meaning of Style*. London: Routledge, 2002 [1979].

SURREALISM

Founded by the poet André Breton in 1924, Surrealism was one of the most influential art movements of the 20th century. An admirer of the revolutionary ideas of Karl **Marx** and Sigmund Freud, Breton defined Surrealism as 'Pure psychic automatism . . . Thought's dictation, in the absence of all control exercised by the reason and outside all aesthetic or moral preoccupations.' Emerging from the Parisian Dada group of the early 1920s, Breton, along with the poets Paul Eluard and Louis Aragon, continued to experiment with various techniques, including automatic writing, trances and the cultivation of dream imagery in order to explore the unconscious systematically, so that a new reality or 'surreality' could be found. This was not intended to be a dream world, but one of surprises, where the most ordinary object could be transformed by the artist's perception.

Surrealism soon became the most vital art movement in 1920s Paris, counting among its number Jean Arp, Joan Miró, Max Ernst, René Magritte, Salvador Dalí, Man Ray and Alberto Giacometti. There was no single Surrealist style, but a tendency to use automatic methods, dream imagery or a startling juxtaposition of objects in painting, poetry or **assemblages**. Freudian concerns, such as fetish, desire, repressed emotions and sexuality, were the focus of much Surrealist work. The anti-Establishment quality of the movement was shown at the 1938 International Exhibition in Paris, which consisted of a total environment designed by Marcel Duchamp, a 'Surrealist street' lined with female mannequins dressed by male members of the group and leading to the main exhibition hall.

Dalí, who joined the movement in 1929, was certainly the most well known Surrealist, largely through his films with Luis Buñuel and his often bizarre public exhibitionism. The Second World War led to most of the group moving to the USA, where the Surrealist Exhibition of

1942 in New York placed them firmly in the annals of modern art. Dalí, by now expelled by Breton for his anti-communist tendencies, nevertheless remained hugely successful as a designer of fashion accessories and the creator of such items as the famous Mae West Lips sofa.

Surrealism's freedom of technique and content had a major influence on young, New York-based artists like Arshile Gorky, Willem de Kooning and Jackson Pollock. It also had a wider international following, and the ideas and methods of Surrealism are now integrated in **advertising**, fashion and design. Indeed, Surrealist techniques are at the centre of the advertising industry, from the groundbreaking 1980s billboard campaign for Benson & Hedges cigarettes to the commercials for Apple iPods in the 21st century. The techniques and devices used by Surrealism to unlock the subconscious are still driving the way many products are marketed to us. The movement's enduring significance was indicated in 2007, when the **Victoria and Albert Museum** held a major exhibition on Surrealist design.

Further reading:

Grant, Kim, *Surrealism and the Visual Arts: Theory and Reception*. Cambridge: Cambridge University Press, 2005.
Wood, Ghislaine (ed.), *Surreal Things: Surrealism and Design*. London: V&A Publications, 2007.

SUSTAINABILITY

A concept that has grown over the last decade to represent and champion a more holistic approach to global resources, people, economics and trade. 'Sustainability' as a term derives from the concept of sustainable development, the notion of development that meets the needs of the present without compromising the ability of future generations to meet their own needs. It achieved international status in 1983 when the World Commission on the Environment and Development was set up by the United Nations. This commission said its central theme was sustainability, safeguarding the earth's resources for future generations. In 1987 a UN publication, *Our Common Future*, used the term to describe the way decision-makers and the public should prioritize the impact economic policies have on the environment, maintaining economic growth without impacting negatively on the ecology of the earth. Sustainability broadens the focus of what might be called '**green**' and '**eco**' thinking to include such issues as social responsibility, ethics and social structures and relations. It provides a more holistic framework for attempting to understand how all these issues relate to each other. This, in turn, has led to a broadening of perspectives in the theory and practice of design.

Sustainability reflects a growing worldwide appreciation that businesses do not operate in isolation and that through their use of materials, technologies and services they impact on the whole of society. This increasing awareness has helped to inform public opinion. There is a growing trend towards corporate social responsibility (CSR), with manufacturers and producers taking into consideration such issues as the environmental impact of their activities, non-exploitative labour, and fair trade with developing countries. In the 1990s, highly influential authors such as Eric Schlosser and Naomi Klein successfully attacked the spread of homogeneous Western culture, and in particular the global domination of brands such as Nestlé, McDonald's and Nike. These writings provided an international focus for the growing unease about the exploitation of developing countries, in particular in relation to working conditions and human rights, which led to widespread condemnation of cheap labour markets. They also stimulated deep concern about the environmental impact of large-scale production on the world's ecosystem. Sustainability was now invoked when discussing deforestation, the use of renewable energy in industrial production, and recycling in **product design** and manufacture.

Sustainability therefore has become a new ethos which has filtered down to the high street with the launch of such brands as American Apparel, which produces clothes that are guaranteed to be made by people who are treated fairly, rather than by exploited sweatshop workers. And its principles have become pivotal to the brands and products that come under the Fairtrade label. Companies are realizing that they need to become more transparent and engage in a global not a local discourse over these issues. Global companies have therefore begun to pioneer projects with a social agenda. Apple, for example, is running a scheme in Recife, Brazil, for people with no access to telecommunications services. Using modified MP3 players, villagers can now listen to personalized webcasts and use voice email. Meanwhile, in Bangalore, India, Philips is selling wind-up radios to villagers at a cost of about thirteen euros, payable in six monthly instalments through a community repayment scheme.

Further reading:

Klein, Naomi, *No Logo: No Space, No Choice, No Jobs*. London: Flamingo, 2001 [1999].

Schlosser, Eric, *Fast Food Nation: What the All-American Meal is Doing to the World*. London: Allen Lane, 2001.

SUSTAINABLE DESIGN

Otherwise known as Design for Sustainability (DfS), this concerns the use of resources, including land and energy, with maximum efficiency and at a rate which does not compromise the ability of future genera-tions to meet their own needs. Sustainable design is linked to **ecodesign** and therefore **green design**, but also to issues of social ethics and equality. It therefore incorporates design best practice and places it in the context of a holistic environmental and social awareness.

The evolution in terminology of what might broadly be called 'environmental design' is characterized by a progression from green to eco- to sustainable design. In this sense, sustainable design is the 'greenest' form of environmental design. This development represents a progressive broadening in scope in theory and practice, and the emergence of an increasingly critical perspective on the relationship between design and the natural environment. While the three terms are sometimes used interchangeably, they can provide anchor points from which to explore the evolution and increasing sophistication of environmental design thinking and practice. Sustainable design's additional commitment to issues of social responsibility and empower-ment has clear parallels with the principles of **inclusive design**, such that good design is not reserved for an affluent and culturally sophisti-cated minority but rather is available to all. It focuses on systems rather than products in isolation, seeking to optimize the delivery of functions and benefits via product service systems (PSS). And it often incorporates dematerialization in delivering benefits that conventionally derived from product ownership but can be delivered more effectively and efficiently via service concepts, such as leasing.

On one level, sustainable design is fundamentally altruistic, in that it represents an investment on behalf of generations to come in a future we might not ourselves live to see. Yet successful sustainable design is also concerned with meeting present needs more effectively. It addresses these needs on a more fundamental level than much conventional design practice, being concerned with radical concept innovation as much as with incremental product improvement. In this sense, it is simply good design.

In 1992 the United Nations Commission on Sustainable Develop-ment was established, and it has since issued guidelines on how businesses may approach sustainability. International companies are exploring new business models that take a longer view and give priority to sustainability. Design and designers are essential in this process.

Contemporary architects have also been in the vanguard of sustainability. The fact that buildings and the processes of constructing and maintaining them have a serious impact on the natural environment and the well-being of their occupants has been addressed in a number of innovative new builds. The Beddington Zero Energy Development (BedZED) is an environmentally friendly, energy-efficient mix of housing and workspace in South London. It incorporates up-to-the-minute thinking on sustainable development in every aspect of the scheme, from the energy-efficient design to the way the houses are heated, demonstrating that an eco-friendly lifestyle can be easy, affordable and attractive. In the corporate sector Foster & Partners' Swiss Re Building (otherwise known as the Gherkin) in London is one of the first in a new generation of more environmentally friendly skyscrapers. Its natural ventilation system dramatically reduces the need for a fuel-gobbling air-conditioning system. Meanwhile, many domestic new builds are incorporating solar panels and good insulation to cut down on fuel **consumption**.

The Freeplay wind-up radio is an example of design that is both environmentally and socially beneficial. Originally developed to meet the needs and circumstances of people in developing countries, it uses simple clockwork technology which eliminates the need for batteries by relying on the user to crank the handle: every sixty turns gives enough power for forty minutes' listening. Another commercial example which displays the influence of sustainable design is the **Ford** Think City electric car. Its clean, non-petrol technology gives it a range of about fifty miles and therefore presents a viable alternative for city transport.

Further reading:

Fuad-Luke, Alastair, *The Eco-Design Handbook: A Complete Sourcebook for Home and Office*. London: Thames & Hudson, 2004 [2002].

Walker, Stuart, *Sustainable by Design: Explorations in Theory and Practice*. London: Earthscan, 2006.

SYSTEMS THEORY

A concept that explores relationships and structures in the widest context. It derives from developments in the world of science in the 1950s that opposed compartmentalization and argued that certain ideas have relevance across a wide spectrum of research. Essentially it argued for the practice of interdisciplinary collaboration, which now forms part of the practice of design but then was very uncommon. Systems theory helped to transform disciplines as well as fostering closer linkages between research projects.

Further reading:

Bertalanffy, Ludwig von, *General System Theory: Foundation, Development, Applications*. New York: G. Braziller, 1968.

Scott, W. Richard, *Organizations: Rational, Natural and Open Systems*. Upper Saddle River, NJ: Prentice-Hall, 2003 [1981].

TASTE

A concept that involves the critical judgement of individuals who look at designed objects and experience pleasure. It suggests a well-trained appreciation of what is aesthetically pleasing and therefore it is a highly contentious area because it is related to education, social background and class issues.

The philosophical arguments about exactly what taste constitutes have a long history. Early theories are linked to the science of aesthetics and the concept of what the Greeks defined as 'the beautiful'. The orator Cicero (104–43 BC) declared: 'There is a certain apt disposition of bodily parts which, when combined with a certain agreeable colour, is called beauty.' For the philosopher Plato (427–347 BC), beauty was associated with what is to be admired and desired. From antiquity, then, principles of taste were developed to help establish what was good. More recently, the 18th century saw the publication of many essays on aspects of taste, including treatises on the picturesque, the sublime and the beautiful. Theories of taste put forward ideals to imitate, such as the Roman villa, the landscapes of Claude Lorrain, Greek sculpture and Arabic pattern-making. Immanuel Kant suggested that taste was subjective.

In the 19th century, and particularly for the **Modern Movement** in the 20th century, these theories of taste were often linked with function. For the Modern Movement, choices and taste in materials and form reflected theories revered as moral truths. With the arrival of **Post-modernism**, taste in its more traditional sense is once more openly discussed. In spite of this, it remains controversial, and the traditional subject of aesthetics is now seldom taught at educational establishments. This is partly due to the widespread belief that good and bad taste are determined by social environment. Taste therefore has strong social and political implications. Many people feel that good taste is largely the preserve of the rich and well educated. Unquestionably, this is not the case. Good taste may be culturally determined, but during the 1960s this idea was fundamentally challenged, with **Pop** artists and designers being prepared to jettison traditional canons of taste in favour of a more populist aesthetic. In the immediate post-war period high and low art occupied two distinct categories, but by the end of the century those distinctions had collapsed. Opera, for example, traditionally a high art, famously crossed the divide when an aria was used as the theme song for the 1990 Football World Cup finals.

Further reading:

Bayley, Stephen, *Taste: The Secret Meaning of Things*. London: Faber and Faber, 1991.

Lloyd Jones, Peter, *Taste Today: The Role of Appreciation in Consumerism and Design*. Oxford: Pergamon, 1991.

Sparke, Penny, *As Long as It's Pink: The Sexual Politics of Taste*. London: Pandora, 1995.

TAYLORISM

A theory of management developed by Frederick Winslow Taylor (1856–1915). Taylor, an American industrial engineer who pioneered time-and-motion studies, wrote an influential book called *The Principles of Scientific Management* (1911) that was widely read by leading industrialists and manufacturers. One of its main ideas was that industrial production could be made more efficient by breaking down the labour process into its smallest component parts, not just on the assembly line, but in the office. Taylorism was intended to be a streamlining of capitalist production which would improve both output and profits, but many European progressives also adopted it as a means of making production benefit working people. Many artists, including Fernand Léger, who used the author's models of production as metaphors in his paintings, read Taylor's book.

His theories also had a direct impact on design and designers. Grete Schütte-Lihotzky famously used Taylorism to develop a modern labour-saving kitchen and more functional domestic appliances. For her pioneer work in 1924 in Frankfurt, she looked at how domestic tasks were undertaken and investigated seemingly obvious but previously neglected issues such as where the sink should be in relation to the cooker. Taylor's ideas also influenced American industrial designers in the 1930s in their creation of the **Modernist** home and the rational redesign of the kitchen.

Further reading:

Doray, Bernard, *From Taylorism to Fordism: A Rational Madness*. London: Free Association, 1988.

Taylor, Frederick Winslow, *The Principles of Scientific Management*. London: Harper & Bros., 1911.

TECHNOCRATS

A group of middle-class professionals working in and around Los Angeles during the 1930s who developed some individual ideas about industrial production. In the main they were industrial technicians who had studied the American capitalist system and concluded that much of the productive capacity was going unused, and that improved efficiency in production techniques would eventually make manual labour unnecessary. The Technocrats, who sped around in grey suits, grey hats and grey cars, envisaged the abandonment of the money economy once the maximum capacity of industry could be unleashed. They were part of the era of **streamlining**, which shaped the New York design practices of such men as Walter Dorwin Teague, and contributed to the debate about the disparity of **consumption** which dominated the 1930s. As a movement, the Technocrats of the 1930s need to be distinguished from the technocrats of today, who believe that the technological management of details, rather than broad ideologies, is the way to improve the world and design.

Further reading:

Teague, Walter Dorwin, *Design This Day: The Technique of Order in the Machine Age*. London: Studio Publications, 1947 [1940].

TIFFANY'S

A world-famous store fixed in popular imagination by *Breakfast at Tiffany's*, written by Truman Capote and subsequently filmed by Blake Edwards. It was founded by Louis Comfort Tiffany (1848–1933), the son of a well-known New York silversmith. During the 1860s Tiffany travelled to Europe and studied painting, but he became increasingly interested in the decorative arts. On his return to the USA, he set up a professional **interior design** firm, Louis C. Tiffany & Associated Artists, in 1879, and experimented with elaborate, iridescent glass design in **naturalistic** forms of flowers and birds. Tiffany glass became one of the best-known products of the **Art Nouveau** Movement, winning prizes at the 1900 Paris Exhibition and at Turin in 1902. For the company, and in the same style, Tiffany also designed ceramics, textiles, electric light fittings and mosaics. After his death in 1933, the Tiffany store specialized in expensive, luxury items.

TRANSPORT DESIGN

The development of mass transportation design began in the 19th century with the development of the bicycle, the steamship and the railway train, and developed in the 20th century with the invention of the car, the supersonic jet and space travel.

Urban transport systems started in Britain with the invention and development of the railway system and, from the 1860s, the development of the underground system in London. In 1883 Gottlieb Daimler produced a single-cylinder engine mounted on to a bicycle; in 1903 the Wright Brothers undertook their pioneering first flight; and in 1930 Frank Whittle patented the jet engine. These events paved the way for two seminal inventions of the 20th century – the mass-produced car and the civilian aeroplane – which would transform the pattern and development of human life. By the 21st century designers were working on superhighways, giant jumbo jets and ever-larger airports.

The design of the first cars relied on the techniques and skills of 19th-century coachbuilders, but in the early 20th century manufacturers started to explore standardization in production techniques to lower the cost for the consumer. This was only possible because of the development of pressed steel. One man above all others changed not only the automotive industry but the whole basis of design production. Henry Ford, at his factory in Detroit, developed assembly-line production systems that became known as **Fordism**. This was the organization of separate processes in a strictly controlled sequence to achieve high quality and quantity in production. By 1928, Ford was turning out 3,000 Model T cars per day at a cost of under $300 to the consumer (less than a third of the price twenty years earlier). It was a phenomenal achievement and established the international standard for car production that was imitated by Citroën in France and Porsche in Austria.

Further reading:

Batchelor, Ray, *Henry Ford: Mass Production, Modernism and Design.* Manchester: Manchester University Press, 1994.
Taylor, Sheila, *The Moving Metropolis: A History of London's Transport since 1800.* London: Laurence King, 2003.

TREND ANALYSIS

A rapidly expanding and highly successful profession which involves analysing data to identify underlying short-, intermediate- or long-term trends: for example, consumer patterns of spending. It is therefore based on the assumption that what has happened in the past will give a guide to what will happen in the future. It is now big business, with growing numbers of forecasters and planners working in every major industry on a global level.

TYPOGRAPHIC/TYPE DESIGN

Typographers arrange and specify type for printing. The arrival of computer typesetting in the late 1980s revolutionized a profession that has been developing since the first books were printed in the 16th century. This meant that it was the first design discipline to be fundamentally changed by the computer. Type designers had traditionally been largely anonymous but in the late 20th century the profession became fashionable and attained a high profile.

Type design has not only been changed by the development of technology but has responded to design movements: For instance, in the 1920s, **Bauhaus** type designers sought to produce a simple sans serif type that reflected a widespread search for a modern idiom across all design disciplines. Other examples of this include Harry Beck's famous London Underground map, inspired by an electrical circuit board, and Penguin Books, a British publishing company with a distinguished design history. During the 1930s, the rise of the Nazi Party caused many leading German designers to flee to Britain or the USA. Among them was Jan Tschichold (1902–74), one of the most influential typographers of the 20th century. His best-known achievement was designing the series style for a whole range of Penguin paperbacks.

Other pioneers of type design included the Swiss typographer Adrian Frutiger, who produced very ordered and disciplined work. Swiss typography was the single most important direction in the post-war years, typified by a search for order, unity and a new start. American typography, meanwhile, was led by the powerful vision of Herb Lubalin and Saul Bass, the latter well known for his inspirational use of type in film credits. Type experiments in 1960s California were a conscious reaction against formal Swiss type. Designers like Rick Griffin explored hand-drawn letterforms inspired by the exaggerated style of **Art Nouveau** posters. These created a distinctive image for the growing **counterculture** of the period, inspired by revolutionary music and **alternative lifestyles**. The counter-balance to this work was the more conservative and commercial type design of companies such as the ITC (International Type Company), which successfully marketed condensed and certified typefaces all over America. In the late 1970s the emergence of **Postmodernism** began to impact on type design. Jamie Reid's legendary album covers for the Sex Pistols used cut-and-paste letters, mixed type and various point sizes to overturn the established and dominant style of typography.

Type design was revolutionized in the 1980s by the introduction of the typesetting software PostScript by the Californian company Adobe Systems. It became the industry standard and brought about the biggest change in printing since the invention of the printing press. The computer has changed the way type designers use language to meet the new demands of **screen design** and web production. At the same time, however, traditional typography and lettermaking live on in artworks and more specialized graphic design.

Further reading:

McLean, Ruari, *Jan Tschichold: A Life in Typography*. London: Lund Humphries, 1997.

ULM

The Ulm Hochschule für Gestaltung (UfG; the Ulm School of Design) opened in 1953 and closed fifteen years later. In that time it became

Germany's most celebrated post-war design school. Its ambition was to take over from where the **Bauhaus** had left off, and it became famous for a rigorous, disciplined and purist approach to **industrial design**. Despite its relatively short life, Ulm is widely acknowledged to be one of the most experimental and influential post-war European design schools. Its history provides a complex and fascinating insight into post-war politics and emerging design theory and practice after the horror and brutality of the Second World War.

The story of Ulm indirectly started with a Nazi atrocity. In 1943, the Nazis brutally executed two Munich University students, Hans and Sophie Scholl, for their role in a resistance movement called Weiss Rose. Their sister Inge survived, and in their memory was inspired to set up a school dedicated to the opposition of **fascist** ideas which would offer programmes in a wide range of subjects, including design. Early supporters of the project included Otl Aicher and the writer Hans Werner Richter Inge. It was this deeply felt commitment to social change that gave Ulm an important focus and also enabled it to acquire funding. For instance, when it opened in the 1950s, Inge Scholl was offered a million marks for the school from John J. McCloy, a former US Assistant Secretary of War and president of the World Bank and at the time US High Commissioner for Germany. This was matched by funding from German industry and local government. The American financial support was forthcoming because the stated political agenda of Ulm, to oppose fascism, fitted the American policy of denazification of Germany. But it compromised the independence of the school and impacted on its future.

When the Swiss designer Max Bill was appointed the school's first director, he was obviously inspired by the Bauhaus and its international ambitions, its curriculum focused on design for industry and its recruitment of high-profile teachers and masters. Under his direction Walter Gropius and László Moholy-Nagy (now both in America) were consulted, and some of Germany's most talented students and designers were attracted to Ulm, including Rams and Hans Gugelot.

The school's buildings were designed by Bill, and it was divided into four areas of specialization: **product design**, architecture, visual communication and information. Bill believed strongly in the creative and individual nature of the designer, ideas that brought him into conflict with a new generation of post-war students and teachers. In this context Thomas Maldonado, an Argentinian theorist, and Giu Bonsiepe were key figures in the institution. Maldonado finally became Ulm's director in 1964, and he believed that design should be explored using teamwork and a much wider range of intellectual enquiry. To this end, he extended the school's curriculum to include anthropology, **semiotics** and psychology. His influence was widespread, and in 1965 L. Bruce Archer wrote *Systematic Method for Designers*, which brought the Ulm approach to London's **Royal College of Art**. Herbert Lindinger was Professor of Design at Ulm from 1962 to 1968, and wrote the definitive history of the school.

Ulm's main achievement was in establishing strong links with post-war German industry, and the school's greatest success story was its collaboration with the Braun Company. Braun employed one of Maldonado's young students, Dieter Rams, who gave the company's household products their distinctive form. In fact, his stylized and formal radios and razors have come to epitomize industrial design in the post-war period. Increasingly, however, internal divisions and funding issues made the future of the school untenable, and it closed in 1968.

Further reading:

Archer, L. Bruce, *Systematic Method for Designers*. London: H.M. Stationery Office, 1965.
Lindinger, Herbert, *Ulm Design: The Morality of Objects*. Cambridge, MA: MIT Press, 1990.

UNDER-CONSUMPTION

A theory which states that what is produced is never matched by what people are able to afford and buy. The term derives from predictions about population growth made by the late 18th-century English economist Dr Thomas Malthus.

The importance of the theory for design began in the economic decline of the USA in the 1920s, when factories were idle and workers impoverished. The **industrial design** profession at the time made a great point of emphasizing that design could effectively solve the problem of under-consumption by stimulating market growth and prosperity. Later, from another perspective, writers such as Vance Packard revived the theory in the late 1950s. In his book *The Hidden Persuaders*, Packard criticized the methods American industry used to generate sales, including the introduction of **planned obsolescence** for such goods as cars, fridges and other domestic appliances.

The theory of under-consumption, however, remains very important because it reinforces the idea that design can solve economic problems by encouraging higher levels of spending and **consumption**. When linked to the doctrine of supply and demand, under-consumption can help to explain some, if not all, of the overall economic picture.

Further reading:

Packard, Vance, *The Hidden Persuaders*. Harmondsworth: Penguin, 1981 [1957].

USER-CENTRED DESIGN (UCD)

Other terms which have a similar meaning include empathic design, participatory design and a Scandinavian approach called cooperative design. All attempt to bring together designers and users, with participatory design (an American term used in product development) focusing on user participation. UCD, then, is a methodology for the commercial development of new products which employs methods from marketing research, anthropology and psychology to connect the designer with the user during the design process. It is also a problem-solving process employed by designers to analyse how consumers use a product in real scenarios. It therefore identifies the needs of the user but also product management, installation and maintenance. The basis of this approach is that designers learn how consumers really use products, as opposed to how the designers would like them to be used. This interaction between the consumer and the product is called the interface. The Canadian **design consultancy** SonicRim has pioneered user-participation methods which help to clarify what it describes as the 'fuzzy front end' of the design development process.

Many examples of UCD come from computer software and web programs (e.g., the Google user interface), where its protocols are more established and well documented, and where positive user experience is crucial. Meanwhile, the Finnish company Nokia has used UCD techniques to improve the user interface of its mobile phones, for example making them easier to use in the dark. And the EU has developed industry benchmark standards which try to ensure that designs meet user's real requirements.

Further reading:

Beyer, Hugh and Holtzblatt, Karen, *Contextual Design: Defining Customer-Centered Systems*. San Francisco, CA: Morgan Kaufmann, 1988.

Jordan, Patrick W., *Designing Pleasurable Products: An Introduction to the New Human Factors*. London: Taylor & Francis, 2000.

UTILITY

The name given to the furniture and household products designed in Britain during the Second World War. When Hitler's bombing campaign began in earnest in 1940, Prime Minister Winston Churchill was anxious that civilian morale should not be further undermined by the prospect of no consumer goods in the shops to replace those destroyed by the bombs. So in 1941 he suggested the Utility scheme, a unique experiment for Britain, in which everyone was given the same choice, at the same price and with a strictly allocated number of coupons depending on your family circumstances, not your income. An advisory board was established, including Elizabeth Denby, whose social research had included a report into working-class housing needs, and Charles Tennyson, who had worked for the design reform group the Council for Art and Industry. For Britain, it was a socialist experiment that could only have been introduced in the direst of wartime circumstances.

The design of Utility goods was placed largely in the hands of a small band of progressive designers who had worked as **Modernists** in the 1930s. In 1943 they produced the first Utility catalogue. One of the group was Sir Gordon Russell (1892–1980), who had grown up in the Cotswolds, where he had gone to school with children whose parents were members of Charles Ashbee's **Guild** of Handicraft. Although he was committed to the principles of industrial production, Russell's furniture for the scheme (two ranges called 'Cotswold' and 'Chiltern' suggest the tone) applied sensible **Arts and Crafts** ideas. In fashion and textiles, top couturiers like Norman Hartnell, Hardy Amies and Victor Stiebel designed clothes for the mass market, while designers like Enid Marx worked on fabrics for Utility sofas and curtains.

Utility was a fascinating design experiment that finally came to an end in 1952. By then, it had ingrained into a whole generation of British people the ethic of 'make do and mend', a slogan taken from a propaganda poster series. Its impact on everyone living through the 1940s and 1950s was profound. Later, with the social revolution of the 1960s, it proved a powerful force against which to rebel. More recently, though, Utility, with its element of recycling and its careful use of materials, has found a sympathetic audience among a new generation of consumers looking for a more responsible approach to **consumerism**.

Further reading:

Geffrye Museum, *Utility Furniture and Fashion, 1941–1951*. London: Inner London Education Authority, 1974.

Sladen, Christopher, *The Conscription of Fashion: Utility Cloth, Clothing, and Footwear, 1941–1952*. Aldershot: Scolar Press, 1995.

VICTORIA AND ALBERT MUSEUM (V&A)

The world's largest collection of decorative art and design. With the support of Prince Albert, it was founded on 6 September 1852 as the Museum of Manufactures in Marlborough House, and Sir Henry Cole was appointed as its first director. The museum's declared purpose was to help educate young designers and the public, and Cole received a grant of £5,000 to buy objects from the **Great Exhibition** of 1851. In 1857 the museum moved to its present site in South Kensington, housed at first in a building of iron and glass, and later in a more permanent building designed by Captain Francis Fowke. In 1899 Queen Victoria laid the foundation stone and declared that the museum should be renamed Victoria and Albert. Owen Jones designed the Oriental Galleries, **Morris & Co.** the Dining Rooms, and Sir Edward Poynter the Grill Room. The museum was imitated internationally soon after it first opened. In 1863 the Paris Union Centrale des Arts Décoratifs opened, and the Vienna Museum of Applied Arts followed the next year.

In the 20th century the V&A design role shifted emphasis. After the First World War its collecting policy concentrated on historical objects and fine-art collections rather than contemporary design. As a result, by the 1960s it had become out of touch and remote. However, in the 1970s Sir Roy Strong brought a different approach and encouraged a policy of limited support for modern design exhibitions and acquisitions. In the 1980s, though, the museum faced a crisis: Government policy required museums to become more financially self-sufficient, and this was linked to a general feeling that they should be more accessible to the public. In 1988 the V&A appointed its first woman director, Elizabeth Esteve-Coll, to introduce radical changes in line with this ethos.

More recently, under the directorship of Mark Jones, the museum has returned to its original commitment of promoting contemporary work through a series of exhibitions. The Contemporary Team at the V&A has also instigated a number of contemporary design projects and commissions that have revitalized the museum.

Further reading:

Lomas, Elizabeth, *Guide to the Archive of Art and Design, Victoria & Albert Museum*. London: Routledge, 2001.

Physick, John, *The Victoria and Albert Museum: The History of its Building*. Oxford: Phaidon, 1982.

VICTORIAN DRESS REFORM

A fashion movement that contributed to the liberation of women. In the 1860s clothes for women were restrictive. The fashion for crinoline was at its most extreme, with skirt hoops reaching a width of six feet, and tightly laced boned corsets obligatory to produce the fashionable nipped-in waist. The reaction against this was the Dress Reform Movement, which advocated loose clothing made of natural materials coloured with vegetable dyes. William **Morris** encouraged his wife to take up the cause, and she was photographed in the style by Rossetti in 1862: lots of gathered fabric, medieval details in the styling and definitely no corsets or waisting. The development of cycling and other sporting activities for women also encouraged change. Women began to adapt items of dress from traditional men's tailoring, which allowed more freedom. Health was another argument raised in favour of dress reform. In 1884 Dr Gustav Jaeger, whose name lives on in a chain of fashion shops, aired his views at an International Health Exhibition held in the Albert Hall. He advocated wool next to the skin to stimulate circulation, absorb perspiration and entice noxious substances from the blood. This theory was perfectly practical, but some of his other ideas were more extreme: for example, five-toed socks; and the idea that you should not wash wool but simply leave it to breathe. He was also firmly opposed to wearing dyed fabric, except in winter, when body perspiration was low.

Men, too, were part of the Dress Reform Movement. The **Arts and Crafts** writer Edmund Carpenter is credited with the invention of open-toed leather sandals for men, an idea he may have picked up from India. Collars were also looser and ties knotted more like scarves. Contemporary photographs of Charles Rennie Mackintosh show off the style. Dress reform of the Dr Jaeger variety, however, was associated with cranks rather than fashion, and this prejudice continued into the 20th century.

Further reading:

Cunningham, Patricia A., *Fashioning the New Woman: Dress Reform – Politics, Health and Art, 1850–1920*. Ohio: Kent State University Press, 2002.

VIRTUAL DESIGN PRACTICE

With the **globalization** of design and manufacturing, designers increasingly have to work in virtual teams that meet and collaborate only over computer networks. The sheer size of design projects and the consequent range of skills required makes such teams essential components of most successful design projects today.

VIRTUAL REALITY (VR)

The name for new developments in media integration, VR was initially developed by the military for flight simulation in the training of astronauts and fighter pilots. As a leisure product it stimulates real-life experiences in which the viewer is no longer a passive spectator but an active participant. Interactive computers now allow the user access to sophisticated technology, including surround-vision helmets with stereophonic sound and gloves studded with motion sensors, to create a tactile, noisy and visually impressive three-dimensional world. Soon students will be able to study Norman England using VR, disabled people will be able to experience the world with no physical obstacles, and **advertising** companies will devise interactive commercials for the consumer.

One system is Dimension International's VR Toolkit, which makes it possible to create three-dimensional objects and place them in a virtual world. The system has already been used to create a British television programme called *Cyberzone*, a game show where contestants' actions are mimicked in the virtual world by cyborgs, which run or walk when the contestant does. Other VR applications, which build and render virtual worlds, are now also widely available, as are virtual binoculars, which offer stereoscopic, computer-generated images with realtime video.

Further reading:

Burnett, Ron, *How Images Think*. Cambridge, MA: MIT, 2005.

VISUAL CULTURE

A relatively new academic discipline that emerged in the early 1990s and investigates visual representations. It developed as a response to the perceived limitations and conservative nature of Art History. As an academic discipline, Visual Culture incorporates Art, Architecture and Design, but its ambition is to extend beyond these areas of study and include new fields of visual imagery, investigating the production, form and reception of images past and present by using a technique called visuality. Visual Culture programmes in universities offer courses which explore the cultural, social and historical contexts informing visual representation in Africa, the Americas, Asia and Europe. This increasingly significant interdisciplinary field is making an important contribution to our understanding of a **Postmodern** society full of images and forms of expression, from architecture to fashion, design and the human body.

Further reading:

Sturken, Marita, *Practices of Looking: An Introduction to Visual Culture*. Oxford: Oxford University Press, 2001.
Journal of Visual Culture. See: <http://vcu.sagepub.com/>.

WEB DESIGN

It is estimated that globally there are over ten billion 'hits' made each day by people to websites. Web design is still relatively new, but it is a rapidly developing design area. It can be defined as the creation of concepts and specifications for Internet/Intranet-enabled products and services. Many designers in this field started their careers as graphic designers in print media, but specific training and education have developed to service this growing discipline, which embraces related fields such as information architecture, interface design, screen graphics, 3D modelling, sound design, video and **animation**.

The inventor of the World Wide Web, which transformed usage of the Internet and consequently our lives for ever, was the British designer Tim Berners-Lee. In 2004 he was awarded Finland's Millennium Technology Prize (and one million euros) in honour of his achievement. His innovation in 1991 was to develop the first website to use hypertext, utilizing email linking to open up the potential of the Internet. Early sites at the end of the 20th century used a basic text script called HTML (HyperText Markup Language) to define what a web page looked like, and allowed the user to open related pages by using individual words linked directly from one page to another. It was a simple and flexible information layout system, which as the technology progressed became visually more sophisticated, allowing the display and linkage of images and photographs, improved **typography**, and simple animation. New programming languages (such as Java) and relatively easy-to-use software programs (such as Flash) have more recently enhanced interactivity.

Every website organizes information and images on its chosen theme. In some ways a website's home page (or index) is comparable to the title and contents pages of a book combined, but from there the analogy falters. Each web page is not just another sheet of paper in a fixed sequence, but an HTML file which has its own unique place, accessible from many other pages, which are typically linked through a common navigation menu. Whereas the text in a book is fixed, the text in a website is flexible and allows form and content to be addressed in a dynamic new way.

Publishing on the Internet can be quite simple and in this form it is effectively available to everyone. Or it can be more complex if what is required is a sound economic model to develop your work. The ease of duplication of digital material via the global network of the Internet has made rights management the Holy Grail of the new economy. In 2001 there was a well-publicized economic crisis for the Internet, which saw a crash in share prices of web-based (dot.com) businesses. That provoked a major re-evaluation of the Internet in terms of its role and its potential. Surprisingly, perhaps, it did nothing to stop the Internet's growth; indeed, thereafter there was a surge in use and development.

The current challenge for web authors and designers alike is a concept called Web 2.0, a term coined by Tim O'Reilly and his company O'Reilly Media in 2003 to indicate the next growth period of the Internet. It involves designing sites that are 'populated' with content by their readers for other readers (peer to peer) and are forever changing and updating as more peer-supplied information appears. This contrasts with conventional publishing, which delivers fixed or static information in one direction – from author to reader – only. Web 2.0 has been marked by the explosion of blogging, self-published diary-like sites which encourage further dialogue with their readers, and by Tim Berners-Lee's concept of Wiki pages. The vast majority of pages on the online encyclopedia WikiPedia are editable by the readers themselves (access to some of the pages has been limited because of malicious, false postings). Hugely successful examples of less academic, 'community' publishing are MySpace, Flickr and YouTube, where everything – text, images and video – is uploaded by the users of the sites, and access rights can be set for anyone or limited to closer associates.

Such developments can only hint at the next direction for web design in the 21st century, which is destined to be liberated still further by enhanced mobile–phone technology and local wireless connectivity between hand–held computers.

Further reading:

Dawes, Brendan, *Analog in, Digital out: Brendan Dawes on Interaction Design.* Berkeley, CA: New Riders, 1997.

WHITE GOODS

The industry term for consumer products such as washing machines, dishwashers and refrigerators traditionally made out of white sheet steel. Although there have been attempts to introduce colour into the design of these domestic products, most notably in the 1950s, white remains the preferred finish. It is a linked term to 'brown Goods', a now defunct description of a range of consumer products for the home dating from the 1930s, with brown referring to the Bakelite radio cases and wooden television cabinets that were then the norm. Later, in the 1980s and 1990s, 'brown goods' was sometimes also used to describe electrical products, such as sound systems, most of which were finished in matt black.

Further reading:

Hardyment, Christina, *From Mangle to Microwave: The Mechanization of Household Work.* Cambridge: Polity Press, 1988.
<www.domotechnica.com>

WIENER WERKSTÄTTE

The German equivalent of C.R. Ashbee's **Guild** of Handicraft. The banker Fritz Warndofer financed the group, which was formally set up in June 1903 as the Wiener Werkstätte Productiv Gemeinschaft von Kunsthand–Werken (the Viennese Workshops Production Cooperative of Art Workmen), with Koloman Moser and Josef Hoffmann as artistic directors. By 1905, it was employing over a hundred workers and had become the Viennese centre of progressive design. They produced small, domestic objects in ceramics, glass, wood and leather, as well as jewellery, none of which was intended for machine production. More importantly, under Hoffmann's artistic direction, the Werkstätte was associated with a distinctive aesthetic, using simple **geometric** forms based on repeated grid motifs and rectilinear shapes. Hoffmann's geometric simplicity combined with decoration produced a rich design heritage of cutlery, glass vases, teapots and furniture which continues to influence contemporary design.

The Werkstätte enjoyed a considerable international profile, with the British magazine *The Studio* lauding its work in a special 1906 edition called 'The Art Revival in Austria', alongside the achievements of other Austrian architects and designers. Retail outlets were subsequently opened in Germany and America to sell the group's products.

In spite of Hoffmann's continuing influence, the Werkstätte later encouraged its craftspeople and designers to develop their own style, unlike Ashbee's guild, where the medieval ideal of the anonymous worker was the norm. After 1915 its objects began to show a more **eclectic** and curvilinear style. Hoffmann himself even moved in this direction, as did fellow designer Dagobert Peche. In general, the work of the Werkstätte was far more **avant-garde** than that of the contemporary British **Arts and Crafts Movement**. One famous design, which gave the group a strong and modern image, was its distinctive rectilinear typeface, attributed to Moser. Another key difference lay in the fact that the Werkstätte was concerned primarily with matters of taste rather than the transformation of society through the **Morris** ideal of joyous labour.

In the 1920s the Viennese design movement was taken to the USA by émigrés, including Hoffmann's son Wolfgang. Here, it was integrated into the Moderne style that dominated American decorative arts at that time. In 1928 the Werkstätte celebrated its twenty-fifth anniversary, but it closed four years later, unable to withstand the economic pressures of the Depression.

Further reading:

Brandstätter, Christian, *Wonderful Wiener Werkstätte: Design in Vienna, 1903–1932*. London: Thames & Hudson, 2003.
Schweiger, Werner J. *Wiener Werkstätte: Design in Vienna 1903–1932*. London: Thames & Hudson, 1984 [1982].

YOUTH CULTURE

In the developed world youth culture leads the demand for consumer products, fashion and new technology. Its study is a post-war element of sociology, encouraged by the emergence of a new category of consumer – the teenager. Changed economic circumstances meant that young people, previously forced to adopt parental norms and **taste**, suddenly had the financial means to develop a lifestyle of their own. This phenomenon, first seen in the USA, quickly spread to Europe during the 1950s, and Britain has played an important role in the emergence of a recognizable youth culture. The 1950s saw a trend for draped jackets, greased-back hairstyles, crêpe-soled shoes and brightly coloured shirts – all elements in the Teddy Boy 'uniform'. This was followed by a series of other British youth cults, including Beatniks, Mods, Skinheads, **Punks**, New Romantics and Acid House.

Sociologists and contemporary culture commentators have studied these youth movements, and their conclusions fall into two camps. The first believe that youth culture is an original, spontaneous development which has its roots in working-class life. The second believe it is the result of commercial manipulation by **advertising** and the media. Whatever the truth, youth culture has affected mainstream design and cultural attitudes. According to Malcolm McLaren, it remains Britain's most original contribution to post-war design, and it is certainly true that images of Punks in their full regalia have become instantly recognizable as British icons.

Over the last ten years the focus for creative youth culture has moved to Asia. Young people in Japan have expressed their feelings about their traditional and structured society through a series of youth cultures. Goth-Loli devotees dress in black, wear crosses and death-inspired accessories and produce websites that focus on cutting and self-harm. On the other hand, some groups of Japanese girls have **appropriated** the clothes, look and toys of younger children to escape moving into the world of adulthood. Youth cultures inspired by social pressures such as these are quickly reflected in commercial products, fashion and **advertising** campaigns.

Further reading:

Aoki, Shoichi, *Fresh Fruits*. London: Phaidon, 2005.

Bennett, Andy and Kahn-Harris, Keith (eds), *After Subculture: Critical Studies in Contemporary Youth Culture*. Basingstoke: Palgrave Macmillan, 2004.

Hebdige, Dick, *Subculture: The Meaning of Style*. London: Routledge, 2002 [1979].

INDEX